The Management of
DEFENSE

The Management

of

DEFENSE

Organization and Control of the U.S. Armed Services

by

John C. Ries

The Johns Hopkins Press,
Baltimore, Maryland

Printed in the United States of America
Library of Congress Catalog Card Number 64–18122
This book has been brought to publication with the
assistance of a grant from The Ford Foundation.

To Fritz
. . . teacher, critic, friend

ACKNOWLEDGMENTS

I can only acknowledge, never repay, the debt incurred during the preparation of this study. To Frederick M. Sallagar of the RAND Corporation, Santa Monica, I owe the debt levied against all who have the privilege of associating with someone who constantly challenges them to proceed beyond "standard interpretations" and to think things through anew. From John C. Bollens of the University of California, Los Angeles, I acquired the debt reserved for those favored with a tireless taskmaster who sets standards which one can never hope to meet, but toward which one will always aspire. Without their inspiration, encouragement, and help, the study would neither have been undertaken nor completed.

Thomas I. Edwards of the RAND Corporation, Washington, D.C., read the manuscript in its entirety. His invaluable criticisms and suggestions improved both its substance and its style. Finally, there is Mrs. Mary Nettuno, patient and long-suffering typist and editor.

JOHN C. RIES

CONTENTS

He who asserts, as is often done, that politics ought not to interfere with the conduct of war, has no grasp of the direction of great war.

War is no independent thing; the main lineaments of all great strategic plans are of a political nature, the more so the more they include the totality of war and the state.

CLAUSEWITZ, *On War*

INTRODUCTION

CRITICS OF DEFENSE ORGANIZATION

When a breathless junior officer reported the enemy had just success-fully launched the first man-made earth satellite, his superior, an Air Force general—so the story goes—blanched and asked which one, the Navy or the Army? The prevalence of such stories indicates both the problems besetting and the diagnosis applied to the national defense establishment. Practically every news commentator, newspaper, and journal has featured the "battle of the Pentagon" at some time during the past seventeen years. "Interservice rivalry" is usually ranked second only to the Civil War as an example of internecine fratricide.

Presidents, secretaries of defense, congressmen, governmental commis-sions, members of the armed services, and a host of self-appointed critics have analyzed the problem of interservice rivalry and have suggested solutions. Their analyses and suggestions are remarkably similar and disarmingly simple. The diagnosis is lack of "unification." The remedy is centralization. All want more "authority" for the secretary of defense, less "autonomy" for the services if not their complete abolition, and a single chief of staff. Recommendations differ only in degree, not in direction. Some would merge the services, others would not go quite so far, but all advocate more centralization.

There is no other subject on which everyone is more willing to express his opinion than organization. And why not? The problem of unification is one of simple common sense. The Army, Navy, and Air Force are out-moded. They are the vestigial remains of the last war. They represent an era that is past—a time when armies engaged armies, navies engaged navies, and aircraft engaged aircraft. Warfare in the nuclear and ballistic age will be different. It will be instantaneous, total, and undeclared. Three separate services tied to outmoded concepts of operation are obviously incapable of meeting the threat of modern war. And since they spend most of their energy fighting one another, they are worse than obsolete. They are wasteful, extravagant, and divisive. They duplicate each other's functions. They simultaneously develop weapons with the same capability. And they can never agree on a common strategy, program, or policy.

The solution is no more difficult than the problem. It is also subject to common-sense analysis. If there is disunity, duplication, and waste under a tri-service system, do away with these evils by doing away with the system. Merge the three services, or, if not that, at least create new ones oriented toward modern needs such as strategic operations, limited war, and home defense. Furthermore, since the military must be subject to civilian control, place a civilian secretary of defense at the top of the merged or reconstituted services and give him real authority to run the department from the top down. Finally, if policy bodies such as the Joint Chiefs of Staff take a service or a parochial view of defense problems, the remedy is as simple as it is obvious. Assign military planning and policy to an officer and a staff freed from parochial interest and make them responsible for creating national policy.

Stated this bluntly, the arguments for centralization sound a bit over-simplified, if not naive, but they *are* logical and compelling. Moreover, they are substantially the same arguments developed by two Hoover Commission task forces, by presidential study groups, and by scholars who have urged, and continue to urge, a greater concentration of functions in the office of the secretary of defense, creation of a single chief of staff, and abolition of the three services. The basic premise of these arguments can be simply stated: centralization means central control.

This study is not a history of American defense organization nor is it a survey of defense strategy. Rather, it is an analysis of some concepts which shape contemporary thinking in both these areas. These concepts include the nature of authority, the policy process, and the effectiveness of centralization. Their tangible manifestations are particular organizational devices that have been advocated and implemented within the defense establishment.

All defense organization proposals have purported to bring about central control. And virtually every specific change in defense structure has been defended as a means to this end. By examining the testimony of advocates of various organizational arrangements, an attempt has been made to determine what defense reformers have sought to do, why they wanted to do it, and how they proposed to bring it about. The substance of defense policy and the history of defense organization are included only as necessary to place reorganization proposals in a contextual perspective.

The first two parts of this study consider the background and early operation of the first attempt to unify the armed services, the National Security Act of 1947. An analysis of the origin and development of centralization as a concept of unification constitutes the first part—Folklore and Unification. The organizational antecedents as well as the early operation of the 1947 act are considered in the second part—An Experiment in Decentralization. And the final portion of this study—Return to Orthodoxy—considers the changes and developments in defense organization since 1949.

FOLKLORE AND UNIFICATION

Everyone considers himself expert in the difficult and complex subject of organization. In fact, a series of common-sense observations have been codified into a set of organizational principles that apply everywhere and at all times. And these clichés on organization, especially those that have the most currency, often turn out to be nothing more than myths rooted in popular folklore.

The folklore symbol of organizational efficiency and control is the all-powerful executive who sits at the apex of a tightly organized, tightly run organizational pyramid—the man who makes all decisions, the man who runs things from the top down. And the history of defense organization in the United States is characterized by repeated attempts to translate this symbol into reality.

The development of unification of the armed services is a study in centralization. It is the study of the single-minded belief that centralization means effective central control. And the roots of this belief run deep into the organizational history of the military establishment.

Congress examined a number of proposals for placing the Army and Navy within a centralized department in the years before it passed the National Security Act of 1947. The War Department has been the major source of support for merger as a concept of unification, and its 1945 proposal, the Collins plan, provides an excellent opportunity for identifying the precepts of organizational folklore.

The Collins plan was both an end and a beginning. It was an end because it represented the culmination of over forty years of organizational development. Into the plan went conceptual formulations developed during a long and bitter struggle between the War Department and the army bureaus for control of the Army. During this struggle, the principles constituting the theoretical foundation of the plan were established. It was a beginning because the Collins plan has served as a model for more recent attempts to centralize the defense establishment.

The Collins plan or any other proposal that views organization as a structural pyramid rests on more than a set of organizational principles. The principles are really prescriptive generalizations based on a view of politics in general and the administrative process in particular. And no analysis of an organizational proposal is complete without a consideration of the behavioral phenomena it purports to explain. There is a direct and an identifiable relation between principles of organization and views of the policy process, the nature of authority, communications, and the nature of control.

AN EXPERIMENT IN DECENTRALIZATION

The National Security Act of 1947 created an organization far short of the ideal advocated by the War Department. It retained the Army and Navy as independent executive departments and added a third, the Air Force. A secretary of defense, operating through four interservice committees, was to exercise central control.

As in the Collins plan, the National Security Act also incorporated a set of principles based upon attitudes about the policy process, authority, communications, and the nature of control. An organizational proposal of the Navy, which eventually became the prototype for the 1947 act, most clearly stated these principles.

The navy proposals were based upon the experience of both American and British agencies of central wartime control. And a survey of both these systems is necessary to uncover the organizational concepts behind the particular structural arrangements implemented by the National Security Act.

Finally, the early history of the defense establishment under the 1947 act demonstrates the extent to which these concepts are responsive to the levies exacted by the American political system as well as the extent to which executive attitudes and preconceptions determine the operation of any organization.

RETURN TO ORTHODOXY

Early secretaries of defense found they could not play the role demanded of an executive by organization folklore. They did not seem to have enough "authority." They did not get the "right kind" of military advice. The services could never agree and they were hard to control. Something had to be done to make unification work better. And there followed, in the eleven years after the passage of the National Security Act, three major defense reorganizations, one in 1949, another in 1953, and the last in 1958.

Because of the relationship between particular structural devices and views of the political and policy process, congressional hearings on each reorganization act make it possible to discover what defense reformers hoped to accomplish. They had decided the defense policy process did not conform to their preconceptions because the structure of the defense establishment was poorly conceived.

Of course, defense reformers have not succeeded in changing the realities of either politics or defense policy-making. Indeed, each reorganization act purported to do the very same thing—give the secretary of defense adequate authority and end interservice rivalry. And in each case this would be done by adding more functions to the office of the secretary of defense. Consequently, defense reformers have succeeded in creating the largest centralized bureaucracy the world has ever seen. The secretary of defense is trying to run an organization of over four million people with an annual budget that exceeds the gross receipts of the ten largest corporations in America.

By 1958, centralization had gone so far that Congressman Carl Vinson warned:

> ... because of the magnitude of this fantastic undertaking, which involves the expenditure of approximately $40 billion annually, it is inconceivable and impossible for any one individual to know every aspect of the functioning of the Department of Defense.
>
> . . . .
>
> It was never intended, and is not now intended that the office of the Secretary of Defense would become a fourth department within the Department of Defense, delving into operational details on a daily basis. The Secretary is supposed to make policy. . . .[1]

Mr. Vinson's warning was somewhat academic because the secretary's office was already, and still is, a centralized operating agency in all but name. It is certainly difficult to imagine a staff of more than 3,000 civilian and military personnel being engaged in policy formulation alone.

But if the secretary of defense is engaged in operations, is he also directing policy? Does he have the time and means to exercise control? Has centralization brought the promised increase in authority? These are the

[1] U.S., Congress, House, Committee on Armed Services, *Report, Department of Defense Reorganization Act of 1958*, 85th Cong., 2d Sess., 1958, H.R. No. 1765, p. 7.

questions to which this study is addressed. Although it is critical of recent trends in defense organization, this study does not presume to offer a final solution to Defense Department problems. It does, however, try to suggest an *approach* to defense organization which will take into account the lessons of the past seventeen years.

PART I

FOLKLORE AND UNIFICATION

I

THE SEARCH FOR
ORGANIZATIONAL CONCEPTS

UNIFICATION AND THE LESSONS OF WORLD WAR II

Identification of the exact time when unification became a major organizational issue is virtually impossible. Some defense historians say that pressure began in the unanswered claim of the prewar army aviators for a commanding position in American military planning rather than with wartime experiences of inefficiency and waste. Unification was the army aviators' only "practicable avenue to independence and authority." [1] And if unification did result from attempts to establish the autonomy of air power, it became a major issue during the early 1920's. Other students of military history feel that the failure of interservice co-ordination at Pearl Harbor and the success of unified command systems developed later in the war provided the impetus for unification.[2] Other military historians point to the degree of actual unification realized by such wartime agencies as the Joint Chiefs of

---

[1] Walter Millis, Harvey C. Mansfield, and Harold Stein, *Arms and the State: Civil-Military Elements in National Policy* (New York: The Twentieth Century Fund, 1958), p. 149. R. Earl McClendon describes the origin and history of the movement to gain equality with the traditional services by air power enthusiasts in *The Question of Autonomy for the United States Air Arm, 1907–1945* (Maxwell AFB, Alabama: Documentary Research Division, Air University Library, 1950). See also Paul Y. Hammond, "Super Carriers and B–36 Bombers: Appropriations, Strategy and Politics," *American Civil-Military Decisions, A Book of Case Studies*, ed. Harold Stein (Twentieth Century Fund, University of Alabama Press, 1963), p. 467.

[2] Timothy W. Stanley, *American Defense and National Security* (Washington, D.C.: Public Affairs Press, 1956), p. 11.

3

Staff (JCS). And they contend that these agencies provided the model for later unification plans.[3] But regardless of its exact beginning in time, unification eventually succeeded in turning defense organization through a full cycle from 1789, when the War Department was divided, and the Navy—like Adam's rib—was removed and given a separate identity.

The issue of unification of the armed services is the product of at least three pressures: attempts to establish the autonomy of air power; the wartime inefficiency and duplication of effort in the Army and Navy; and the success of wartime experiments in interservice co-ordination. However, the plea of aviators for coequal status with the other service arms was, and is still, a major commitment of the proponents of unification.

In late 1945, two years before the enactment of the National Security Act, the status and role of air power were declared to be involved inseparably with the issue of unification. In the words of General of the Army Henry H. Arnold:

> It is now, in my opinion, basic to proper organization of our armed forces, that fundamental air power be established as coequal partner with land power and sea power. All must be directed and the relative emphasis to be given each must be determined by supreme command or authority.[4]

General George C. Kenney put it this way:

> When the air arm is subordinate to any other there cannot be free and unhampered development of airborne craft and weapons.... An equal status under an over-all, single department is, I am convinced, a prerequisite to national security.... Primary responsibility for air warfare must rest with the coequal Air Force, whatever the character of the earth's surface underneath.[5]

Nor were such views restricted to persons directly committed to air power because of their membership in the Army Air Forces. Secretary of War Robert P. Patterson averred that: "we recognize now that the basic air power of the United States must be established as an arm of

[3] Millis, Mansfield, and Stein, *Arms and the State*, p. 105.

[4] U.S., Congress, Senate, Committee on Military Affairs, *Hearings, Department of Armed Forces, Department of Military Security*, 79th Cong., 1st Sess., 1945, p. 69. Cited hereafter as Senate Committee on Military Affairs, *Hearings, 1945*.

[5] *Ibid.*, pp. 232–33.

our national defense coordinate with our land power and our sea power—all, of course under supreme direction." [6]

The way air enthusiasts proposed to accomplish air force autonomy is more interesting than their arguments in favor of air power. Notice that all of the preceding arguments identify unification with a supreme command and a single department. Such an identification was held to be an obvious lesson of World War II.

The Lessons of World War II

The lessons of World War II were that slow and costly mobilization, limited intelligence as to the designs and capacity of potential enemies, "prodigal" use of resources, lack of unity of command in the Pacific, and duplicating supply lines—all these undesirable conditions—resulted from the existence of two separate service departments. And these conditions could be eliminated by merging the two service departments.

The creation of a single service department would bring many advantages. One department meant one department head. One department head meant unified direction. The argument was simple, logical, and compelling, especially to wartime field commanders who saw their plans for victory deterred by delay, wrong decision, or no decision at all. Grafted on to this argument was one supported by the Army Air Forces that the role of air power was so irrefutably demonstrated during the war that it must never again risk domination by either land or sea power. Therefore, unification must "triplify" as well as "unify." If the independence of air power and the lessons of wartime "disunity and duplication" were accepted, only one answer was possible: three services, land, air, and sea, under one department. So the argument ran, and such was the thinking during the summer of 1945.

Trends in Organization Theory

It would be misleading to view in isolation these organizational attitudes of defense reformers. To do so would overlook the prevailing attitude of students of government about organization and the nature of administrative authority. Since the turn of the present century, organization theory had been dominated by "New Hamiltonianism," as

[6] *Ibid.*, p. 11.

Leonard D. White termed the concept.[7] Developed in reaction to the corruption and irresponsibility prevalent in administrative organizations that had been characterized by extraordinary dispersion and disintegration of authority, it involved concentrating administrative authority, that is, legal authority, in chief executives: mayors, city managers, county managers, governors, and the President. With both military and civil administrators, this notion was translated into the "principle" of unity of command. To implement this concept, organizational structure was viewed as a pyramid through which authority and decision flowed down from the top, while responsibility and information flowed up from the bottom. These lines of authority and responsibility could be traced on a chart from the chief executive down to the lowliest private or civil servant. Authority, unity, and efficiency were equated with hierarchy, chain of command, and bureaucracy.[8]

In fact, the proposals for defense organization that appeared during World War II could well have been written by the President's Committee on Administrative Management which published its findings on executive organization in 1937. As was the case in military organization, the President's Committee stipulated certain

> assumptions and presumptions about the way government ought to be organized, formulating proposals for change which would bring the actual arrangements into conformity with the announced assumptions and presumptions, and exhorting all who had authority and influence . . . to put the recommendations into effect.[9]

[7] Leonard D. White, *Introduction to the Study of Public Administration* (3d ed.; New York: The Macmillan Co., 1950), p. 18.

[8] No attempt will be made to trace the development of what today is referred to as the orthodox model of organization. Throughout the remainder of this and the following chapter, evidence will be offered to demonstrate the complete compatibility of the "principles" of military organization and management and the "principles" of what has now come to be called the "classical," "hierarchical," "pyramidal," "orthodox," or "Weberian" model and/or schools of organization and management. Literature describing and criticizing these schools abounds. A representative sample would include: Peter M. Blau and W. Richard Scott, *Formal Organization: A Comparative Approach* (San Francisco: Chandler Publishing Co., 1962), pp. 27–36; Peter M. Blau, *Bureaucracy in Modern Society* (New York: Random House, 1956), pp. 28–36; Alvin W. Gouldner, "Metaphysical Pathos and the Theory of Bureaucracy," *American Political Science Review*, XLIX, No. 2 (June, 1955), 496–507; Talcott Parsons, *The Social System* (Glencoe, Ill.: The Free Press, 1951), pp. 507–8; Herbert A. Simon, *Administrative Behavior: A Study of Decision-Making in Administrative Organization* (New York: The Macmillan Co., 1951), *passim;* and John M. Pfiffner and Frank P. Sherwood, *Administrative Organization* (Englewood Cliffs: Prentice-Hall, Inc., 1960), *passim.*

[9] Charles S. Hyneman, *Bureaucracy in a Democracy* (New York: Harper and Bros., 1950), p. 254.

The principles of organization and management formulated and defended by such authorities as J. D. Mooney, Lyndall Urwick, Leonard D. White, W. F. Willoughby, and Luther Gulick formed the theoretical foundation of most early unification proposals.

EARLY ADVOCATES OF ONE DEPARTMENT

Between June 30, 1941, and December 12, 1945, three major proposals were made for consolidating the two service departments under a single military staff headed by a single chief of staff.[10] And during congressional hearings on one of these proposals, the McNarney plan,[11] most military witnesses testified in favor of merger as a concept of unification. Those who did not asked only for postponement of a final decision and further study, not for rejection.

In October, 1945, when the Senate Military Affairs Committee opened hearings on two bills[12] for the creation of a single department of armed forces composed of three equal services, air, land, and sea, witnesses invariably equated unification with a single department headed by a single chief of staff. Furthermore, they equated unification with the results they expected such centralization would bring.

In addition to establishing air power in its proper role, ten other benefits were cited in support of unification. (1) It would insure the required teamwork of all components of the armed forces in wartime.[13] (2) It would provide the peacetime training for exercising and operating

[10] For a detailed account of all U.S. unification attempts up to 1947, refer to Lawrence J. Legere, Jr., "Unification of the Armed Forces" (Ph.D. dissertation, Harvard University, 1951).

[11] This plan was submitted by Air Force General Joseph T. McNarney, with War Department approval, before a select committee on postwar military policy. The plan called for a single department and a single chief of staff. Further description of this and the other two early unification proposals can be found in Paul Y. Hammond, *Organizing for Defense: The American Military Establishment in the Twentieth Century* (Princeton: Princeton University Press, 1961), p. 191; Millis, Mansfield, and Stein, *Arms and the State*, p. 146; and Stanley, *American Defense*, p. 72.

[12] Senator Edward C. Johnson of Colorado introduced a bill for creation of a Department of Armed Forces (Senate 84), and Senator Lister Hill of Alabama introduced a bill for the creation of a Department of Military Security (Senate 1482). Discussion of these bills gave way to consideration of a War Department proposal submitted at the hearings by Lt. General J. Lawton Collins and a Navy Department proposal submitted by Secretary of Navy James Forrestal.

[13] Senate Committee on Military Affairs, *Hearings, 1945*. See the testimony of General Dwight D. Eisenhower, p. 363; General Douglas MacArthur, pp. 24–25; and General George Kenney, p. 234.

unified commands.[14] (3) It would give the military establishment an organization prepared for the events of war.[15] (4) It would make possible the speed and flexibility required in modern warfare fought with modern weapons.[16] (5) It would assure the necessary impetus for adequate research and development of weapons.[17] (6) It would bring about the proper co-ordination of military programs with other governmental programs.[18] (7) It was necessary for the development of comprehensive military plans and programs.[19] (8) It would provide the best means for over-all presentation and consideration of the budget.[20] (9) It would reduce the waste inherent in the present duplication of services and facilities.[21] (10) It would eliminate undesirable interservice competition and rivalry for goods and man power.[22] These benefits were alleged to be the direct consequences of creating a single service department headed by a chief of staff.

The equation of goals with particular structural arrangements has strongly characterized all defense organizational proposals since 1945. For example, the National Security Act of 1947, which created an organizational structure far different from the one under consideration in 1945, was going to bring about

> optimum efficiency of military operations and the closest integration of national security organization with other departments and agencies of government concerned with the national security . . . as well as the maximum economy compatible with military efficiency.[23]

[14] *Ibid.* See the testimony of Secretary of War Robert A. Patterson, p. 17; General J. L. Devers, p. 312; General Henry H. Arnold, p. 80; and former Secretary of Navy Josephus Daniels, p. 183.

[15] *Ibid.* See the testimony of General Dwight D. Eisenhower, p. 360; General Carl Spaatz, p. 342; General Omar N. Bradley, p. 355; and Secretary of War Robert A. Patterson, p. 17.

[16] *Ibid.* See the testimony of Secretary of War Robert A. Patterson, p. 22; General Henry H. Arnold, p. 77; General Carl Spaatz, p. 341; and former Secretary of Navy Josephus Daniels, p. 181.

[17] *Ibid.* See the testimony of General J. Lawton Collins, p. 313; Secretary of War Robert A. Patterson, p. 14; and General J. L. Devers, p. 313.

[18] *Ibid.* See the testimony of Secretary of War Robert A. Patterson, p. 18.

[19] *Ibid.* See the testimony of Secretary of War Robert A. Patterson, p. 12; General George C. Marshall, p. 50; and General J. L. Devers, p. 314.

[20] *Ibid.* See the testimony of General J. L. Devers, p. 314; Secretary of State James F. Byrnes, p. 191; and General George C. Marshall, pp. 52, 59–60.

[21] *Ibid.* See the testimony of Secretary of War Robert A. Patterson, p. 15; General George C. Marshall, p. 51; and General Brehon Somervall, pp. 371, 639.

[22] *Ibid.* See the testimony of Secretary of State James F. Byrnes, pp. 190–91; General J. Lawton Collins, p. 160; General Dwight D. Eisenhower, p. 371; and General M. G. White, pp. 322–23.

[23] U.S., Congress, Senate, Committee on Armed Services, *National Security Act of 1947*, 80th Cong., 1st Sess., 1947, Rept. No. 239 to accompany S. 758, p. 3.

Similar claims were made for the defense reorganizations of 1949, 1953, and 1958.

In view of the goals inherent to the early centralized plans for defense organization and those used to justify far different organizational concepts in subsequent years, the significance of goals as operative devices for measuring specific organizational proposals is subject to question. Unification advocates should not be severely criticized for stressing goals, or for the inconsistency of some of their goals, however. Few reorganization plans in government or business have avoided superficiality and ambiguity in goal specification. If some goals emphasize *speed* of decision, while others emphasize *accuracy* of decision, and still others emphasize *economy* of execution, it is probably because organizational planners want all these objectives attained, even if, for practical purposes, they are incompatible.

Even when organizational reformers can agree on a single consistent set of goals, knowledge of methods for achieving them is limited. Administrative science has not progressed very far. And there is no way to be certain of the consequences of decisions relating to organization. Not only is knowledge of consequences limited, but the effectiveness of any particular allocation of activities is often impossible to measure. Administrative measurement is one of the most backward of all administrative arts.[24]

If the consequences of specific organizational decisions are unclear, at least agreement can be reached on the goals. Those who testified on behalf of unification in 1945 thought they were certain of their goals. Unfortunately, the equation of a particular organizational structure with a set of goals did, and still does, produce some distressing side effects. First, those who question the desirability of a chosen structure are subject to the accusation that they oppose the goals, and their objections are therefore discounted.[25] Second, insufficient consideration is given to means. The goals are somehow considered to be self-executing.

No serious consideration was given to questions of organizational operation (means) as distinct from organizational goals (ends) until late in 1945 during the hearings before the Senate Military Affairs Com-

[24] Herbert A. Simon, Donald W. Smithburg, and Victor A. Thompson, *Public Administration* (New York: Alfred A. Knopf, 1950), p. 176.

[25] For examples see Stanley, *American Defense*, p. 74; Hammond, *Organizing for Defense*, pp. 188, 222, 226; Millis, Mansfield, and Stein, *Arms and the State*, p. 150; and Senate Committee on Military Affairs, *Hearings, 1945*, pp. 441–42.

mittee.[26] The change in focus was gradual but certainly began with the submission of a plan for national security organization by Secretary of Navy James V. Forrestal in October, 1945. Defenders of the Navy plan began to question the relationship between the goals of previous proposals and the organizational devices which purported to make them operative.[27]

Plans presented by the War Department and the Navy Department in 1945 represent the extreme positions of defense organization, with respect to both co-ordination among national security agencies and principles of management. They have to a considerable degree set the framework within which issues of defense organization have been later discussed. And in a large measure, they reflect the variations to be found in organization theory, both public and private. Furthermore, in their original conception, before compromises effected in 1947, they represent two opposing models of organization. Analysis of these two models will be useful in studying and analyzing later organization of the national military establishment.[28]

THE COLLINS PLAN

Lt. General J. Lawton Collins presented the War Department plan for unification to the Senate Committee on Military Affairs.[29] The plan called for a single department of armed forces composed of three services, land, sea, and air, with an agency of common supply. A secretary of armed forces, assisted by an undersecretary and four assistant secretaries, would head the department. The four component agencies would report to the secretary through a chief of staff. And the chiefs of the three service agencies, the armed forces chief of staff, and the military adviser to the secretary would sit as joint chiefs of staff.

[26] For a contrasting interpretation see Hammond, *Organizing for Defense*, p. 222. Professor Hammond feels the significant dividing line is between discussion of "general structural questions" and the "practical and profoundly political questions about forces, functions, and status of the Navy." While these hearings did mark the beginning of the roles and missions dispute, earlier consideration was not devoted to structure, but rather to goals. The significance of the roles question, while obviously important, cannot be used by itself to explain the entire case which the Navy presented during the hearings. Indeed it might well have been the motive behind the Navy case, but its case against merger is a good one, not to be discounted simply because one disagrees with the Navy's ulterior purpose.

[27] Senate Committee on Military Affairs, *Hearings, 1945*, see the testimony of Admiral Chester W. Nimitz, pp. 383–434, and Assistant Secretary of the Navy H. Struve Hensel, pp. 469–73.

[28] The Navy plan is discussed *infra*, Chapter IV, pp. 53–55.

[29] Senate Committee on Military Affairs, *Hearings, 1945*, pp. 155–80.

Fig. 1

THE COLLINS PLAN

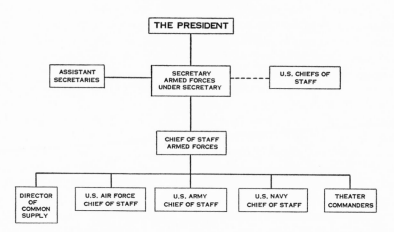

Structure and Organizational Goals

Structurally, the Collins plan was quite precise. It could be, and was, presented as a neat organizational pyramid with clear lines of authority and responsibility. Advocates of the plan testified that it provided an organization that would realize all the goals of unification. But the plan was primarily defended in terms of what it would accomplish. Little consideration was given to how the proposed structural arrangements would actually operate. For example, General Collins never did explain the responsibilities or the control devices available to the secretary. He was simply the "head." Apparently nothing more was considered necessary.

General Collins was more specific when he discussed the duties of other structural elements of the proposed department. And some of these specific descriptions are worth considering because they reflect the emphasis placed on desired organizational outcomes. In some respects a kind of "word magic" was at work, or so it seemed. Activities and goals were assigned to particular units because some of the same words were used in describing the activity and goal and the unit. Consider the following proposals of the Collins plan.

Assistant Secretaries.—Assistant secretaries would have functional responsibilities, under the secretary, for the "co-ordination of scientific research and development," for the supervision of "procurement and

industrial mobilization, legislative affairs, and public information." [30]
For example, the assistant secretary for procurement and industrial
mobilization would *supervise* all procurement matters and prepare
mobilization plans. Operating under the secretary, "but with direct
channels of communication to the Air, Army, and Navy components,
and with the Director of Common Supply and Hospitalization," the
assistant secretary would be responsible for eliminating "wasteful inefficiency and duplication in the business management of the department." [31]

Direct lines of communication with subordinate agencies would seem
to violate the hierarchical position of the chief of staff. Would the
assistant secretary give orders to the service agencies? Would he give
orders to the chief of staff? These questions were neither raised nor
answered. Apparently *co-ordination* of research and development
would come about simply by appointing a *co-ordinator.*

Chief of Staff.—The chief of staff would be the "principal military
adviser and executive" for the secretary.[32] Would this mean that the
chief of staff advised the secretary or that he ran the department for
the secretary? General Collins said that the chief of staff "undoubtedly"
would need a "small staff to assist him in the establishment of over-all
policy on military personnel matters, military intelligence, joint training, and logistics." [33] Would the chief of staff and his "small staff"
stand between the service agencies and the secretary? If so what did the
secretary and his assistants really do? General Collins did not go into
this.

United States Chiefs of Staff.—The armed services chief of staff and
the chiefs of staff of the air, army, and navy divisions would constitute
the United States chiefs of staff. One of its major functions would be
to "integrate" the peacetime budget. In the event there was disagreement, the minority view would be forwarded, along with the majority
view, to the President after the secretary had an opportunity to *append*
his comments.[34] The secretary would not even be able to resolve disagreement in the United States chiefs of staff committee. At best the
role and authority of the secretary and his assistants seemed obscure.

[30] *Ibid.,* p. 157.
[31] *Ibid.,* p. 159.
[32] *Ibid.,* p. 157.
[33] *Ibid.,* p. 161.
[34] *Ibid.,* pp. 157–58.

THE COLLINS PLAN AND PRINCIPLES OF ORGANIZATION

Although the matter of organizational operation was not treated in the Collins plan, the principles of organization were not neglected. Indeed the major elements of the plan conformed almost exactly to contemporary principles of organization theory.[35]

Unity of Command

The accepted principle is that "no subordinate shall be subject to the orders of more than one superior." [36] A single chief of staff was to head each service component according to the Collins plan. Each service chief of staff reported directly to the armed forces chief of staff. The armed forces chief of staff reported to the secretary of armed forces. The secretary reported to the President. At any point in the chain of command responsibility could be identified.

Span of Control

This principle warns that "there are limits to human capacity and ... when attention is spread too thinly over too many circumstances, unsatisfactory results occur." [37] In the Collins proposal, the secretary had only six persons reporting to him: his four assistants, his undersecretary, and the chief of staff. The chief of staff had only four persons reporting to him; they were the three service chiefs of staff and the director of common supply. Presumably this process of limiting the number of subordinates reporting to any one superior would continue on down the organizational pyramid.

Hierarchical Conformation

"[Hierarchical Conformation] in essence consists in the universal application of the superior subordinate relationship through a number of levels of responsibility reaching from the top to the bottom of the

[35] The following elements or principles of organization theory are taken from White, *Public Administration*, pp. 29–39. They could have been taken from a number of texts published before World War II. For a summary of the approaches used by White see Pfiffner and Sherwood, *Administrative Organization*, pp. 41–65.

[36] White, *Public Administration*, p. 33.

[37] *Ibid.*, p. 36.

structure." [38] Each position has its place in the hierarchy, indicated by a distinctive title, with the authority to give orders to subordinates and responsibility to obey orders from a superior. At each level, the superior's authority flows from law, organizational status, his disciplinary power, and his presumed superior knowledge and ability. Thus, according to the Collins plan, the secretary at the top of the hierarchy had all authority while the private at the bottom had none.

This principle probably explains why General Collins did not find it necessary to describe the authority and responsibility of the secretary. He was at the top of the organizational pyramid and therefore had all authority.

Co-ordination by Staff

"Coordination is the adjustment of the function of the parts to each other, and of the movement and operation of parts in time so that each can make its maximum contribution to the product of the whole. . . . A staff is an effective coordinating organ. . . ." [39] In the Collins plan each commander at each level would have his own staff to "coordinate" the various parts of his organization. Indeed, the component commanders were designated chiefs of staff. The staff would not violate the principle of unity of command because the staff only "supervises" or "advises"; it never issues orders.

Departmentalization by Major Purpose

"Principal subdivisions . . . are ordinarily organized on the basis of major substantive purpose, and are concerned 'with the content matter' of their field." [40] Under the Collins plan, major subdivisions would be the three services, each concerned with fighting in a given medium of warfare—land, air, and sea. Added flexibility would be gained by establishing composite units for areas of combat. These theater commands also help square the requirements of functional specialization by the service components with the requirements for unity of command in an operational area.

[38] *Ibid.*, p. 33.
[39] *Ibid.*, p. 36.
[40] *Ibid.*, p. 29.

Specialization in Auxiliary Services

"Over a period of years, the 'major purpose' departments have been losing part of their responsibility for carrying on their auxiliary or secondary services . . . in response to the pressure of specialization and presumed economies." [41] In order to gain the advantages of central purchasing and supply, as well as the economies of a single hospital system, the Collins plan called for a separate "auxiliary" department of supply and hospitalization.

Neither the structure nor the supporting principles of the Collins plan were radical or peculiar to the military environment. However, particular items could not be explained solely in terms of the "principles" of administration. The relationship of the armed forces secretary and the chief of staff was not made clear. The position of the chiefs of the service components as subordinates within the departmental hierarchy, but equals on the United States chiefs of staff, was a peculiar arrangement at best. Finally, the control which the United States chiefs of staff had over the budget seemed in conflict with the hierarchical position of the secretary. These particular arrangements could be understood only in terms of the history of the War Department during the present century.

WAR DEPARTMENT ORGANIZATIONAL HISTORY [42]

In many respects the problems facing reformers of the organization of the War Department at the beginning of the twentieth century were not unlike those facing reformers of the organization of local, state, and national government. In each case, at that time, responsibility was dispersed, authority disintegrated, and organization consisted of many layers of independent or semi-independent bureaus and agencies. The analogy cannot be carried too far, however, because the War Department had certain peculiar problems. In wartime it was the focus of attention, appropriations, and highest national policy. In peacetime it was subject to almost no public notice. In peacetime, the department

[41] *Ibid.*, p. 30.
[42] There are two detailed histories of War Department organization from the beginning of the twentieth century. Although both defend the general staff system, they are well documented. Otto L. Nelson, *National Security and the General Staff* (Washington, D.C.: Infantry Journal Press, 1946) and Paul Y. Hammond, *Organizing for Defense.*

carried out essentially non-military functions: feeding, clothing, curing, arming, and housing troops. These functions were divided among various bureaus or divisions (the special staff) such as Ordnance, Engineers, Signal Corps, and Quartermaster.[43] Officers who had spent their entire careers within the bureau and who served as commanders without limit of time commanded the bureaus. "Some of them had lived in Washington and presided over their separate duchies for two or three decades." [44]

The inability of the system to mobilize forces and to train, dispatch, and then supply them in a theater of combat was dramatically demonstrated during the Spanish-American War.[45] After this conflict, Secretary of War Elihu Root (1899–1904) pushed for reorganization and a general staff. In his report to Congress in 1902, Root recommended the organizing of a group of professionals "that would give continuous substance and meaning to the work of military planning and direction." [46] The general staff, authorized on August 15, 1903, never succeeded in realizing its ideal or in consolidating its power over the bureaus.[47] That this should happen is not surprising. The bureau chiefs and individual members of Congress were natural allies against the general staff. For example, in 1911, the Army, about 75,000 strong, was scattered about the country in forty-nine posts, located in twenty-four states and territories, "in accordance with the strategic requirements of Indian fighting." [48] Congressmen representing these districts were at least as interested in the money the Army could bring into their districts through payroll, armories, and development of rivers and harbors as they were in preparedness for war.

[43] Combat forces (infantry, cavalry, and artillery, and so on) were organized into seven geographical departments: East, Missouri, Dakota, Colorado, California, Texas, and Platte. These seven geographical departments bear a striking resemblance to the eight unified commands within the present Defense Department. See infra, Chapter X, pp. 188–90.

[44] Elting E. Morison, Turmoil and Tradition: A Study of the Life and Times of Henry L. Stimson (Boston: Houghton Mifflin Co., 1960), p. 148.

[45] The Dodge Commission on the conduct of the War Department in the war with Spain issued a report indicting the bureau system. A summary of its findings can be found in Philip C. Jessup, Elihu Root (2 vols.; New York: Dodd, Mead and Co., 1938), I, 241 and J. D. Hittle, The Military Staff: Its History and Development (Harrisburg: The Military Service Publishing Co., 1949), pp. 174–82. See also Leonard D. White, The Republican Era: 1869–1901 (New York: The Macmillan Co., 1958), pp. 134–53.

[46] Morison, Turmoil and Tradition, p. 149. See also Henry L. Stimson and McGeorge Bundy, On Active Service in Peace and War (New York: Harper and Bros., 1947), pp. 31–33.

[47] Ray S. Cline, Washington Command Post: The Operations Division (Washington, D.C.: Department of Army, 1951), pp. 16–17.

[48] Morison, Turmoil and Tradition, p. 146. See Nelson for distribution of troops in 1896, National Security, pp. 12–13.

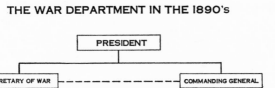

Fig. 2

THE WAR DEPARTMENT IN THE 1890's

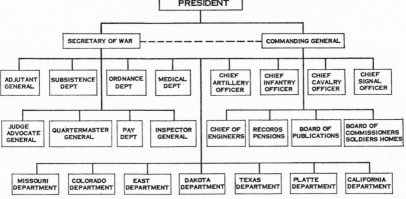

In view of their congressional strength, bureau chiefs, regardless of the hierarchical position of the chief of staff and the general staff, could and did ignore efforts to control them. They represented authority in the present, that is, authority to build bridges, dredge harbors, buy food, and spend money. The General Staff represented a remote and distasteful contingency—war. As expected, the contingencies, rather than the principles of organization were controlling. The high-water mark of the power of the General Staff was World War I. The rest of the period between 1903 and 1941 was marked by a struggle in which bureaus and divisions more than held their own.[49]

A new alliance developed between the chief of staff and the secretary of war out of this struggle between the general staff and the bureaus. In peacetime, caught between the bureaus and Congress, the secretary and the chief of staff formed an alliance for their mutual protection. And in wartime, the secretary found himself imposed between the President and his generals. He then sought the alliance to avoid being completely bypassed.[50] However, the *legal* relationship was one of subordination. Only the secretary could command; the chief of staff could merely supervise, but he had direct access to the President.

[49] Arthur Maass has prepared an authoritative study of the power base from which an Army bureau operates, *Muddy Waters: The Army Engineers and the Nation's Rivers* (Cambridge: Harvard University Press, 1951). Problems of control were not limited to the Army. Robert G. Albion discusses similar problems in the Navy, "The Administration of the Navy, 1789–1945," *The Navy: A Study in Administration* (Report No. 95; Chicago: Public Administration Service, 1946).

[50] Morison, *Turmoil and Tradition*, pp. 601–4.

The Collins plan reflected these trends in War Department experience. The emphasis on the role of the chief of staff is unmistakable. He was to be not simply the advisor to the secretary, but his "military executive." The relationship of the secretary to the chief was undefined because it had always been undefined. And what of the bureaus, the prime rivals of general staff authority? They were eliminated. There would be no bureaus. The traditional sources of strength for the bureaus were to be handed to a department of common supply and hospitalization. This particular solution to forces which promote disintegration and disunity was in keeping with the prevalent recommendations of students of public administration. Just as municipal reformers recommended centralization under a manager or a strong mayor, and just as the President's Committee on Administrative Management recommended consolidation and centralization, so did the proponents of the Collins plan.

The political implications of this move should not go unnoticed. This was an attempt, through structural arrangement, to transfer the level at which Congress would control the military from bureau level to departmental level. What additional consequences this might have apparently were not considered.[51]

During World War II, President Roosevelt developed the practice of dealing directly with the chiefs of staff and frequently did not bother to inform the service secretaries of major plans and developments.[52] As mentioned previously, this accounts in part for the alliance between the secretary and the chief. It also continued the practice of developing direct access between the commanding generals and the President. Just as Stanton could not stand between Lincoln and his generals, and Baker and Daniels (secretaries of war and navy, respectively) could not stand between Wilson and the military, so Stimson and Knox (secretary of the navy) could not stand between Franklin D. Roosevelt and the wartime joint chiefs of staff.[53] This circumstance might be attributed to the personalities involved, but it seems more probable that it was

[51] In reference to a bureau chief who had developed great power, one general is quoted as saying: "He understood . . . that the War Department was . . . something that stood between the Army and Congress; that the way to get legislation for the Army was not to educate Congress and the people to Army methods, but to educate the War Department to congressional methods." Quoted in Morison, *Turmoil and Tradition*, p. 151. This might well be considered a timeless prudential tip.
[52] *Ibid.*, p. 602. The relationship of the President to the military and the entire issue of integrating military plans with national policy during the twentieth century is discussed by William Y. Smith, "The Search for National Security Planning Machinery, 1900–1947" (Ph.D. dissertation, Harvard University, 1960).
[53] *Ibid.*, p. 601.

also the product of a wartime situation.[54] Whatever the cause, the Collins plan sought to perpetuate in peacetime the practices of two wars.[55]

Added to this arrangement of access to the President and the resulting ambiguous position of the secretary was the role which the wartime chiefs of staff played with respect to Congress. As noted earlier, before the War Department reorganization of 1942, the secretary of war stood between the President and the chief of staff. The job of supervising the bureaus (to the extent that the War Department could supervise them) was shared by the chief of staff, the secretary, and the assistant secretary. After 1942, strategic matters moved away from the secretary's office and became the function of the chiefs of staff.[56] Increasingly, the secretary became a "housekeeper" for the department.[57] To some degree this arrangement ratified the existing relationship between the chief of staff and the secretary. In theory, the chief of staff only supervised the General Staff while the secretary actually gave orders. In wartime, the secretary was in fact bypassed, while in peacetime the military functions became "civilian" in nature. The cement of the secretary–chief of staff relationship was the threat to control that the bureaus represented to the War Department. Remove this and there is little reason for the chief of staff to maintain the alliance. Along with this shift, there was a shift in budgetary control. The chiefs of staff presented and explained the wartime budget to Congress.

The provisions of the Collins plan, which vested responsibility for integrating the military budget with the chiefs of staff, merely reflected the practice developed during the war.

The wartime role of the joint chiefs of staff and the evolving position of the secretary probably contain the explanation for the vague treatment given by the Collins plan to the powers and duties of the secretary. In strategic matters, the military has primary responsibility and must deal directly with the President. In civil (housekeeping) matters, the secretary has prime responsibility and must deal directly with the President. Such an arrangement certainly follows the historical development within the War Department, but it fails to take into account the fact that the conditions underlying the trend would be substantially changed by the new organization. The bureaus, the forces which bound

[54] Both David Lloyd George and Winston Churchill acted as their own minister of defense and insisted on dealing directly with their generals.

[55] Hammond, *Organizing for Defense*, p. 225.

[56] Morison, *Turmoil and Tradition*, p. 601.

[57] *Ibid.*, p. 602.

the secretary and the chief of staff together, would be consolidated under the director of common supply and hospitalization, who reported to the chief of staff. What then would be the function of the secretary under the Collins plan? [58] If civilian control depended upon the ability of the secretary to dominate his chief of staff, civilian control would be tenuous indeed.

From the history of the War Department emerges a partial explanation for the dedication to merger, pyramidal structure, and general staff as a solution to the problems of disunity. Just as the War Department had sought to solve the problem of bureau independence through the general staff system, so it proposed the same solution to the problem of service independence. What deviations existed between the Collins plan and contemporary organization theory can be explained in terms of an attempt to solve the riddle of civilian supremacy by adjusting relations between the secretary and the chief of staff. But the deviations between the two were far less than the points of agreement. Both agreed on the essential point that diversity could only be offset by centralization and centralization could only work through the staff system.

As a solution to organizational problems, the hierarchical general staff approach underwent two important tests. The first was its operation in the War Department during World War II. The second, the analysis of organizational behavior in both public and private administration, is still in process. The findings of both must be applied to military organization before final judgment on the hierarchical model can be made.

[58] Some members of the Senate, considering a later version of the Collins plan, expressed fear that the secretary would become the captive of the chief of staff, and that civilian control would be preserved in name only. U.S., Congress, Senate, Committee on Armed Services, *Minority Report, Department of Common Defense*, 79th Cong., 2d Sess., 1946, the S. Rept. 1328 to accompany S. 2044, p. 3.

II

THE WAR DEPARTMENT
IN WORLD WAR II

THE GENERAL STAFF[1]

The National Defense Act of June 4, 1920,[2] established the War Department structure that existed until World War II. One of the important changes made by this act was designed to limit the strength of the bureaus. A consolidated promotion list was provided; it took promotional authority away from the bureau chiefs and insured greater rotation of assignment. The General Staff was organized into five units: G–1 (Personnel), G–2 (Intelligence), G–3 (Mobilization and Training), G–4 (Supply), and War Plans Division.[3]

Legislation could not change the power base of the bureaus or quell the enthusiasm of military innovators, who quickly learned that there were sources of power other than hierarchical position. The struggles of the Air Corps, the Field Artillery, the Infantry, the Coast Artillery, and the Cavalry for appropriations invariably placed them in competition with the General Staff. The pre-World War I problem of power

---

[1] The standard works on the general staff are J. D. Hittle, *The Military Staff: Its History and Development* (rev. ed.; Harrisburg: Stackpole, 1960), and Nelson, *National Security.* A good short summary is by Dallas D. Irvine, "The Origins of Capital Staffs," *Journal of Modern History,* X, No. 2 (June, 1938), 161–79.

[2] U.S. Statutes at Large, XLI, 759.

[3] For details see Nelson, *National Security,* pp. 274–313, Cline, *Washington Command Post,* p. 19. The General Staff was responsible for "recruiting, mobilizing, supplying, equipping, and training the Army for use in national defense." U.S., Statutes at Large, XLI, 759, sec. 5.

bases reasserted itself.[4] Once again the General Staff represented a future condition while the bureaus represented elements of political power in the present. Limited budgets only increased the tendency of the bureaus to institute their own claims for resources rather than follow the prescriptions of programs developed by the War Department.

By 1940, the situation was such that one author was prompted to comment:

> The military establishment had grown into a loose federation of agencies—the General Staff, the Special Staff for services, the Overseas Departments, the Corps Areas, the exempted stations. Nowhere in this federation was there a center of energy and directing authority. Things were held together by custom, habit, standard operating procedure, regulations and a kind of genial conspiracy among the responsible officers. In the stillness of peace the system worked; but in the turmoil of war the system disintegrated in 1917 as it did again in 1941. And it was not a system that could be used to prepare an army effectively for war.[5]

Although in practice the hierarchical positions of the secretary of war, the chief of staff, and the General Staff were able to contribute little or nothing to the power of the War Department against the bureaus, a body of doctrine was developed to perpetuate the myth of hierarchical authority. Between the two wars, this notion was codified into a series of principles of command, not unlike the principles of administration being codified by scholars.

In the system of service schools which flourished between the wars, the notion of command received extensive treatment.[6] It came to mean "in charge of" and it included planning, operations, and communications. "In this context the chain of command is a chain of military ideas expressed in the form of orders." [7] Command involved both strategy (the prescription of objectives) and tactics (specification of maneuvers to accomplish objectives). A commander really "ran" his command. However, it was recognized that a commander needed assistance. This assistance was provided by the staff. Its function was to gather information, offer solutions, recommend concrete lines of action, and oversee the execution of the resulting orders.[8]

[4] Mark S. Watson, *Chief of Staff: Prewar Plans and Preparations* (Washington, D.C.: Department of Army, 1950), p. 37.
[5] Morison, *Turmoil and Tradition*, p. 488.
[6] Cline, *Washington Command Post*, p. 4.
[7] *Ibid.*, p. 5.
[8] *Ibid.*, p. 6.

This view of the staff sees it as a part—an extension of the personality—of the commander. It is from this notion that the fiction of staff supervision arises. As *part* of the commander, the staff cannot usurp his authority to command. All orders, even those involving minute details to lower echelons, are given in the name of the commander. The fiction that the staff officer does not command does not alter the fact that he not only plans and issues orders, but he also directs the details of execution, insofar as the commander permits.[9]

In larger commands where communications are not personal and direct, a chief of staff co-ordinates the work of the staff in behalf of the commander. When a chief of staff is appointed, he becomes an executive agent of the commander.[10]

This doctrine buttresses the notion that the commander, whether he commands a squad or the Army Ground Forces, does so personally. It also provides the underpinning for the notion that the staff officer does not command, whether he is the company S–3 or the army chief of staff. It must be stressed that these notions were in no way peculiar to the Army. Consider the desire of the President's Committee on Administrative Management to make the President a real manager. Consider the fictions that exist with respect to the President's executive office. Consider the functions of a Sherman Adams.[11]

THE REORGANIZATION OF 1942

The War Department entered World War II within this environment and with this doctrinal heritage. The first problem facing the department was a series of command breakdowns.[12] It became apparent that top echelons would need extensive reorganization of the immediate needs of the war effort were to be handled. Not only were delays in execution of orders occurring, but it was impossible to discover the reason for them.[13] The alternatives included strengthening the General Staff or substantially changing its concept of operation. As Chief of Staff George C. Marshall put it:

[9] *Ibid.*, p. 25.
[10] *Ibid.*, p. 6.
[11] Richard E. Neustadt considers the possibility of a presidential chief of staff in *Presidential Power: The Politics of Leadership* (New York: John Wiley and Sons, Inc., 1960) pp. 159ff.
[12] Cline, *Washington Command Post*, pp. 75–78.
[13] *Ibid.*, p. 73.

Careful consideration has been given to the idea of reorganizing the staff. This would virtually eliminate GHQ and provide a small staff, but it would still be an operational staff, and the Chief of Staff and the Deputies would still be troubled by pressure coming towards the top. While they would be freed of much detail, the proposed staff reorganization would not provide a complete solution.[14]

The Chief of Staff pinpointed two serious problems of the hierarchical general staff system. In the first place, the staff was trying to direct operations. It was commanding.[15] The consequence of command is detail. Decisions must be made within the context of specific problems. Thus, when circumstances—war—tipped the balance of power in favor of the General Staff, the channels of command became clogged. "It had become necessary in 1940 and 1941, for the Chief of Staff to employ three deputies, each with itemized duties, responsibilities, and authority, to handle the ever increasing press of business referred for decision to the General Staff." [16] When one considers there were 40 large commands and 350 small ones reporting directly to the chief of staff, it is hardly surprising that the chief of staff needed help.[17]

General Marshall had raised a very pertinent issue, one that the hierarchical approach often overlooks. It may be possible for the commander to administer the details of his command (by means of his

---

[14] *Ibid.*

[15] This contradiction with the principles upon which the general staff is founded is partly explainable by the fiction that no matter what the staff does, it, by definition, does not operate. So, even when it operates, this is called either "supervising" or "coordination." But there is another reason for the situation in 1941. It stems from the "lessons" of World War I. Up until Pearl Harbor, War Department organization and plans alike were prepared for a one-theater war. Developed as early as 1921 and implemented in embryo from 1932, a general headquarters (GHQ) was to direct operations in that one theater. In the event of mobilization, War Plans Division of the General Staff was to be transferred to GHQ as the nucleus of an operating staff. The general staff under the chief of staff would stay in Washington and direct home efforts. GHQ and a commanding general would direct operations in the theater. It was planned that the chief of staff would become the commanding general.

Unfortunately, World War II refused to fit the plan. Attempts to activate GHQ aborted. The general staff thus became the only point at which co-ordination and control could be exercised. This entire episode is some sort of a commentary on the vicissitudes of planning. For a detailed account of these happenings see Frederick S. Haydon, "War Department Reorganization, August, 1941–March, 1942," *Military Affairs*, XVI, Nos. 1 and 3 (Spring, 1952, and Fall, 1952), 1–11, 97–114.

[16] Cline, *Washington Command Post*, p. 94.

[17] *Ibid.;* and Haydon, "War Department Reorganization, August, 1941–March, 1942," p. 103.

staff), but does he really want to? The price of concentration on operational detail, among others, is a lack of time for the broader problems of command. A choice must be made. Either the commander will delegate a large measure of command detail to subordinate commanders, or he must run the risk of allowing long-range planning to go begging because his staff is absorbed with trivia. But how can an orderly delegation take place when there are 390 subordinate commands?

Marshall chose to free the War Department from minutiae and reorganize the entire department so that top levels could deal with the broader aspects of planning. To do this, delegation was not enough. Something had to be done to decrease the number of agencies reporting directly to the chief of staff.

The War Department reorganization of 1942 sought to attack the problem which Marshall pinpointed. Consolidating the many agencies into three major commands, it delegated command functions downward to these commands.[18] All combat components were grouped into the Army Air Forces and the Army Ground Forces. The many bureaus and special staffs were consolidated into the Services of Supply (later called the Army Service Forces). Each of these major components had its own headquarters, staff, and "within the sphere of their respective command responsibilities, the commanding generals . . . made policy as well as carried out programs." [19]

The Army Air Forces "had virtually complete control of the development of its own special weapon, the airplane." [20] It organized its own units, trained its own personnel, and established its own system of supply. The Army Service Forces took responsibility for administrative and technical services, including those of the Signal Corps and the Engineers Corps. It also assumed the planning functions of G–1 and G–4 of the General Staff.

This much of the plan attacked the problem of consolidation and decentralization, but the question of the General Staff and how it was to link the more detailed aspects of command with the broader ones was still to be met. To form the link, the War Plans Division of the General Staff (renamed the Operations Division—OPD) was developed into a central command post. No attempt was made to separate its policy and administrative functions. It came much closer to the ideal

[18] Only the major features of the 1942 reorganization will be considered here. For a detailed account of these changes see Cline, *Washington Command Post, passim;* and Haydon, "War Department Reorganization, August, 1941–March, 1942," pp. 1–11 and 97–114.

[19] Cline, *Washington Command Post*, p. 94.

[20] *Ibid.*, p. 93.

Fig. 3
THE WAR DEPARTMENT IN 1942

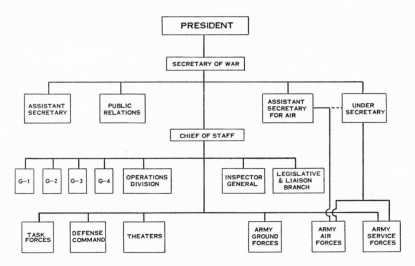

of central control than the General Staff had succeeded in doing. Here is how it worked.

The Operations Division (OPD) would establish requirement objectives in light of requests coming from theaters of operation. This was probably its most important function, for here priorities were set for theater[21] requests in light of the Joint Chiefs of Staff (JCS) and Combined Chiefs of Staff (CCS)[22] decisions as to the relative emphasis to be given the several theaters. The three army commands would then make their own policies in the process of performing the day-to-day task of filling the requirements established in OPD and sent to them.[23]

The flow of information and requirements worked two ways. The OPD relied on the "advice and assistance" of specialists in the three army commands. For example, in the case of the air forces, the procedure was as follows: "1. AF *will give* Expert Advice toward workable directives to Chief of Sections [of OPD] Concerned. 2. WPD [OPD] will issue directives. 3. AF will carry them OUT." [24]

[21] A description of the origin of "theaters" can be found in Legere, "Unification of the Armed Forces," pp. 208–30.

[22] The combined chiefs of staff is discussed in Chapter IV. Additional material can be found in Cline, *Washington Command Post*, pp. 110–11, 116.

[23] *Ibid.*, p. 116.

[24] Taken from memo for the record between OPD and Army Air Forces, 16 March 1942, cited in Cline, *Washington Command Post*, p. 116. A general description of AAF organization can be found in McClendon, *The Question of Autonomy*, pp. 190–94, 214–32.

This linkage, which tied requirements to policies to directives, involved more than the operation of a staff. It actually brought the operators into the policy process. The cross-check of requirements to feasibility was a constant process. The formulation of ends or goals was always done through a careful specification of the means designed to accomplish them. To facilitate the linkage, attempts were made to provide equal representation for the air and ground officers on the OPD. And the procedure applied "regardless of whether the action resulted from decisions reached by the Chief of Staff, the J.C.S., or the C.C.S." [25]

This arrangement gained the acceptance and co-operation of the various components. Although legal or hierarchical authority for direction of air units, for example, in theater operations resided in OPD, in practice this authority was exercised only upon "the data and recommendations from General Arnold's [Air] staff." [26] General satisfaction with this system is attested to by the fact that neither the air staff nor General Arnold ever challenged OPD or General Marshall's pre-eminence or superior legal authority. Indications are that the authority and discretion of the Army Ground Forces and the Service Forces, although less than the Air Force, were considerable. [27]

As the war progressed, theater staffs began to displace the OPD in establishing theater requirements and operational planning, completing the cycle of decentralization. Through its theater sections, OPD merely monitored theater planning. They became concerned only when theater requirements hinged on world-wide strategy being considered in the JCS–CCS system. [28] The only control OPD attempted to exert over theater commanders was to appraise them of what they could expect and inform them of the kinds of decisions they would have to make. [29]

As theater headquarters were able to acquire more experienced staffs later in the war, operational requirements were determined and implemented there at the scene of actual combat. By this time the OPD was relieved of all detail, and it became a monitor of the theaters on the one hand and the three home commands on the other. Decisions were made at the operational level in accordance with the guidelines established at the top. [30]

The sources of influence of the OPD should be carefully noted. In terms of hierarchy, it was the only agency responsible for army-wide

[25] Cline, *Washington Command Post*, p. 116.
[26] *Ibid.*, p. 117.
[27] *Ibid.*
[28] *Ibid.*, pp. 168–69.
[29] *Ibid.*, p. 184.
[30] *Ibid.*, p. 210.

activities. But by purging itself of all operational and support details, it maintained control by dealing only with the broadest policy outlines and by providing a link between goals and the instrumentalities to achieve these goals. Although it ordered and issued directives, it did so based on the requirements coming from the theaters and the feasibility information coming from the three home forces. It was the agency by which the operators were made part of the policy process.

In addition to being the link between combat theaters and service forces, it was the link between the Army and the Navy, the Army and the JCS–CCS system.

> As the strategic planning staff for General Marshall in his capacity as both Chief of Staff of the Army and member of the JCS and the CCS, OPD helped lay down the foundations of strategy and military policy which, once approved by the Chief of Staff or the JCS or the CCS, provided a frame of reference for the guidance of Army activities both in the theaters of operation and in the zone of interior. Having helped to formulate these interservice and international policies, OPD was the only Army agency that could issue Army directives designed to carry out joint and combined decisions.[31]

The above description constitutes a perceptive insight into the nature of authority and the policy process. It points out that authority is more a circular than a hierarchical process and that policy-making is a continuum. To describe the authority flow one must merely intrude into the cycle rather than start at the top. By its knowledge of strategic objectives, OPD could provide the three home services with the demands they must meet. By getting feasibility data from the three services, it could keep strategic objectives within feasibility requirements. By its knowledge of feasibility it could formulate strategic objectives. Having participated in strategic formulation, it could provide guidance to theaters. It could assist the services in supporting theaters by its knowledge of theater requirements and strategic objectives. At this point the cycle started over again. This circular flow of information made the system work. The influence which OPD exercised resulted from its ability to assist this flow rather than from its position in the hierarchy.

One can argue that OPD's ability to assist the flow of information resulted precisely from its position in the hierarchy. Those who raise

[31] *Ibid.*, p. 118.

such an objection must stop to consider one point. If the OPD maintained its same position, but attempted to (1) gather all feasibility data through its own staff and (2) make all decisions necessary to relate requests to resources to strategy objectives—could the system have worked? The General Staff attempted to do this during 1940 and 1941, but the channels became so clogged that the staff had no time to make decisions. The key to the OPD system was in making decisional centers coincide with communications centers.[32]

One can only speculate what might have happened had Marshall made the decision to reorganize and increase the size of the General Staff. The experiences of 1940 and 1941 are suggestive, however. The more decisions the staff seeks to make, the more detail it must absorb. The more detail it absorbs the more decisions it must make. Details begin to force out, by sheer weight of numbers, the major decisions. And what is more, control is lost even over the detail. Note what was referred to earlier as "command breakdown." Decisions were made but no one could discover why they were never carried out.

The most obvious characteristic of the system which Marshall established was that operators were brought into the policy process. Those who were going to have to carry out the decisions were forced to make the decisions—the three services and the theaters. In matters of major strategy this also held true. Since OPD was to be responsible for carrying out army commitments to over-all strategy, OPD was brought into the over-all policy process. Policy, then, was made at all levels. No distinction was made between policy and execution, but a distinction was made in levels or breadth of policy matters. This distinction is more a matter of emphasis than an actual separation. OPD emphasized larger, long-range, army-wide matters. Theaters devoted themselves to the details of applying force in the area of operations. The three services devoted themselves to the details of meeting theater requirements. OPD served as the link to make sure demands and resources

---

[32] What happened to the General Staff can be illustrated by comparing the size of its various divisions during the war.

	Jan 31, 1942*	April 30, 1942	June 30, 1943	Nov 30, 1944
G–1	149	35	41	100
G–3	195	51	46	83
G–4	287	37	54	82
OPD	132	335	483	540
TOTAL	763	495	624	805

* Before reorganization. Numbers include officers, civilians, and enlisted clerks. Ratio of officers to other personnel was approximately 2–3. Based on Nelson, *National Security*, pp. 390–92. Between 1942 and 1944 the Army increased from 1,679,000 to 8,113,000 men.

meshed. The process is in marked contrast to the one envisioned by the notion of command which sees the commander performing all of these activities through a functional staff at the top.

The 1942 reorganization effected these changes within the framework of a hierarchical structure. Through the three years the system was used, it did not operate in accordance with the principles of the hierarchical concept. Nor did the change come at once. In the beginning, while the services and theaters were locating and training adequate staffs of their own, OPD involved itself in much more detail than it did later.

Although the general staff sections were decreased in size, G–1, G–2, G–3, and G–4 still existed. These remnants of the hierarchical concept created some confusion. Although the Army Service Forces absorbed, for example, most of the army-wide functions of G–1 and G–4, as late as 1943, G–1 "was still screening requests for the addition of a single soldier at a particular field installation." [33]

The delegation of planning functions in the area of services and supply to the Army Service Forces dealt the final blow to bureau independence. "General Somervell's headquarters staff had succeeded in supervising, coordinating, and in fact dominating the work of the administrative and technical staffs, the old 'bureaus,' in a way the General Staff had never done." [34] General Somervell proposed the consolidation of this gain over the bureaus by complete abandonment of the general staff concept and the assignment by law of G–1 and G–4 responsibility to the Army Service Forces (ASF). This proposal was rejected as gaining decentralization at the cost of co-ordination! In fact, it should be noted that OPD and ASF had divided G–1 and G–4 functions between them on the basis of the degree of detail involved. OPD had replaced the General Staff and substituted a system of vertical rather than horizontal delegation. The headquarters staffs of the air forces, the ground forces, and the Army Service Forces *were* the War Department staff. The OPD was the agency of staff co-ordination. The system achieved a remarkable linkage between policy and operations. [35]

[33] Cline, *Washington Command Post*, p. 111.

[34] *Ibid.*, p. 271. It must also be remembered that total war conditions completely undermined the Congress-bureau alliance which was the peacetime source of bureau strength.

[35] This, perhaps, is the beginning of what today is called the "two-hat" concept. One person both directs an agency and acts as part of the staff for a higher agency. At any rate, the "two-hat" concept was not the monopoly of the JCS. In the Army Service Forces this concept was carried out among its own major subordinate units. See John D. Millett, "The Organizational Structure of the Army Service Forces," *Administrative Management in the Army Service Forces* (Report No. 90; Chicago: Public Administration Service, 1944), pp. 14–27.

POSTWAR TRENDS IN ARMY ORGANIZATION

Ray S. Cline, the historian of the OPD, begins the final chapter of his work with the words: "It [this chapter] may be more nearly an epitaph, memorializing the gone and soon to be forgotten." [36] He goes on to describe the postwar reorganization of the War Department. His story begins with the Patch Board.[37] In its report, this board concluded that the General Staff should not again become devitalized as it had during the war. It stipulated the following principle as the key to preventing the future breakdown of the General Staff:

> [There should be an] aggressive application of the principle of decentralization . . . no function should be performed at the staff level of the War Department which can be decentralized to the Major Commands or the Services without loss of adequate control of operations by the Staff.[38]

The report went on to say:

> The old theory that a staff must limit itself to broad policy and planning activities has been *proved unsound* in this war. . . . Unless a staff officer is able to assist his commander in getting things done, in addition to coordinating, planning and policy making, he is not serving his full usefulness. In short a staff is a commander's principal means for determining that his orders, instructions, and directives are being carried out as he intended.[39] [Italics added.]

If, by this, the Patch Board meant that the commander must consider his major subordinate commanders as his staff, this was a good description of what happened during the war. But, if the board was referring to OPD and the other parts of the General Staff, the analysis seems somewhat out of touch with reality. The specific organizational recommendations of the board removed any doubt as to which case maintained:

> Pursuant to this concept, the Patch board recommended allocating the "operating" functions of the Army Service Forces, an organization which it did not propose to perpetuate, among the General Staff Divisions, each supervising the work of the administrative and

[36] Cline, *Washington Command Post*, p. 352.
[37] *Ibid.* A committee, under the direction of Lt. General Alexander M. Patch, studied the organizational lessons of World War II and made recommendations for organizational revision.
[38] Quoted in *ibid.*
[39] *Ibid.*, p. 352.

technical services in so far as they fell within their respective spheres of functional responsibility. This arrangement plainly put the weight of responsibility for the execution of orders on the General Staff. It went considerably farther than giving the General Staff directors permission to "operate" if necessity arose. It made them take "operating" responsibility for the work of the "operating" agencies of the Army. [Cline concludes by remarking:] How this procedure could in practice be reconciled with the principle of decentralization was open to question.[40]

Cline notes that the recommendations of the Patch Board were greeted with "surprise and dismay."[41] A new board, headed by Lt. General William H. Simpson, was constituted to make further studies. Although not reaching quite to the extreme position of the Patch Board, Cline notes, it departed from wartime experience in two major respects:

The General Staff directors were made responsible for "operating" duties rather than made free to supervise in as much detail as necessary the execution of such duties by "operating" agencies in conformity with General Staff instructions. This strong emphasis on "operating" achieved the desired result as far as supervision of execution of orders was concerned, but it also made the General Staff directly responsible for the performance of duties that were likely to interfere with the formulation of general plans and policies. It tended to run counter to the injunction to decentralize duties and *it overlooked the extent to which OPD had depended on merely monitoring the activities of Army agencies to pick the critical points for staff action rather than engaging in routine duties.*[42] [Italics added.]

It left open the question of how coordination among the staff divisions would be achieved. The Chief of Staff himself would find it hard to absorb and evaluate the mass of details necessary for such coordination. *He would need a staff.* . . . Prompt and efficient coordination, however, might prove as difficult between five coequal "operating" staff divisions as it had between five coequal "nonoperating" staff divisions in 1941. . . . The Chief of

[40] *Ibid.* One might add there may be some difficulty reconciling this with the principle of unity of command as well.

[41] It should be noted that these recommendations were made shortly after the McNarney plan and shortly before the Collins plan were presented to Congress.

[42] Cline, *Washington Command Post*, p. 356.

Staff, with such help as his deputy could give, still would have to try to bring about this final co-ordination himself.

On this problem the Simpson Board, like the Patch board report, was silent.[43] [Italics added.]

By executive order of May 13, 1946, and War Department Circular 138, the War Department was reorganized along the lines recommended by the Simpson Board. A five division General Staff was created with responsibility to "plan, direct, coordinate, and supervise," as well as "assist the Chief of Staff in getting things done, in addition to coordinating, planning, and policy making on an Army wide level "—all this, but also with responsibility to, "by means of direct contact with the troops, determine that orders, instructions, and directions are being carried out as the Chief of Staff intended!" On the heels of these responsibilities came the prescription: "They will follow the principle of decentralization to the fullest degree." [44]

In addition to the five division General Staff, there was a ten division Special Staff, reporting to the deputy chief of staff on such matters as public relations, military history, and budget. Finally there were five "administrative services" and eight "technical services." [45] The reorganization circular concluded with the observation:

The two functions of staff and command, although vested in a single individual, are separate and distinct in that each involves different responsibilities and duties, and the exercise of one is not to be confused with nor permitted to interfere with the exercise of the other.[46]

Cline concludes his remarks on the War Department postwar reorganization with the following observation:

All of these arrangements, plus the establishment of two or three special offices or committees and the organization of the Army Air Forces on a virtually autonomous basis, gave the reorganized Army

[43] *Ibid.*, p. 357.
[44] *Ibid.*, p. 360. The misunderstanding of the lessons of the war and the reorganization of 1942 must, to some extent, be explained in terms of the vision of those who analyzed them. Although the fact of decentralization was observed and recognized, the methods by which it was accomplished were not. Indeed one student of military organization hailed the wartime experience of the War Department as proof of the fact that the general staff must serve as an alter ego of the commander. This confusion in understanding was equalled only by the confused and downright contradictory recommendations which purported to consolidate these gains. See Nelson, *National Security*, Chapter 11.
[45] *Ibid.*
[46] *Ibid.*

an extraordinarily complex structure at the War Department level. The chart showed twenty-nine individual staffs reporting directly either to the Chief of Staff or his deputy.[47]

The only conclusion that can be drawn from the extraordinary happenings in the War Department during and after the war is that experience made no impact whatsoever on the Army's thinking about reorganization. It is probably as good a commentary on the strength of ideas, in spite of reality, as it is on organization. The lessons to be gained from the success of OPD were either not realized, ignored, or purposely rejected.[48]

It will be recalled that this excursion into the organizational history of the War Department was made in order to cast light on the Collins plan and to seek evidence about the actual operation of the hierarchical general staff concept. Wartime operation of the General Staff seems to indicate that the proponents of the Collins plan must rest their case on devotion to the ideal of hierarchy, rather than on evidence of its workability. The General Staff failed to function during peacetime because of the greater strength of the bureaus, and it failed to function during wartime because it could not accomplish its self-imposed task—to run the Army from the top. The little item of "command failure" appears to be the key weakness of the hierarchical system. Decisions can be made at the top, but decisions are not self-executing. Command, authority, or decision-making, to mean anything, must be effective. It must be able to alter behavior, load ships, train recruits, deploy troops. The early war period demonstrated conclusively that such actions do not happen simply because someone at the top gives an order.

The uncritical acceptance of the hierarchical general staff system by the War Department, the advocates of the Collins plan, and many students of public and private administration, in spite of the wartime experiences of the General Staff, deserves special note. The reason for their endorsement of the system seems to be the conviction that it meant real control for the man at the top. If the advocates of unification proposed the re-institution of a system that they had abandoned during

---

[47] *Ibid.*, p. 361.

[48] In debates over organization during congressional hearings, officers, War Department leaders, and civilian authorities "frequently pointed to the experiences of the armed forces in overseas operations under unity of command as a compelling argument for unification of the *high command* of the armed forces." An example is President Truman's message to Congress of 19 December 1945." Ray S. Cline and Maurice Matloff, "Development of War Department Views on Unification," *Military Affairs*, XIII, No. 2 (Summer, 1949), 67. Many of those who testified spent the war in combat theaters, *supra*, Chapter I, p. 8.

the war, it is probably because administrative analysis was, at that time, far behind administrative experience.

Another factor must also be considered. Tradition has been found to play a major role in both organizational operation and organizational change.[49] There is little doubt that tradition has had a deep influence on War Department thinking. For forty years the Chief of Staff and the General Staff had been the symbols of hope that the chaotic bureau system might someday be overcome. Reverence and devotion to symbols can be quite unrelated to the actual operation which the symbol represents. The association, developed in practice and codified in theory, between the notion of General Staff and the hope of central control, probably played a large role in early unification proposals.

A symbol such as the General Staff is easy to represent and locate on an organizational chart. Its functions can be readily defined, and rules can be formulated to insure its position as an agency of control. This approach to organization can lead to an oversimplification of organizational operation, to an overemphasis on formal control, and to a neglect of actual organizational behavior. The elaboration of formal controls which characterized the general staff system before the war, when measured against the operation of the department, indicates that there is no necessary relation between formal roles and organizational behavior. In fact, the elaboration of controls resulted from the very resistance of the bureaus to central control. In this context, the prewar organizational charts which showed 390 commands reporting to the chief of staff was really a picture of what in practice was a very decentralized structure. Although it may be no more than a common-sense observation that formal structure and organizational behavior may vary sharply, the notion that centralization equates with control does not allow for this.[50] For example, in testifying before Congress in 1937, Louis Brownlow stated: "We believe that the Chief Executive should

[49] Eli Ginzberg and Ewing W. Reilley, *Effecting Change in Large Organizations* (New York: Columbia University Press, 1957), pp. 5, 132; and Pfiffner and Sherwood, *Administrative Organization*, p. 198.

[50] Herbert Kaufman, after studying the U.S. Forest Service made this observation: "The elaboration of formal controls may indicate only that field men in the organization in question are not responsive to central leadership, and that previous attempts by the leadership to influence their behavior have failed, necessitating still more and tighter efforts at direction; thus, the seemingly centralized organization may, from a behavioral standpoint, be more decentralized than one lacking the traditional procedural manifestations of centralization." *The Forest Ranger: A Study in Administrative Behavior* (Baltimore: The Johns Hopkins Press, 1960), p. 231. One should consider the recommendations of the Simpson Board in light of this statement.

be given more authority over the management of the Executive branch in order to make that authority more commensurate with his responsibility." [51] In order for the President to be able to fulfill his responsibilities (for example, control the administration), he had to be given more "authority" over management. The committee sought to provide this by enlarging the establishment in and around the White House (a general staff?), and making the President an "administrative manager."

One critic of the committee's recommendations raises two pertinent questions: (1) Can the President make personal judgments on each administrative issue? (2) If he can, does he want to? Instead of enabling the President to "direct and control administration," should not methods be sought "to relieve him of the necessity for doing so?" [52] This goes to the core proposition of the hierarchical general staff concept—centralization means control.

If the President's committee can be taken as representative of the thinking of administrative analysts, Marshall's decision to decentralize was a rejection of contemporary organizational principles. In its report, the committee stated:

> With the development of central or over-all management of the Government, it is equally important to develop within each department corresponding facilities for administrative management. This requires the development of managerial agencies under the Secretary dealing with such matters as finance, personnel, and planning, and centralized institutional services for legal advice, supplies, records, correspondence, and information.
>
> These managerial and institutional agencies should be under the direction of a single executive officer. . . .[53]

This prescription, to centralize all staff and service activities under one man, rests on a series of assumptions about organizational behavior. And no consideration of the hierarchical general staff system would be complete without considering them. They constitute the subject of the next chapter.

[51] U.S., Congress, Joint Committee on Government Organization, *Hearings, Reorganization of the Executive Departments*, 75th Cong., 1st Sess., 1937, p. 12.

[52] Hyneman, *Bureaucracy*, p. 256.

[53] The President's Committee on Administrative Management, *Report of the Committee* (Washington, D.C.: U.S. Government Printing Office, 1937), p. 39.

III

PREMISES OF THE HIERARCHICAL
GENERAL STAFF CONCEPT
OF ORGANIZATION

As indicated in the two preceding chapters, merger was offered as a means of unifying the armed services because students of both military and civilian organizations viewed organization as a tightly structured pyramid under the direction of a powerful executive. And a hierarchical structure directed by a single administrator with the assistance of a general staff seemed an ideal way of meeting the requirements of this view of organization.

Advocates of the hierarchical general staff system are characterized by their tendency to explain and justify their organizational proposals in terms of the "principles" of organization. But these "principles" are based upon a series of assumptions, often unstated, about organizational goals, executive control, communications and the nature of the policy process.[1] When measured against findings of contemporary studies in organization behavior, many of these assumptions seem to be based on nothing more than popular folklore.[2]

[1] These principles can also be reduced to a set of hypotheses about human behavior. Chris Argyris has made this translation and finds the resulting assumptions about human rationality are "half-truths and incomplete." See *Interpersonal Competence and Organizational Effectiveness* (Homewood, Ill.: The Dorsey Press, Inc., 1962), pp. 28–37.

[2] James W. Fesler provides a lucid description of the several schools of administration in "Administrative Literature and the Second Hoover Commission," *American Political Science Review*, LI, No. 1 (March, 1957), 135–57. William R. Dill describes the "classical" notions about the advantages of the pyramidal form of organization in "Administrative Decision-Making," in Sidney Mailick and Edward H. Van Ness, eds., *Concepts and Issues in Administrative Behavior* (Englewood Cliffs: Prentice-Hall, Inc., 1962), pp. 36–41.

ORGANIZATIONAL GOALS

The hierarchical general staff concept of organization seems to assume that goals can be achieved only by making them the responsibility of some official or office. In fact, this is the very foundation of the general staff system. If personnel activities are to be controlled, then a personnel officer (G–1) must be appointed to control them. If the task is beyond the capability of any one person, responsibility will have to be divided among a number of people, each with responsibility to pursue an appropriate subgoal, all held together and directed by a unilateral chain of authority from top to bottom. This premise fashions organizational attitudes into a set and highly predictable mold. If there is a general staff function, there must be a general staff. This is not limited to staff functions. It applies to operational ones as well. If there is a strategic function, there must be a strategic military command, and so on.[3]

In addition to placing undue emphasis on organization as the only means of achieving social goals, this notion implies other assumptions. One is that, if given the legal authority and sufficient resources, an office can accomplish an objective, regardless of the magnitude or complexity of the task, regardless of counterforces which might thwart the effort. For example, a chief of staff is expected to pull together or co-ordinate the work of the other staff divisions of a general staff. If organization is small enough, and the number of decisions which the chief of staff must make are few, perhaps one man can accomplish this. But in large organizations—for example, the Navy Department—the illusion of continuous co-ordination and close control is frequently mistaken for the reality.[4] The consequence is a congestion of unrelated memoranda, studies, requests, and orders at the top.[5] The bottlenecks, or log-jams, which characterize top levels of large organizations are relatively un-

[3] See, for example, the arguments of the air power enthusiasts, *supra*, Chapter I, p. 4. C. E. Lindblom points out that this notion, "in extreme form ... degenerates into a proposition that most of us would reject at once—that only do-gooders do good." "Bargaining: The Hidden Hand in Government," The RAND Corporation, RM–1434–RC (February 22, 1955), p. 7.

[4] Schuyler C. Wallace, *Federal Departmentalization: A Critique of Theories of Organization* (New York: Columbia University Press, 1941), p. 59.

[5] As one navy secretary lamented to President Theodore Roosevelt: "My duties consist of waiting for the Chief of the Bureau of Navigation to come in with a paper, put it down before me with his finger on a dotted line and say to me 'Sign your name here.'" See also comments by Army Chief of Staff Marshall with respect to the mass of details with which he became involved. Haydon, "War Department Reorganization August, 1941–March, 1942," p. 98. Albion, *The Navy*, p. 7.

known in small ones but are the result of attempting to run large organizations like small ones.

Another premise lying behind the attitude which views organization as the sole or primary means of achieving goals is that decision-making is confined to the formulation of over-all policy. To hold this premise is to consider declarations of policy as obvious, mutually consistent, and readily accepted by all. Once top management decides objectives, the matter of "getting them done" is viewed as a routine process readily deduced from the objectives themselves.[6] The goal is considered given, developed through the "political process" (that is, by Congress, the President, or the department head, but no lower). The job of the staff is to decide "how" the value or goal will be accomplished. The operator merely performs the mechanical task of "doing." [7]

THE POLICY PROCESS

Assumptions as to organizational goals become premises for the policy process. If goals are external to the organization (that is, provided for the organization), then the job of the organization is primarily that of administration. The staff seeks complete "rationality" by selecting those means which come closest to achieving the goal. But few organizational goals are as operational or as obvious as this assumption suggests.

The General Staff still lives in the world of pure staff planning. It is almost socialist in its metaphysics. It is at least utopian. It stakes its chances of success on the notion that if any project is given enough top-level direction, it just won't dare fail. Every program or project must be minutely planned from the beginning. The future holds no uncertainties, or if it does, they must be anticipated and treated as certainties.[8] One of the basic faiths of the hierarchical general staff system is that there are no insoluble problems. Goals are viewed as puzzles for which there is only one right answer. The answer may not be obvious, but there is no doubt that it exists. If only enough analysis,

[6] Simon, *Administrative Behavior*, p. 1; and Argyris, *Interpersonal Competence*, p. 28.

[7] Simon, Smithburg, and Thompson, *Public Administration*, pp. 488–89.

[8] Cf., *supra*, Chapter II, p. 24, the War Department plan for one theater of operations prior to World War II. For further elaboration of bureaucratic methods of dealing with uncertainties refer to Edward C. Banfield, "Ends and Means in Planning," *Concepts and Issues*, Mailick and Van Ness, eds., pp. 70–80.

thought, expertise (the "stuff" from which staffs are made) are brought to bear on the goal, problems will be solved and success achieved.[9]

To offset the tendency of isolating planning from the tasks of doing, staff agencies at the top of the pyramid usually develop some independent channels of communication with operating echelons. This not only provides them with channels of communication which are more direct and unclogged than those available through the steps of the hierarchy, but also gives them better opportunity for control at lower levels.[10] On organizational charts, this is reflected by a General Staff in miniature at all levels of organization, and dotted lines of "co-ordination" indicating the flow of information.

The relationship between General Staff and lower echelon staff agencies is usually called "co-ordination" so as to preserve the integrity of the principle of unity of command. Yet the fact that this is a control relationship does not go completely unnoticed. In fact, it has a name— informal organization. Somehow this is excused as not being a usurpation of operating functions by staff agencies.[11]

Some have referred to the principles upon which the general staff system is based as the "myths of staff work" and the "proverbs of organization." [12] They include the following assumptions: Staffs do the knowing-thinking-planning. Line does the work. Staffs cannot issue orders to line officers. Staffs prescribe methods. Line decides when the act shall be performed. Anything specialized, aside from major operating functions, is staff.[13]

In spite of these principles, there seems to be an inherent conflict

---

[9] Those who might consider this statement an exaggeration with respect to contemporary organization are advised to read Burton Klein, "A Radical Proposal for R and D," *Fortune*, LVII, No. 5 (May, 1958), 112–226.

[10] Simon, Smithburg, and Thompson, *Public Administration*, p. 293; and Blau and Scott, *Formal Organization*, pp. 167–76.

[11] As recently as 1956, Lyndall Urwick set out to prove that staffs exercise no command authority. He did this by showing that staffs only handle details for the commander, "The Manager's Span of Control," *Harvard Business Review*, XXXIV, No. 3 (May–June, 1956), 39–47. See also Paul H. Appleby, "Organizing Around the Head of a Large Federal Department," *Public Administration Review*, VI, No. 3 (Summer, 1946), 205–12. For a brief description of the line-staff conflict see Pfiffner and Sherwood, *Administrative Organization*, pp. 177–80.

[12] Simon, *Administrative Behavior*, pp. 20–44. Alvin Gouldner observes that "we do not make a commercial contract with a theory in which we agree to accept only the consignment of intellectual goods which has been expressly ordered; usually we take also the metaphysical pathos in which the theory comes packaged." "*Metaphysical Pathos and the Theory of Bureaucracy*," p. 498.

[13] Robert C. Sampson, *The Staff Role of Management* (New York: Harper & Bros., 1955), pp. 41–42.

between line and staff activities.[14] In the first place, their functions largely overlap. The only way "doing" can be distinguished from planning is to say that doing never involves discretion. In the second place, the staff must be able to justify its existence. But when it gets involved in "doing," the line challenges this as undermining its authority. To say that a staff does not exercise authority is a difficult proposition to defend.

If the operational officers never accept staff recommendations, staff existence is not justified. When the executive follows staff advice, the legal authority is his, but the judgment is that of the staff.[15] As a matter of fact, this is the very justification of a staff. It is expected to influence the decisions of the executive and the organization. Hence, the staff always exercises authority in the sense of providing judgments for the executives. And when the staff creates counterparts at lower echelons, through which it enforces these judgments, it encroaches upon the authority (legal or otherwise) of lower echelon executives. Since few executives are willing to accept this amicably, the system provides built-in resistance to all new plans, regardless of their merits, for each one is accompanied by a potential threat to the prerogatives of lower echelon executives. This does not bridge the gap between policy and operations; it walls them off from one another. The myth that staffs exercise no authority, thus is necessary and serves a useful purpose. It disguises the contradiction and preserves the principle that each subordinate reports to only one superior.[16]

Even though the general staff system frequently expresses the sincerest affirmations that operations must be decentralized, the forces in the system pull toward centralization. A staff unit, such as a personnel section, is expected to bring its special competence to bear throughout all phases of an organization's activities. Its job is to see that sound personnel premises are used by operators in making decisions. This involves developing sound rules, communicating them, and seeing that they are enforced. This is usually done by issuing a regulation, and it is the job of the personnel office to insure uniform compliance, so far as

[14] Melville Dalton, "Conflict Between Staff and Line Managerial Officers," *American Sociological Review*, XV, No. 3 (June, 1950), 342–51; and Rensis Likert, "A Motivational Approach to a Modified Theory of Organization and Management," ed. Mason Haire, *Modern Organizational Theory: A Symposium of the Foundation for Research on Human Behavior* (New York: John Wiley and Sons, Inc., 1959), pp. 195–96.

[15] Herbert A. Simon, "Staff and Management Controls," *The Annals of the American Academy of Political and Social Science*, CCXCII (March, 1954), 99.

[16] Simon, Smithburg, and Thompson, *Public Administration*, p. 262.

is possible. It is very difficult to distinguish the pursuit of uniformity from the assurance that sound personnel premises are being used. Frequently the two are equated. Sometimes, perhaps, the pursuit of uniformity "may provide the overhead unit with a plausible substitute for a real goal."[17] In either case, uniformity can be achieved only by centralizing responsibility for personnel in a top-level staff unit or by a centralized personnel agency. Uniformity may or may not be important in personnel, but if it is to be had, it must be purchased at the price of centralization.[18] The cost, at a minimum, is reduction of the executive's discretion by the centralized agency or staff. The coin is usually charges of interference and resistance to policy by line officers.

Uniformity in some areas may be cheap at the price, but the price cannot be disguised by saying that the staff never issues orders or usurps line authority. If authority is defined as ability to influence or exact obedience, "it is clear that overhead units do exercise authority; they do control and command." [19] In some cases, as in the postwar reorganization of the War Department, this cost is not even disguised. It is demanded, by insisting that the staffs "operate."

Those who accept centralization as the price of the general staff system do so because they believe the staff, lacking dedication to narrow, departmental, or special interest will always seek to serve the over-all, or, in the case of defense organization, the "national" interest.[20] As a matter of fact, War Department officers who had previously defended the Collins plan, accepted the National Security Act of 1947 because it provided a secretary of defense, who would be above service interest. He would make decisions with an eye to national issues.[21]

Can a person, and especially a staff, be expected to take a "national" view of problems, just because they are located at the top of the pyramid? Aside from the difficulty of determining what is national and what is parochial, this notion assumes that the staff will be loyal to and identify with its executive superior.[22] This overlooks the fact that, as they grow in size, staff units become complex organizations. They specialize and set up a hierarchy within the hierarchy. The Bureau of the Budget, for

[17] *Ibid.*, p. 278.
[18] The converse also appears to be true, that is, centralization encourages the growth of staffs. Herbert Kaufman, "Emerging Conflicts in the Doctrine of Public Administration," *The American Political Science Review*, L, No. 4 (Dec., 1956), 1066–67.
[19] Simon, Smithburg, and Thompson, *Public Administration*, p. 286.
[20] Morris Janowitz, *The Professional Soldier: A Social and Political Portrait* (Glencoe: The Free Press, 1960), pp. 271–72.
[21] Simon, "Staff and Management Controls," p. 100.
[22] See Janowitz, *The Professional Soldier*, p. 293.

example, employs over 500 persons assigned to divisions of estimates, administrative management, legislative reference, fiscal analysis, statistical standards, to the field service, and to a personnel office. These divisions are further divided into branches. The office of assistant secretary of defense, International Security Affairs, employs over 325 persons assigned to four major divisions, which are in turn divided into ten sections and five regional directorates. Personnel of these units are as likely to identify with their units as with the assistant secretary (or director of the budget bureau), let alone the executive for whom they are presumably staff.

If operations divisions are subject to parochial views, what can be expected from staff units? What magic keeps them from developing group values, accepted ways of doing things, a policy of their own? One observer of this phenomenon points out that they do much worse than this. They "develop strong tendencies to harmonize . . . present decisions with past ones, and both present and past decisions with future ones. A body of rationalizing principles develops which reconciles past and present." [23]

This rationalizing tendency and the emphasis upon uniformity noted earlier combine to add an extremely high price tag to the employment of the hierarchical general staff concept. To the extent that staffs become preoccupied with enforcing uniform standards and defending their own integrity, their policy orientation is undermined by emphasis on mere management. [24] As mere management replaces policy orientation, the staff starts to develop an immunity to policy change. Furthermore, mere management can readily become bad management. The very agencies developed and designed in the name of insuring policy control and direction can become obstacles in the path of policy development.

Action by operators in the name of policy tends to disturb the smooth functioning of the bureaucratic machine. In these circumstances, the staff can develop a preference for the sin of omission rather than commission. [25] When this happens a typical reaction of the top executive is to appoint a "co-ordinator" or a special agent to get on-the-spot information. The temptation is to direct operations by special co-ordinators,

[23] Simon, Smithburg, and Thompson, *Public Administration*, p. 543; also see Simon, "Staff and Management Controls," p. 100.

[24] William N. Hogan, "A Dangerous Tendency in Government," *Public Administration Review*, VI, No. 3 (Summer, 1946), 237; Peter M. Blau, *The Dynamics of Bureaucracy, A Study of Interpersonal Relations in Two Government Agencies* (Chicago: University of Chicago Press, 1955), pp. 231–41; and Blau, *Bureaucracy in Modern Society*, p. 86.

[25] Hogan, "A Dangerous Tendency in Government," p. 238.

who short-circuit the entire hierarchy, in the interest of getting "results." The lower operating executive, already constrained by the policies enforced through staff agencies, is now faced with a new threat. He must either resist the special agent or abdicate still further. "Abdication means misplaced responsibility and unsound administration. Resistance means lack of effective cooperation and 'bickering.' " [26]

Although the situation may not always deteriorate to the point just described, the sources of the possibility are to be found in the myths of the hierarchical concept. Regardless of position, line or staff, people who control services and who have access to top authority can hinder, expedite, or harass the policy and decisions of operators.[27]

The very logic and justification for staffs can be used to criticize them. The value of a staff rests on the claim that a small group, close to the executive, without any assigned interest of its own, is more likely to identify with over-all purpose and the responsibilities of the executive than are line departments with their narrower responsibility, bureaucratic purposes, and parochial attitudes.[28] If this is so, the effectiveness of a staff should be inversely proportional to its size and degree of internal specialization. If it is large, it will have its own problem of internal bureaucratic control. If it is overspecialized, it loses its over-all viewpoint. A quick look at any General Staff dissipates any thought that the system meets its own requirements for effectiveness. If, then, staffs are large and specialized, exercise control, and give commands, the real price of a staff is diffusion and confusion of authority and responsibility —a price not frequently found among explanations and defenses of the hierarchical general staff system.

[26] *Ibid.* Using military research and development activities as his example, Burton Klein provides an excellent example of what can happen when the top executive assigns someone from his staff to find out "what's going on below": "When he [the secretary of defense] adds two people to look into a project, each of the armed services has to add about ten people to its top-level ... staffs to gather material to answer questions. And each of the agencies lower down has to add about thirty. Because it is not possible to bring new people in at the bottom of the pyramid as fast as they are added to the top, the bottom gets narrower and narrower relative to the top. People at the bottom—those who are directly in charge of the project— spend more and more of their time answering questions." "A Radical Proposal for R and D," p. 112.

[27] One observer formulated this phenomenon as follows: "Whoever controls the mechanics of administration is in a position to influence its policy and its function.... He who has access to top authority then comes to speak in the name of that authority." Hogan, "A Dangerous Tendency in Government," pp. 235, 237.

[28] Archie J. Knight and Allen F. Herzberg, "A Proposal for the Next Step in Defense Reorganization," *Air University Quarterly Review*, XII, No. 2 (Summer, 1960), 69; and Anthony L. Wermuth, "A General Staff for America in the Sixties," *Military Review*, XXXIX, No. 11 (February, 1960), *passim.*

CONTROL

The hierarchical general staff concept of organization relies heavily upon the principle of subordination. Varying amounts of power are distributed throughout the system, and each subordinate reports to one superior. The superior being higher, presumably has more power; he at least has more legal authority. This tendency to equate hierarchical position with power, as seen earlier, leads to the myth that a junior officer on a high-level staff does not give orders to a superior officer who occupies a lower position in the command hierarchy. He either coordinates, advises, or acts in the name of the chief of staff. In addition to ignoring the real power of staff agencies, this notion tends to view organization as a closed system.[29] But authority is a much more complex phenomenon. Legal authority (the right to demand obedience), cannot be confused with influence or power (the ability to obtain obedience).[30] The chief of staff in the War Department reorganization of 1903 held the highest position in the Army. He was to be obeyed when he acted in the name of the secretary of war. Yet both the highest military authority and the highest civilian authority in the department suffered many defeats at the hands of subordinate bureau commanders.

If the experience of the chief of staff proves anything, it proves that "simply being in an executive hierarchy does not mean that one can direct freely those below him." [31] Since the bureaus could gain control over the chief of staff by their alliances in Congress, the chief of staff had to make his own alliances to fight a recalcitrant subordinate. In 1911, for example, the controversy between Chief of Staff Leonard Wood and Adjutant General F. C. Ainsworth was settled in favor of General Wood only by the direct intervention of the President and members of Con-

[29] As Simon put it: "They seem to assume that organizations are antiseptically clean of influences from outside." Quoted in Pfiffner and Sherwood, *Administration Organization*, p. 334.

[30] Here and throughout the book the term authority is used to mean "legal" authority or "right" to command. The usage roughly corresponds to Max Weber's concept of rational authority and to Harold Lasswell's, Abraham Kaplan's, and Herbert Simon's concepts of influence based on legitimacy. No distinction will be observed between the terms—real authority, power, control, or influence. They will be used interchangeably, and they will approximate Herbert Simon's concept of power. See Max Weber, *Theory of Social and Economic Organization* (Glencoe, Ill.: The Free Press, 1947), pp. 324–91; Harold D. Lasswell and Abraham Kaplan, *Power and Society* (New Haven: Yale University Press, 1950), pp. 83–92; and Herbert A. Simon, "Notes on the Observation and Measurement of Political Power," *Journal of Politics*, XV, No. 4 (Nov., 1953), 500–16.

[31] Simon, Smithburg, and Thompson, *Public Administration*, p. 404.

gress.[32] Control then can operate both ways. If a hierarchical superior wishes to control his subordinates, he must use more weapons than his legal authority.

Not only can subordinates appeal to external power sources to control their superior, but they can manipulate their superior through other devices. As one proceeds toward the top of the hierarchy, a superior has time for only the most cursory review of his subordinates' decisions or his staff's judgments. The variety, complexity, and number of decisions that reach the top conspire to reduce the executive's ability to influence more than a very few aspects of the action of his subordinates. "Tremendous volumes of technical staff work will be reduced to a single recommendation by the time a problem reaches an executive only moderately far up the line." [33]

For these same reasons, most decisions are in fact made at lower echelons. More frequently than not an executive must rely on his confidence in the staff rather than any deep knowledge of the merits of their judgments.[34] The executive then is trapped by the size of his organization. If he tries to develop a staff as large and complex as the organization he is trying to control, he is unable to control the staff. The alternatives offered seem to resolve themselves into one core dilemma of control: either the executive will be unable to control his line subordinates or his staff. In either case he cannot really control.[35]

The implications of this dilemma are far-reaching. The executive is reduced, in general, to endorsing the proposals of either his line officers or his staff officers. In either case he has precious little control beyond indicating general approval. The means to carry out the program will rest in either the hands of the staff or the line. But are the means of any consequence?

[32] Nelson, *National Security*, pp. 151–66; Morison, *Turmoil and Tradition*, pp. 150–70; and Stimson and Bundy, *On Active Service*, p. 522.

[33] Simon, Smithburg, and Thompson, *Public Administration*, p. 533. See also Janowitz, *The Professional Soldier*, p. 431.

[34] It is more realistic to speak of a "line of confidence" from the top to bottom than a "line of command," Simon, Smithburg, and Thompson, *Public Administration*, p. 533.

[35] There are several criticisms of the "classical" concept of authority which are much more extensive than the brief critique offered here. Especially recommended are: Blau, *Bureaucracy in Modern Society*, pp. 34–36, 70–83; Alvin W. Gouldner, *Patterns of Industrial Bureaucracy* (Glencoe, Ill.: The Free Press, 1954), *passim*; Blau, *The Dynamics of Bureaucracy*, pp. 207–28; and Blau and Scott, *Formal Organization*, pp. 183–209.

MEANS AND ENDS AND POLICY-MAKING

To appreciate the significance of means in pursuing organizational goals, reference must be made to the point at which this discussion of the assumptions of the hierarchical model began, namely, are goals obvious, consistent and generally accepted? If an executive can expect to influence only minimally the discretion of his subordinates, line or staff, how can he be sure they understand the goals as he does? Can he safely assume that his goals will be somehow translated into specific actions at lower echelons? [36] The hierarchical concept would seem to answer affirmatively. As noted above, the staff is supposed to translate goals into specific actions; the line is supposed to perform these actions. This attitude puts enormous demands on the staff, for they are expected to come up with a program that will, for example, bring about a maximum of deterrent force for a minimum cost.[37] Yet even when goals are consistent and generally agreed upon, the instruments of policy, the conduct of it, the form it takes and the assignment of credit for it, all matter as much as the policy objectives.[38]

Goals, such as those involved in defense, are frequently non-operational. They do not contain measuring rods for comparing alternative solutions, "but can only be related to specific action through the intervention of subgoals." [39] Now the relation of these subgoals to the broader goals is usually not subject to proof. For example, can a given weapons system accomplish a specified level of air defense? There is no answer to this question. The only answer that can be given is that weapons system X will cost more or less than weapons system Y, or that it is better or poorer than weapons system Y.[40] The task, then, of selecting the subgoals becomes the most significant part of the policy process. Now the subgoals, for example, building and maintaining a given number of super-carriers, is operational and can be judged ob-

[36] See Kaufman, *The Forest Ranger*, p. iv.

[37] For a full discussion of this problem of conflicting goals in defense see Alain Enthoven and Henry Rowen, "Defense Planning and Organization," The RAND Corp., p. 1640 (July, 1959), *passim;* and Charles J. Hitch and Roland N. McKean, *The Economics of Defense in the Nuclear Age* (Cambridge: Harvard University Press, 1960), pp. 158–77.

[38] Neustadt, *Presidential Power*, p. 46.

[39] James G. March and Herbert A. Simon, *Organizations* (New York: John Wiley and Sons, Inc., 1958), p. 156; and Hitch and McKean, *Economics of Defense*, pp. 128–31.

[40] Hitch and McKean, *Economics of Defense*, pp. 105–33.

jectively. But the heart of the problem is which subgoals shall be pursued? [41]

There is another side to this process of establishing subgoals. If, in fact, the subgoals do not satisfy the general goal, until these subgoals are altered, they collectively add up to *the* policy. Now if policy is the product of the subgoals, those who control them, control policy. The question of agreement on policy becomes agreement on subgoals. If, for example, Polaris missiles, B–52's, super-carriers, and Redstone missiles are all weapons which can attack a potential aggressor, they are all means for accomplishing deterrence. But is there general agreement as to which of these should be brought into play, and in what quantities? These are the operational goals and these are the *real* policy problems.[42] Furthermore, factors which might control the choice of these weapons are not all in the hands, or capable of being in the hands, of any executive official. Congressmen, aircraft companies, shipyards, electronics firms, even cities, and a host of others care about which means will be selected.[43]

Since selection of means, or subgoals, takes place at various levels within an organization, policy can hardly be viewed as a process flowing from top to bottom. It flows in at least two directions, if not from the bottom up. And to the extent that groups within the organization make alliances with external power sources, policy control is further diluted. Top management must compete internally and externally for control. The policy process extends well beyond the confines of what can be controlled by an executive from his hierarchical position.

[41] The problem of non-operational goals and the end-means sequence can be demonstrated as follows: The statesman may say our policy is to resist communist aggression. This does not tell the soldier whether South Korea should be evacuated or reinforced. If the Communists should invade South Korea, the soldier has to wait for an order to resist by force. But even this "means" is not operational. What kind of force? Not until force is translated into troops, carrier task forces, or the Strategic Air Command—all possible "means"—is an operational goal reached. So, although resisting an aggressor is an "end," it has little meaning for South Korea until a decision to use force is made. Although force is an "end," it has little meaning until which and how much force is specified.

[42] Morris Janowitz discusses the end-means aspects of policy in terms of contemporary military strategy. He divides strategists into two groups, the "absolutists" who consider the end as given, and the "pragmatists" who insist that ends must be conditioned by military means. This distinction approximates the distinction discussed in the text. However, military strategists do not seem to divide on the organizational issue in the same way they do on strategic issues. See Janowitz, *The Professional Soldier*, pp. 264–77, 350.

[43] Such problems are not confined to national defense. See, for example, David Lilienthal's findings with respect to TVA. *TVA—Democracy on the March* (New York: Harper and Bros., 1953).

COMMUNICATIONS AND POLICY

Since the selection of means plays such a large part in the policy process, those who have knowledge and control of means play one of the most crucial roles in policy-making. They play this role primarily through the process of internal communications. The hierarchical model of organization sees a two-way flow throughout the structure. Authority and orders flow downward, while information flows upward. As noted above, authority is subject to no such law of organizational gravity, and neither is communication.

Where the hierarchy is used as an information network, each step in the communication chain acts as a screening point to decide how much information will flow upward.[44] This happens because subordinates can not pass up the line all the details available to them. In order to reduce communications to tolerable size, a subordinate must synthesize and summarize the facts available to him. Facts, then, are transformed into judgments. If the chain of communications is very long, each link must take the judgments of lower echelons and use them as its facts.

This process of substituting inferences or judgments for facts has been called "uncertainty absorption." [45] And this can be used consciously and unconsciously as a technique of acquiring and exercising power. Preservation of influence upon decisions higher up depends upon communicating as many judgments and as few facts as possible.

This phenomenon has many consequences. Agencies make interpretations of information coming up to them. Once an appraisal of a situation has been made through this process, isolated facts running counter to the appraisal tend to be discounted, regardless of how well substantiated these facts are. One author attributes the success of the Germans in the attack which led to the Battle of the Bulge in 1944 to this process. Intelligence at army level predicted the attack several days in advance. Because this prediction did not square with the estimate of the situation made at higher echelons, higher headquarters reversed this judgment, and, in turn, "reported that the Germans were most probably only strengthening their defensive positions." [46]

Furthermore, through this process, communications moving upward tend to get sugar-coated. A subordinate is much more likely to report

[44] Simon, Smithburg, and Thompson, *Public Administration*, p. 245.
[45] March and Simon, *Organizations*, p. 166.
[46] George Pettee, *The Future of American Secret Intelligence* (Washington, D.C.: Infantry Journal Press, 1946), p. 8.

improvements and successes than failures.[47] Also, the specialized activity that a person is engaged in, along with the particular organizational subgoal he is identified with, help determine the frame of reference he will use in interpreting facts and making judgments. Some distortion is inevitable.

When communications are required to follow the hierarchical channels, the crosswise flow of communications becomes impeded. Communications must proceed upward until a common superior is found. The common superior can either approve and pass on the information without adequate review, or he can edit it with the attendant costs in distortion, accuracy, and time.

As the above comments show, the higher up the pyramid one proceeds, the more difficult rationality becomes. Judgments replace facts; the specific becomes abstract; the definite becomes vague. Improved communications promise to offset some of this, but there is little evidence that it can overcome all. Therefore, just as the top executive has really minimal control over the discretion of his subordinates, he is also a victim of "uncertainty absorption." The individual who occupies the top position in a hierarchical structure is much more isolated, powerless, and dependent than the advocates of the hierarchical model believe.

The single-dimensional view of organization which characterizes the hierarchical general staff approach to solving organizational problems seems, at best, excessively narrow, at worst, dangerous. This danger does not lie simply in the bureaucratic tendencies of the pyramidal structure; it lies in the loss of control at the top.[48]

But simply to note the limitations of the hierarchical model is not to offset them. An attempt must be made to determine if there are any alternatives. To be of value, any alternative must take into account the elements of organizational behavior which the hierarchical model neglects. Most of all it must promise the possibility of central control.

[47] For example, compare the first report of the Secretary of Defense on the progress of unification in 1948 with the report of the Hoover Commission task force six months later.

[48] Morris Janowitz points out the extent to which modern technology has exacerbated the military commander's dillemma of control at all levels in *Sociology and the Military Establishment* (New York: Russell Sage Foundation, 1959), pp. 26–34.

PART II

AN EXPERIMENT IN
DECENTRALIZATION

IV

A DECENTRALIZED
APPROACH TO UNIFICATION

THE NAVY PLAN

On October 22, 1945, Secretary of Navy James Forrestal submitted a unification plan that was in complete contrast to any previous proposals. It certainly bore no resemblance to the various War Department proposals, or the Collins plan.[1] In fact, the Navy plan paid little attention to the "principles" of administration and attacked the concepts of merger and centralization.

Leaving the existing departmental structure intact was an integral part of the Navy plan for unification. A series of committees would not only co-ordinate the activities of the War and Navy departments, but also would integrate military policy and programs to the requirements of national policy, foreign and domestic.

The Navy plan proposed four major committees: a national security council, a national resources planning board, a joint chiefs of staff, and a military munitions board. Each of these committees would consist of representatives of existing executive departments. And their purpose was to integrate and co-ordinate the activities of the executive departments concerned with various aspects of national security.

---

[1] The Collins plan was actually submitted shortly after James Forrestal submitted the Navy plan. However, for purposes of developing the background of the National Security Act of 1947, it is convenient to reverse the chronological order.

The National Security Council

The National Security Council (NSC) would consist of the secretaries of State, War, and Navy, and the chairman of the National Security Resources Board. The President would act as chairman. The purpose of the council was to advise the President on foreign and military policy. It would have a small permanent secretariat to prepare agenda and monitor policy implementation.

The operational concept of the NSC, as well as other committees proposed in the Navy plan, was remarkably simple. Those who had responsibility for implementing national security policy should assist the President in making it. The committee system was used to match responsibility with decision-making authority.

The National Security Resources Board

The National Security Resources Board (NSRB) would consist of the heads of various cabinet departments, such as Treasury, Interior, Agriculture, and so on, concerned with the mobilization of national resources, manpower, and production. A chairman appointed by the President would preside.

Both the NSC and the NSRB would be concerned with the broader aspects of national security policy. Both would consist of the heads of existing departments. And neither would have corporate authority. They would advise the President and integrate the activities of their

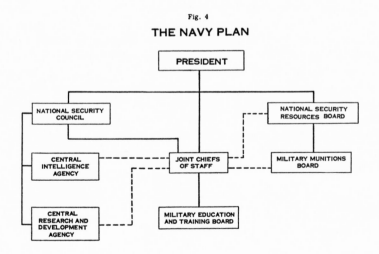

Fig. 4

THE NAVY PLAN

component agencies. The Navy plan proposed a comparable set of committees for the narrower subject of defense policy.

The Joint Chiefs of Staff

The military chiefs of the armed services would constitute the Joint Chiefs of Staff (JCS). And the JCS would prepare strategic and logistic plans as well as provide strategic direction of combat forces. It would advise the NSC on defense policy and co-ordinate its planning with the NSRB.

Military Munitions Board

The Military Munitions Board (MMB) would consist of the under-secretaries of War and Navy, and the chairman of the Maritime Commission. A chairman appointed by the President would preside. It would prepare joint plans and co-ordinate procurement, production, and distribution between the service departments. It would develop its plans on the basis of JCS logistic policy.

CONTROL BY COMMITTEE

The Navy plan sharply contrasted with the Collins plan and other proposals for unification through merger and centralization of the War and Navy departments. First, the plan rejected the concept of co-ordination and control by placing agencies under one administrative head. Second, committees were offered as devices of control. The assumptions which underlie control by committee differ radically from the assumptions which support the notion of control by administrative centralization. And in contrast to the Collins plan, justification for the Navy plan was less in doctrine than in the experience of World War II.

The Navy plan evolved from a study conducted under the direction of Ferdinand Eberstadt, at the request of Secretary of Navy James Forrestal.[2] The only significant difference between the Eberstadt report and the Navy plan was that the latter proposed to continue the two military departments and the former recommended separation of the

[2] U.S., Congress, Senate, Committee on Naval Affairs, *Unification of the War and Navy Departments and Postwar Organization for National Security, Report to Hon. James Forrestal, Secretary of the Navy*, Committee Print, 79th Cong., 1st Sess., 1945, pp. 1–2. Hereafter cited *Eberstadt Report*.

Air Force from the Army and its establishment as a third, coequal department.

The opening paragraph of the Eberstadt report noted an important distinction. It stated that the report dealt with the question of unifying the War and Navy departments—"the great administrative organizations that make plans and preparations for our defense and that train our forces and marshal our resources." [3] It continued by stating that *"unified command* in the *zone* or *theater* of *operations"* was a lesson of both military history and the "late war" to be accepted "without question." [4] [Italics added.] Having made this distinction between combat operations and departmental organization the report went on to spell out the perspective from which it viewed defense problems:

> Military organization involves the position of military power in a free society; it is affected by the nature of modern warfare and the all-embracing demands that it makes. It involves the adjustment of the military profession to the rest of society, and vice versa. Analysis of military organization must, therefore, be concerned with the wide implications of these interrelations.[5]

For the first time, a unification proposal indicated an awareness of the political consequences of military force and its institutional arrangements. The Eberstadt report pointed up an aspect of organizational behavior that eluded the framers of contemporary, and many subsequent, unification proposals. "Even where highly effective organizations are planned and set up in advance, personality and *environment* remain as variable and unpredictable factors which can undo the most carefully conceived administrative plans." [6] [Italics added.]

The report then proceeded to list the assumptions and goals which would govern its proposals:

> (a) That the authority of those in control be firmly and clearly established;
>
> (b) That those responsible for decision and action be fully, promptly, regularly, and conveniently informed on the facts and *influences affecting,* and, in turn, *affected* by their decisions and actions; [Italics added.]
>
> (c) That appropriate means be devised for the prompt and accurate dissemination of decisions and information which are essential to effective group action; and

[3] *Ibid.,* p. 2.
[4] *Ibid.*
[5] *Ibid.,* p. 30.
[6] *Ibid.,* p. 31.

(d) That lines of coordination as well as authority be clearly established and constructively cultivated.[7]

The above stipulations are unusual proposals for defense organization. The particular choice of words in item (b) suggests that authority may involve more than hierarchical position, and it might defy any assumed organizational law of gravity. It might flow up as well as down. Further evidence of this notion is found in item (d), where authority is referred to as something which must be "cultivated." Such views of authority are rather commonplace today, but as factors which must be taken into account in defense organization, they are as novel today as they were in 1945.[8]

Since committees were offered in place of a staff and a chief of staff, for central control, the report included an analysis of effective committee operation. It listed a staff and an executive as equally important committee devices. Between them they should: (1) prepare agenda; (2) supply essential data; (3) press for action on deferred matters; and (4) see that decisions and policies are brought to the attention of all concerned. In recommending various boards, the report repeated, in each case, the importance of having an adequate secretariat. In every instance it recommended a secretariat to record and distribute board decisions.[9]

The emphasis upon the requirement for an executive should be noted. All committees, except the JCS, were to have a chairman with "full power of decision." [10] Furthermore, every committee member was the head of an operating agency. The credentials of membership, then, were operating responsibility and operating knowledge. The credential of the chairman was formal decision-making authority. These boards were doubtlessly intended to avoid conditions that have led many administrators to consider all boards long, narrow, and wooden.

The notions which the Eberstadt report sought to realize in defense organization were: (1) The importance of bringing operators into the policy-making process; (2) use of committees to establish this link between policy and operations; and (3) the importance of an executive and staff to make committees function. Although this analysis of policy-making and policy machinery demonstrated a clearer insight into or-

[7] Ibid.

[8] See, for example, Hammond, Organizing for Defense, p. 206.

[9] The importance of this requirement for the successful operation of any decision-making body is attested to by the fact that the initial order of Mr. Churchill, upon becoming prime minister, was "that all decisions be put in writing." Mr. Dean Acheson who recounts this instance, goes on to say that "to many of us this innovation ranks in importance with the discovery of the wheel." "Thoughts about Thought in High Places," New York Times Magazine, October 11, 1959, p. 86.

[10] Eberstadt Report, pp. 9–10.

ganization than the Collins plan, the report left unanswered (and un-
raised) the problem of the board chairman's ability to resolve conflict
among board members.

In the case of the NSC, disagreement would be no problem. The
President would be chairman. It was also possible that the chairman
of the NSRB could gain influence by his access to the President. But
what of the lower echelon boards, and especially the JCS? Decisions
made by fiat are difficult to enforce as the War Department learned in
its struggle with the bureaus. Board members could outdo the chairman
in knowledge, responsibility, and influence—in a word, power. If the
chairman tried to develop his staff to combat the superior knowledge
of board members, he destroyed the premise upon which the committee
system was based, that is, the contribution which each member was to
make. Unless the chairman had some way of "influencing" board members, it would be as easy for board members to disagree as to agree, to
logroll or compromise as to find common ground.

In the case of the JCS, the plan was even more defective. Assuming
that the NSC provided the kind of policy goals which the plan required,
there was still the matter of translating these policy goals into operational strategic plans and logistic requirements. And who would provide authoritative interpretation in case of disagreement? If every dispute had to be resolved in the NSC, there would be time for little else.
These obvious defects in the plan along with the novelty of the idea of
control by committee, subjected both the Navy plan and the Eberstadt
report to serious criticism.

Unlike the War Department proposals, there was no body of military or administrative theory to lend doctrinal support to the idea of
control by committee. But similar to the War Department proposals,
the Eberstadt report was attempting to analyze and project the organizational lessons of World War II. Although the Collins plan focused on
unified commands in theaters of operations, the Eberstadt report focused on devices of higher control. Every agency proposed by the report
had its counterpart in actual wartime administration.

WARTIME AGENCIES OF HIGHER CONTROL

The National Security Council had its wartime counterpart in the
State-War-Navy Coordinating Committee (SWNCC) created in 1944.[11]

[11] For a description of SWNCC see Smith, "The Search for National Security Planning Machinery, 1900–1947," pp. 363–67.

The National Security Resources Board was a "logical outgrowth of the Office of War Mobilization and Reconversion." [12] The Military Munitions Board had its counterpart in the Joint Army-Navy Munitions Board created in 1922.[13] The Joint Chiefs of Staff, of course, was an exact carry-over of the wartime institution.

State-War-Navy Coordinating Committee

The SWNCC was created as a temporary response to a pressing wartime need. Because the surrender of Germany became imminent much earlier than anticipated and because no plans for surrender, occupation, or long-range plans of any type existed, Secretary of State Edward R. Stettinius, Jr. suggested a committee of those most vitally concerned with these issues. When the committee began operations in December, 1944, it consisted of three assistant secretaries. The board was to assist the secretaries of State, War, and Navy in handling "politico-military matters" and in co-ordinating the views of the "three departments on matters in which all have a common interest, particularly those involving foreign policy and relations with foreign nations." [14] The board was composed of civilians and not the military because H. L. Stimson had objected to the direct consultation between the State Department agencies and the JCS, bypassing the service secretaries.[15] In operation, the SWNCC papers were circulated to the JCS for comment. The major role the SWNCC played in co-ordinating occupation policy both in Europe and Japan indicated the success it had in integrating foreign and military policy.[16]

The SWNCC was a co-ordinating rather than a policy-deciding agency. It thus did not attempt to approve or modify plans, but rather to "mesh" or "integrate" policy proposals developed, staffed, and approved within the three departments. This process was accomplished through negotiation until agreement was reached. Under the press of wartime needs, the process was eminently successful. Wartime success, however, contained no guarantee that a peacetime extension of the SWNCC would function. Therefore, the report recommended that the NSC be chaired by the President. The idea was to have someone force

[12] *Eberstadt Report*, p. 8.
[13] U.S., National Military Establishment, *First Report of the Secretary of Defense, 1948*, I, 92.
[14] Cline, *Washington Command Post*, p. 326.
[15] *Eberstadt Report*, p. 53–54.
[16] *Ibid.*, p. 54; and Cline, *Washington Command Post*, p. 327.

negotiation in the absence of the external pressures provided by the war effort.

In listing the duties of the NSC, the report recommended that it "formulate" as well as "coordinate" policy. If these provisions meant that the NSC was to suggest and staff rather than amend or approve plans developed by the participating agencies, a significant change from the SWNCC was introduced. For in practice the SWNCC would seldom, if ever, initiate policy proposals. Instead, problems originating within a department or in the JCS would be submitted to the SWNCC through its secretariat. These problems usually involved either a departmental action which would effect the acts (or depend upon the acts) of other departments, or a JCS decision which depended upon foreign policy premises. A subcommittee of the SWNCC, consisting of representatives of all three departments, would report to the SWNCC after "ascertaining the views of all the appropriate agencies within their respective Departments." [17] Staff work, then, was done in the departments, not by the SWNCC staff. Negotiation or decision, or both, took place after staffing was accomplished, not during the process. This brought differences of opinion to the top.

The report noted and corrected the weaknesses of the SWNCC, however. Department heads replaced assistant secretaries on the NSC. Thus members could commit their agencies. Negotiation could still go on, but it would be subject to presidential control. Because of the combination of negotiation and presidential control, the NSC would have authority, whereas the SWNCC's decisions were subject to the individual ratification of each department head. And, finally, an adequate staff and secretariat were recommended.

Office of War Mobilization and Reconversion

During the first year of the war there was no agency of central control to supervise the allocation of resources between the civilian and military sectors of the economy. During 1942 and 1943, the War Production Board (WPB) was the central agency of economic mobilization, but it was not the only agency which distributed resources. And not until May, 1943, was the Office of War Mobilization (later called the Office of War Mobilization and Reconversion) created as a device for co-ordinating all agencies of resource distribution.[18] Both the War Production Board

---

[17] *Eberstadt Report*, p. 54.

[18] The background and operation of agencies for economic mobilization is discussed in Smith, "The Search for National Security Planning Machinery, 1900–1947," pp. 339–46.

and the Office of War Mobilization and Reconversion operated on the same principle. They did not attempt to establish a master production and resource plan. Rather, they adjusted specific conflicts between claimant agencies, and, in the process, gradually developed a comprehensive system of allocations.[19]

The National Security Resources Board and the Military Munitions Board proposed by the Eberstadt report represented a postwar extension of the wartime control agencies. The NSRB would be the peacetime counterpart of the Office of War Mobilization and Reconversion to adjust conflicts and co-ordinate the plans of agencies concerned with resources and production. The MMB would be the postwar successor to the War Production Board which had, among other activities, co-ordinated procurement, production, and distribution of resources between the military services.

As in the case of the NSC, both the NSRB and the MMB would continue the tradition of the wartime boards. They would be negotiating rather than operating agencies. A chairman would have power to resolve disagreement and to give authoritative approval to board decisions. And the boards themselves would consist of the responsible heads of those agencies who had operating responsibility. The duty of the boards and their chairmen would be to harmonize operating policy and programs, not to direct operations.

In the case of the Munitions Board, policy premises would have to be provided by the JCS. In matters of logistics, decisions as to who gets what are crucial. And these decisions were to be the responsibility of the JCS. Without JCS guidance the MMB would have no basis upon which to develop its production plans. Its success, then, would depend entirely upon the success of the JCS.

The Joint Chiefs of Staff

The JCS was a direct outgrowth of the British-American strategy conference (ARCADIA) which was held in December, 1941, and January, 1942. Arrangements for this meeting included a provision that the British chiefs of staff for Air, Army, and Navy meet together with their American counterparts as the combined chiefs of staff. Hence, the JCS was a child of circumstance. It came into being with no formal charter, executive order, or even letter. The JCS, which first met on February 9, 1942, consisted of General George C. Marshall, chief of staff Army, Ad-

[19] A description of the role played by the WPB secretariat can be found in Robert L. Hubbell, "Techniques of Making Committees Effective," *Public Administration Review*, VI, No. 4 (Autumn, 1946), 348–53.

miral Ernest J. King, chief of naval operations, and General Harold H. Arnold, chief of staff Army Air Forces. Admiral William D. Leahy, chief of staff to the President, presided, but he did not vote on any measure under consideration. He served as a link between the JCS and the President.[20]

The functions of the JCS developed out of the exigencies of war. Since its decisions were translated into commands to the two services, it had the power of command. A series of joint subcommittees were developed to handle logistics, intelligence, transportation, communications, munitions allocations, meteorology, and civil affairs.

There was precedent for the JCS and its supporting staff system in the Joint Army-Navy Board created by agreement between the secretaries of War and Navy in 1903. The purpose of the board was to secure co-operation and co-ordination in all policies involving joint action by the Army and Navy. It was not a strategic planning agency and had neither corporate character nor decision authority. It was simply a committee of service representatives.[21]

In 1939, the Joint Board was placed under the "direction and supervision" of the President. This change and the approaching hostilities transformed the operation of the board. It undertook many studies and it prepared a number of joint strategic plans which brought together and defined general, and specifically interservice, elements in Army and Navy plans for identical operational situations. By December, 1941, with the establishment of a Joint Intelligence Committee, a real interservice high command was developing. But after its formation in early 1942, the JCS quickly displaced the Joint Board.

Whereas the JCS became the military staff of the President, the Joint Board never took this form until after 1939. It was simply an interservice committee to make recommendations. It never succeeded in reaching decisions on matters where the two departments were in substantial disagreement. Its rulings had only such authority as its members chose to exercise independently in their own agencies. The only exception to this was in those urgent cases where it was possible to get formal presidential approval.

Since its creation, the Joint Board always had a planning staff. After

---

[20] *Ibid.*, p. 107; and Cline, *Washington Command Post*, p. 105.

[21] Descriptions of the Joint Army-Navy Board can be found in Cline, *Washington Command Post*, pp. 44–45; and *Eberstadt Report*, pp. 57–58. Louis Morton provides an analysis of State-War-Navy relations and early operation of the Joint Board in "Army and Marines on the China Station: A Study in Military and Political Rivalry," *Pacific Historical Review*, XXIX (Feb., 1960), 51–73. Also see Smith, "The Search for National Security Planning Machinery, 1900–1947," pp. 260–62.

1939, however, this staff was reduced to only two members who supervised a joint strategic survey committee composed of officers assigned to the Army's and Navy's war plans divisions. Thus the Joint Board sought to use the knowledge of existing service staffs rather than develop its own independent staff system.

It is clear that the JCS and its supporting staffs evolved directly from the system which grew up under the Joint Board after the 1939 reorganization. British influence might have provided the final impetus, but the system was not foreign to the military high command.

The Joint Board system was characterized by the same procedure which later developed in the OPD, the SWNCC, and the War Department reorganization of 1942. Staff work was delegated vertically to major operating divisions. The heads of the agencies which were to have responsibility for the implementation of policy were brought directly into the decision-making process. The committee system was typical of the entire top structure of governmental control during the war. The Eberstadt report is a fair projection of actual wartime organization and operation into a system of both service unification and foreign-military-domestic policy co-ordination and control.

The Joint Board system did not accomplish much (except when the services were in agreement) prior to the stress of impending hostilities. The General Staff was impotent prior to the pressure of the war effort, and it broke down under the pressure of the sudden upward flow of decisions. In contrast, the committee system, although ponderous, operated. But in the case of both the Joint Board and the General Staff, the opportunity for control was less institutional devices than external forces of overwhelming proportions.

The Eberstadt report found much to criticize in the wartime operation of the various committees. It particularly criticized the failure of the system to relate requirements to production in spite of the multiplication of committees under the WPB, particularly the interservice committees which were developed for procurement, purchasing, contracting, and so on.

COMMITTEES AND CONTROL

In spite of the limitations which the Eberstadt report found with respect to the operation of the wartime system, the report indicated that the system, however imprecisely, contained an essential element of control unavailable in the hierarchical system. This element has been overlooked by most analysts of military organization. It can be elucidated by referring back to the changes in the Joint Board system in 1939.

When the President elevated these boards to his Executive Office and had them report directly to him, he made them presidential agencies. In addition to transforming the boards from departmental co-ordinating committees, he altered their very nature. They were no longer simply agents for the military departments; they were made into a part of the war-policy process. And President Roosevelt followed this pattern of policy-making with respect to all wartime agencies of control.[22]

This pattern had enormous consequences for the policy process (civil-military relations) throughout the war. Although, in the words of Henry L. Stimson, "inherently disorderly," this system of splitting organizations right down the middle was the key to presidential control. Both the War and the Navy departments were split by this maneuver because, it will be recalled, the service secretaries did not sit on the Joint Board. Although maintaining responsibility for their departments, Knox and Stimson lost control over their military chiefs. Their loss was the President's gain. One observer described the resulting situation as follows:

> If the service secretaries are indeed the principal agents of civilian control over the military, it would seem that in strategic matters the chiefs . . . were under no civilian control whatever, *apart, of course, from that exercised by the President himself.*[23] [Italics added.]

The net effect was to increase the President's control. As the sole co-ordinator of military, logistics, mobilization, and foreign policy, the President was in a position of control unequaled by the head of any other government. Certainly the price of this control was a great deal of duplication, failure to co-ordinate (those matters in which the President was uninterested), and constant and, at times antagonistic, squabbling caused by overlapping jurisdiction. But whatever the apparent or real chaos, the effect was to increase, and frequently disguise, presidential power.

The beneficial results of this increase of presidential power should not go unnoticed. It assured the President that all major issues would come directly to him for decision. But along with this, it assured the President that the issues would be brought by those who had (or thought

[22] William Emerson, "Franklin Roosevelt as Commander-in-Chief in World War II," *Military Affairs*, XXII, No. 4 (Winter, 1958–59), 183–84; and Smith, "The Search for National Security Planning Machinery, 1900–1947," pp. 303–5.

[23] Emerson, "Franklin Roosevelt as Commander-in-Chief in World War II," p. 183.

they had) the responsibility to implement the decision once it was made.[24] Now this circumstance had important consequences. First, scattered responsibility seldom failed to bring important issues up for consideration. But, just as important, information on these issues was brought from different sources with differing points of view. Second, the issues of "what" should be done and "how" came at the same time from those who thought they ought to "do" it. This arrangement provided the President with alternative means as well as alternative ends. His choice would include selection of both ends and means, enabling the subordinate to have a real understanding of goals in terms of the specific operations planned as well as the ends desired. This took place without a large staff, without prescription of detail, without the services of an intermediary to filter the flow of information.

Most important of all, the process gave the President real power of decision, not just apparent power. To place anyone between himself and these competing sources of information and action, the President would have had to be willing to share his power with him. Whether it be a military chief of staff, a civilian secretary of defense, or the service secretaries, whoever resolved the dispute, or summarized the dispute, before it reached the President would be in fact exercising presidential power. During war it is doubtful that any President would knowingly permit this.

The Eberstadt report discovered this concept of control in the otherwise confusing, disorganized system of committees which operated during the war. Its recommendations sought to preserve the concept while making its operation more orderly. It sought to preserve presidential control without the confusion and lack of co-ordination that accompanied it. But in attempting to preserve presidential control, it overlooked something else.

Whereas in wartime, the President's willingness to devote himself full time to matters of defense is beyond question, would such be the case in peacetime? Some approach had to be made to resolving conflict short of the President. Because this would be a usurpation (or exercise) of presidential power, the solution would have to take this into account, and bring it about in such a way as to be acceptable to the President.

Furthermore, any attempts to make the system more orderly at lower levels would have to be careful not to eliminate aspects of "disorder" which contained the very substance of control, overlapping responsi-

[24] See Janowitz, *The Professional Soldier*, p. 369.

bility. On the other hand, to preserve these sources of presidential control seems to suggest a preservation of forces too strong for anyone short of him to handle. It was on the horns of this dilemma which the Eberstadt report and subsequently the Navy plan became impaled.

Civilian Control

Since the elevation of the Joint Board, and later the position of the JCS, succeeded in isolating the service secretaries, the question of civilian control resolved itself into the relationship between the JCS and the President.[25]

Some students of defense organization have pointed out that the JCS-President relationship upset the chief of staff-secretary alliance which had developed in the War Department and which had at times developed in the Navy Department.[26] The issue of civil-military relations, as they see it, must be solved in terms of this relationship. Accordingly, one of three alternatives is possible: the chief of staff dominates (absence of civilian control), the secretary dominates (rather unlikely), or an alliance is formed which makes the two mutually interdependent. The rise of the JCS and its relation to the President destroyed the possibility of the continuance of such a state of mutual independence. It followed that any solution to the question of unification which included a JCS, no matter how organized, would present an insoluble dilemma: "How to get a departmental organization which . . . [would] not supersede the JCS or, on the other hand, remain in its shadow?" [27]

The Eberstadt report refused to frame the problem of civil-military relations in these terms. If one chooses to consider the problem in terms of a pyramidal organization, leading up to a chief of staff, only then is this formulation necessary. But not only is the JCS-secretary relationship insoluble, the chief of staff-departmental secretary relationship also seems insoluble.

If, on the other hand, one views the issue in terms of its solution under President Roosevelt, other formulations become possible. The President's control resulted from his position above the JCS as the

[25] Much material is available on this relationship. Perhaps the best known works are Millis, Mansfield, and Stein, *Arms and the State*, and Hammond, *Organizing for Defense*, cited previously; and Samuel P. Huntington, *The Soldier and the State* (Cambridge: Harvard University Press, 1957). But no list would be adequate without reference to Emerson's brilliantly perceptive study "Franklin Roosevelt as Commander-in-Chief in World War II," pp. 181–207.

[26] See, for example, Hammond, *Organizing for Defense*, pp. 222–26.

[27] *Ibid.*, p. 222.

agency for decision and co-ordination. Anyone placed between the President and the JCS would share that control. So the formulation becomes, what can be placed between the JCS and the President? It was this question which the Eberstadt report raised, and sought, however inadequately, to answer.

FAILURES OF THE EBERSTADT REPORT

Under the system proposed in the report, service secretaries would sit as equals on the National Security Council (NSC), the service chiefs of staff would sit as equals on the JCS, service representatives would sit as equals on the Military Munitions Board (MMB). The President could be expected to have sufficient power to resolve dispute and end negotiation on the NSC, but where would the chairmen of other boards acquire similar power? If foreign policy goals should be developed at NSC level, who would provide authoritative interpretations in case of disagreement at the JCS level? Since the JCS was to assign logistic responsibilities for the services, and these assignments were to be the premises of the MMB, how could the MMB operate in the absence of JCS agreement? What would happen if the chairman of the MMB should attempt an interpretation of JCS decisions which one or more of the services felt was in error? Would the dispute in this interservice board have to go directly to the NSC or the President for solution?

The decentralization of staff and operational functions envisioned in the Eberstadt report is completely dependent upon solution to these major decisional problems. If, during World War II, it took a combination of direct participation by the President and the overriding goal of victory to make the semi-independent boards operate, what could be expected in peacetime? Reduced military budgets, presidential preoccupation with other matters, and the lack of clear foreign policy objectives (all characteristics of the period between wars) could be expected to make the services warring factions, fighting over their respective claims on the budget, using these boards as their battlefields. The chairman of the MMB, as well as the lofty goals of unification, could be counted upon to be among the first casualties.

V

BRITISH DEFENSE ORGANIZATION:
A MODEL OF
DECENTRALIZATION AND CONTROL

The Joint Chiefs of Staff which replaced the rapidly expanding Joint Board system was formed in response to the need for a counterpart of the British Chiefs of Staff Committee. The Eberstadt report included a brief survey of British military organization and asserted the applicability of some of its concepts of operation to American defense needs. Since the British system operated successfully during peace as well as war, it might offer an answer to the problem of providing central control in the absence of the unifying pressures of war.

THE COMMITTEE OF IMPERIAL DEFENSE

The British origins of the committee system in defense date back to 1902. The British had an experience similar to our own during the Spanish-American War. After the Boer War a committee, organized under the chairmanship of Lord Esher, to study the reorganization of the War Office pointed out there were

"no means for co-ordinating defense problems or for dealing with them as a whole." They suggested that apart from any question of War Office reform, it was essential to set up machinery which could obtain and coordinate "for use of the Cabinet, all information and expert advice required for the shaping of national policy in war, and for determining the necessary preparation for peace."

They added that "such information and advice must necessarily embrace not only the sphere of the War Office but also the sphere of the Admiralty and other offices of State." [1]

The Esher Committee suggested the reconstitution of a cabinet committee established by Lord Salisbury in 1895. This committee was to be advisory and consultative. "As the corner stone of the whole edifice there was to be a small Permanent Secretariat. Mr. Balfour at once adopted this proposal, and the Committee of Imperial Defense was brought into existence by a Treasury Minute dated the 4th of May 1904." [2] From that day, the Committee of Imperial Defense has constituted the main instrument of government preparation for war during peacetime, and supreme control in time of war.

Since the form and membership varied from time to time depending upon the will of the prime minister, a detailed discussion of the Committee of Imperial Defense from its creation in 1904 until its wartime operation under Mr. Chamberlain will be omitted. It is omitted, however, with some misgivings, recalling the comment by Lord Hankey, when asked how the teamwork and loyalty among ministers, military staffs, and civil servants in Britain was accomplished. To this he replied

by telling the old story of the American visitor to Cambridge, who asked the gardener of one of the Colleges how the flawless grass in the court had been achieved, and received the reply: "By mowin' and rollin' and rollin' and mowin' for about three hundred year." [3]

It was by some such process that the British committee system had been evolved—an answer which one might consider discouraging, but which underscores the importance of experience in the structure of government. But the experience which stands between 1904 and 1940, represented a practice in co-operation and teamwork which the British capitalized on during World War II.

In its operation as a peacetime agency, the Committee of Imperial Defense (CID) evolved a standard form. The prime minister served as chairman, and the minister of defense was deputy chairman. The lord president of the council, foreign secretary, chancellor of the exchequer, service ministers, minister of labor and the minister of supply were

[1] Lord Ismay, *The Memoirs of General The Lord Ismay* (London: Hinemann, 1960), p. 45.

[2] Lord Hankey, *Government Control in War* (Cambridge: Cambridge University Press, 1945), p. 23.

[3] *Ibid.*, p. 16.

members. The chiefs of staff and other experts attended as requested. Although granted no corporate executive power, CID members were ministers.[4]

World War I Changes in CID

During World War I, the committee was transformed into the War Cabinet. The nucleus of members was the same. It did not meet daily, but in the words of Mr. Asquith, it was summoned "when serious questions involving new departures in policy or joint strategic operations arose." [5] In the event of special actions such as those in the Dardanelles, a special committee was formed. In some respects the special committee was an improvement on the War Council because it met more frequently and took charge of the day-to-day running of the war as a whole.[6] Under Lloyd George, the War Cabinet was reduced to five: the prime minister, leader of commons, chancellor of exchequer, plus one or two others. The number never exceeded seven. A participant observed that "the system was essentially flexible, and subjects were redistributed to meet changing circumstances. That method is preferable to any rigid distribution of subjects between members. . . ." [7] The War Cabinet became a supreme council of control with the prime minister as dominating and directing force. The system was characterized by decentralization and "delegation, which provided a safeguard against congestion of business." [8]

In 1919, the Committee of Imperial Defense was re-established and it operated through a series of subcommittees, whose actions were supervised by a Co-ordination Committee. These subcommittees developed a complete set of war plans and policy which were integrated by the Co-ordination Committee into a document called the *War Book*.[9]

---

[4] Franklyn A. Johnson, *Defense by Committee: The British Committee of Imperial Defense, 1885–1959* (London: Oxford University Press, 1960), p. 340.

[5] Hankey, *Government Control*, p. 36.

[6] *Ibid.*, p. 38.

[7] *Ibid.*, p. 41.

[8] Lord Hankey felt that this system met his test for control in war: "Efficiency in war or in any Cabinet business depends on reducing every process to the shortest possible time, on synchronization, on accuracy, on secrecy, and other details." *Ibid.*, p. 45.

[9] *Ibid.*, p. 27.

Fig. 5

THE BRITISH WAR CABINET

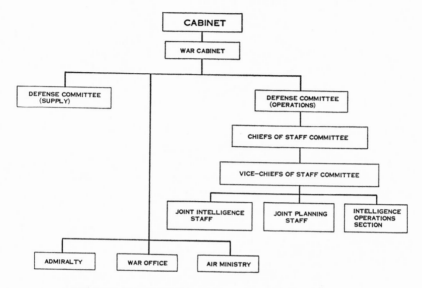

CENTRAL CONTROL IN WORLD WAR II

Again in World War II, the War Cabinet replaced the Committee of the Imperial Defense and the chiefs of staff moved into a key role. Mr. Chamberlain created the Committee of Vice-Chiefs of Staff to take some of the burden from the Chiefs of Staff Committee. Upon assuming the premiership, Mr. Churchill reconstituted the machinery under the War Cabinet. He set up a Defense Committee which operated through two subcommittees, one for operations and one for supply. They replaced the Committee of Imperial Defense's subcommittees for supply and operations. The entire committee machinery was reduced to the minister of defense (chairman of the Defense Committee), the chiefs of staff, and a small military staff. The chiefs of staff, in practice, were the Defense Committee (Operations).[10] Chairmanship was rotated among the three service chiefs. The chief of staff to the defense minister played the key role of bringing an interservice viewpoint. His function of conciliating conflicting views called for the greatest tact and diplomacy.[11]

[10] Johnson, *Defense by Committee*, p. 287. Although this occurred in fact, the minister of production and the ministers of War, Admiralty, and Air still maintained their positions as members of the committee.
[11] *Ibid.*, p. 294.

Defense Committee Operations

The Defense Committee (Operations), was chaired by the prime minister or the deputy to the prime minister, with the three service ministers and later the foreign secretary as members. Other ministers such as war transport or home secretary were in attendance when appropriate. The chiefs of staff always attended.[12]

Chiefs of Staff Committee

The Chiefs of Staff Committee, which was composed of the chief of staff to the minister of defense, the three service chiefs of staff, and the chief of combined operations, was the key to the entire structure. In the words of Mr. Churchill:

> I do not, of course, conduct this war from day to day myself; it is conducted from day to day, and in its future outlook by the Chiefs of Staff Committee. . . . These officers sit together every day, and often twice a day. They give executive directions and orders to the Commanders-in-Chief in the various theatres. They advise me, they advise the Defense and the War Cabinet on large questions of war strategy and war policy.[13]

In 1941, Mr. Churchill presided at only 44 of 462 meetings. Because of its prewar responsibilities for planning, its comprehensive annual review of the military situation as a whole (in light of the international situation as viewed by the Foreign Office), and its standing interservice organization, the Chiefs of Staff Committee gained a competence in interservice and intragovernmental teamwork which made the efficient wartime operation possible.[14]

Vice-Chiefs of Staff Committee

This committee was created to ease the burden of the chiefs of staff who not only had responsibility to advise the government on defense policy as a whole, but also to direct the activities of their own service. The vice-chiefs acted as *alter ego* to the chiefs, and they held meetings at which they dealt, in the name of the chiefs, with matters delegated to them.[15]

[12] Ismay, *Memoirs*, p. 159.
[13] Hankey, *Government Control*, p. 62.
[14] *Ibid.*, p. 57.
[15] Ismay, *Memoirs*, p. 160.

Joint Intelligence Committee

A foreign officer counsellor presided over the Joint Intelligence Committee. The three service directors of intelligence and a representative of the Ministry of Economic Warfare served as members. The committee was aided by a small Joint Intelligence Staff (on which there was a representative from the Foreign Ministry and Economic Warfare Ministry) and Intelligence Operations Section.[16]

Secretariat

The Secretariat was small (about 300 in 1940) and performed the important function of collecting data, under the direction of a minister, on any question to be solved. All solutions were made in the War Cabinet. "The secretariat was performing certain preparatory operations, and was then charged with seeing that all those concerned were informed—and assumed the responsibility of acting upon the decision when taken." [17] The Secretariat performed the function of follow-up and review so crucial to a decentralized operation.

Broad policy considerations were formulated and decided in the War Cabinet, presided over by the prime minister. The Secretariat acted as planning agent and executive supervisor for decisions, once made. The defense activities of planning, intelligence, and operations were handled by the chiefs of staff.

ORGANIZATIONAL CONCEPTS

The resemblances between the British CID-War Cabinet machinery and the proposals of the Eberstadt report are unmistakable. A careful analysis of the concepts and operation of the British mechanism might help elucidate the defects already noted in the Eberstadt-Navy plan.

It was as natural for the British to establish a committee to fill the needs of central control in 1904 as it was for the United States War Department to seek central control through a chief of staff.[18] The solution to the problems of control proposed by the Esher Committee was designed "not [to] run counter to current conceptions of Cabinet

[16] *Ibid.;* and Hankey, *Government Control*, p. 57.
[17] Johnson, *Defense by Committee*, p. 291.
[18] For an authoritative description of how the committee system operates at all levels of government in Britain see K. C. Wheare, *Government By Committee* (Oxford: Clarendon Press, 1955).

Government, and . . . not [to] interfere with the collective and individual responsibilities of Ministers to Parliament." [19] This explains why the CID was created as an advisory body. It could not be allowed to usurp Cabinet responsibility. The CID was not a corporate body, collectively responsible to Parliament. If so, considering the strength of the Cabinet, how could an advisory committee reasonably be expected to exert any influence on policy? The answer to this was in the membership of the committee. The prime minister was made chairman and was the only permanent member. He had absolute discretion in determining who would attend meetings. This arrangement assured the CID of considerable influence. Authority and responsibility rested with and only with, the prime minister.

Although the CID might be able to provide the policy premises upon which the two services could develop their strategic plans, it had little success in developing any machinery for interservice planning. Consequently, early operation of the CID, even during World War I, was characterized by a complete lack of service co-ordination. With the separate establishment of a third service, the Royal Air Force, the need for interservice co-ordination was emphasized. This resulted in the creation of the Joint Staff under the Chiefs of Staff Committee in 1924.

There was no Ministry of Defense. The CID was simply a committee to advise the prime minister with respect to the military and mobilization implications and constraints on foreign policy objectives. Note the contrast to American thought in the means used. The CID might be considered as performing the function of a general staff. It enabled the prime minister to make foreign policy decisions. It provided him with detailed information. But the requirement for general staff work significantly did not result in the creation of a general staff. The heads of the major operating agencies, Foreign Office, Service Ministries, Ministry of Supply, acted as the staff of the prime minister. This responsibility was separated from their individual responsibility to Parliament for the administration of their separate ministries and their collective responsibility as members of the Cabinet. Indeed, non-Cabinet members were frequently called on to attend meetings and render advice.[20] The CID performed the function of a staff by being a committee!

[19] United Kingdom, "Central Organization for Defense" (White Paper, Cmd. 6923), reproduced in H. G. Thursfield, ed., *Brassey's Naval Annual, 1947* (New York: The Macmillan Co., 1946), p. 272. Hereafter cited as *White Paper on Defense, 1946.*
[20] *Ibid.,* p. 272.

During World War II, the CID was transformed into a War Cabinet. The prime minister took the additional title of minister of defense, and the new machinery operated much the same as in the American war effort under the emergency powers granted the President. The major difference was that British co-ordination started at the top and continued on down, whereas President Roosevelt attempted co-ordination of the War Production Board, State Department, and the services, and so on, personally. These agencies were forced to develop such temporary devices as the SWNCC and the service committees under WPB for lower level co-ordination. The British, on the contrary, formalized but did not render inflexible these lesser avenues of co-ordination. At all times, the Defense Committee (Operations) consisted of those the prime minister chose to have attend. And the functioning of the system depended completely upon the willingness of the chief executive to use it.

The temptation is great for those who are keenly aware of the striking differences between the operation of the cabinet system and the presidential system to explain the successful operation of the British CID and the War Cabinet in terms of the phenomena of collective responsibility and fusion of power. To end the explanation there is as superficial as it is inaccurate. Those who have participated in the operation of the system are ready to explain its success otherwise. First, it filled a need. Second, it worked.

The need was the same one which prompted the United States War Department to adopt a General Staff. It was the same need which prompted the War Department reorganization in 1942, the creation of WPB and other emergency agencies during the war—effective control at the top.[21]

But if the system worked, what were the elements of its operation? As has already been noted, committee members were executive heads of ministries. They could commit their agencies. They were the ones who would have to take action once a decision was made. When a number of different executive agencies required concerted action, the British brought the heads of these agencies together in committee. The

[21] F. G. Lee and Roger Stevens, "Coordinating Policy and Operations in Government of the United Kingdom," *Public Administration Review*, VI, No. 4 (Autumn, 1946), 354–61; Ismay, *Memoirs*, p. 45; and Hankey, *Government Control*, pp. 22–24. This need is not restricted to democracies. Ludendorff, commenting on government control in Germany during World War I, stated: "The various departments worked side by side without any real sympathy or cohesion, and there was infinite 'overlapping.' The left hand often did not know what the right was doing. A Bismarck could have made these departments co-operate properly, but the task was beyond our War Chancellors." Quoted in Hankey, *Government Control*, p. 15.

British find two ingredients necessary for the successful conduct of committee business: adequate leadership and decisional authority; and a permanent, adequately manned, committee secretariat.

The functions of the CID–War Cabinet secretariat have already been described, but some of them are worth repeating. Although a data-gathering agency, it does not attempt to formulate a committee position. Members of the committee develop their views, plans, and positions within their own agencies. The Secretariat is a link between agencies, not a replacement for agency staffs.[22] Furthermore, it does act as a follow-up agency for the committee, reporting non-compliance or problems back to the committee.[23] The Secretariat reported to and worked under the minister of defense. But too much stress cannot be placed on the fact that it was not his advisor, military or otherwise.[24]

Each major policy-making committee during the war had the same chairman, the prime minister. This built leadership and decision into the system. But in the United States, although the SWNCC resembled the British Defense Committee (Operations), the crucial element of decisional authority was absent. And various emergency agencies such as WPB, frequently were composed of those who could not commit their agencies. Furthermore, there was no co-ordination of all these agencies short of the President. In Britain, the prime minister could control the entire war effort through three committees. In the United States the President had to deal with dozens.

Of all the American wartime committees, it was the JCS which developed the closest resemblance to the British model. In both Britain and the United States, the chiefs of staff rapidly developed in prestige and importance. In each system, the chiefs of staff became the executive body, issuing orders and supervising theater commanders. Each developed a subcommittee system called the Joint Staff, which was manned by officers from the three services. Yet, in both instances, the Joint Staff did not attempt to handle the details of service planning. It restricted itself to the joint aspects of service planning; thus it was an agency which connected the services horizontally rather than giving staff direction vertically.[25]

A major point of contrast between the two systems was that the British COS had its political premises provided or endorsed by the War Cabinet. In the absence of comparable machinery in the United States,

[22] Hankey, *Government Control*, p. 47.
[23] Johnson, *Defense by Committee*, p. 289.
[24] *White Paper on Defense, 1946*, p. 274.
[25] Michael Howard, "Central Defense Organization in Great Britain, 1959," *The Political Quarterly*, XXXI, No. 1 (Jan.–Mar., 1960), 69.

the JCS had to develop its own political assumptions.[26] This produced the direct relationship between the President, the State Department, and the JCS. The service secretaries never played the role in policy development which their British counterparts enjoyed. Consequently, the JCS was projected into matters of economic, social, and political significance unheard of in the British COS.[27]

The top agencies of control in both Britain and the United States, then, were marked by resort to the "two-hat" concept. Each served the purpose it was designed to accomplish. The British system, however, attained a much higher degree of co-ordination throughout because all war agencies were brought together in the two defense committees. The JCS and the COS (and their supporting staff systems) functioned similarly, although the JCS absorbed by default functions which normally would be considered political and civilian in character. Both depended greatly on the direct participation of the chief executive, both benefited by the unifying forces which a war effort brings, and both, it might be suspected, would have similar problems in converting to peacetime operations. In fact, British conversion to peacetime organization was accompanied by some of the same problems and transitions.

POSTWAR TRENDS IN BRITISH DEFENSE ORGANIZATION

In a white paper on defense, British organization in peacetime was declared deficient because there was an

absence from the machinery of the Committee of Imperial Defense of a guiding hand to formulate a unified defense policy for the three Services. . . . There was no provision within the central organization for a regular examination of Service programmes to ensure that, if war came, we should be ready in all important respects to meet it.[28]

This observation capsulizes a great deal of information about the CID as a system. While the CID could be effectively transformed into an

[26] Huntington, *The Soldier*, p. 323.
[27] Professor Huntington quotes an American officer as remarking that "these non-military problems were handled by other British agencies which furnished guidance to the British military. In some cases the British officers 'didn't even know how some of the subjects handled by our planners were dealt with in the U.K.'" Huntington, *The Soldier*, p. 323. The Eberstadt report recognized this by prescribing the functions of the JCS in such a way that their duties would involve strategy and logistics. The political premises would be provided by the NSC.
[28] *White Paper on Defense, 1946*, p. 275.

instrument of wartime control, and although the CID had provided the services with foreign policy premises, it did not provide any method for allocating resources among the services so that the individual programs added up to a desired defense posture. Although the CID structure facilitated interservice co-ordination and helped develop service-Foreign Office teamwork, it did not bring about central control in peacetime.

The paper went on to say that "during the war a unified defense policy was achieved by the assumption of executive control by the Prime Minister. . . . How was it to be achieved in peacetime?" [29]

One of the alternatives considered and rejected was the development of an over-all general staff. The reason for its rejection was clearly stated:

> It has always been a cardinal principle of the British organization that, alike in the Chiefs of Staff Committee and in the Joint Staffs, it should be the men responsible in the Service Departments for carrying out the approved policy who are brought together in the central machine to formulate it.[30]

The paper went on to note that the general staff system used in the German *Oberkommando der Wehrmacht* failed precisely because this principle was ignored. Staffs were not drawn from the service headquarters.

> The plans they produced had later to be handed to those headquarters for execution, and were often found to be unrealistic. The cleavage between planning and execution set up dangerous antagonisms and entirely nullified any theoretical advantages of the German system.[31]

The solution which the White Paper selected was the appointment of a minister of defense. Although the prime minister was to retain "supreme responsibility for defense," and he would continue to preside over a reconstituted CID (called simply the Defense Committee), the new minister would see to (1) allocating resources among the services; (2) establishing general research and development policy; (3) settling questions of general administration on which a common policy for the services is desirable; and (4) administrating interservice agencies.[32]

The Defense Committee would continue its function of providing or

[29] *Ibid.*
[30] *Ibid.*, p. 276.
[31] *Ibid.*
[32] *Ibid.*, pp. 275–76.

endorsing political premises for the service departments (strategy goals). As with the CID, its membership would be flexible, but among the regular members were: lord president of the council, foreign secretary, chancellor of the exchequer, service ministers, minister of labor, minister of supply, and the chiefs of staff. Preparation of plans would be by the individual departments through a system of subcommittees.[33]

The minister of defense, then, was to provide for the element missing from the earlier CID system, interservice control. He would not stand between the services and the Defense Committee. The White Paper spelled out his responsibility as follows. For allocation of resources and research and development policy he would be responsible to the Cabinet, and would answer questions in the Parliament on these as well as on items common to the three services. The individual service ministers would be responsible to the Cabinet and Parliament for the execution of approved programs and the use of assigned resources.

It is also important to notice what was not included in his responsibility. He was not expected to run the three service ministries.[34]

To accomplish the allocation of resources among the services, the minister of defense was to take the strategic advice of the COS as translated into requirements for men, money, and supplies by the individual service departments. Then, with the assistance of the COS and the service ministers, he would prepare a program for submission to the Cabinet.[35]

A standing committee of the service ministers was to undertake the resolution and standardization of common administrative problems. There would be a ministerial production committee (service ministers, ministers of supply, and labor) to handle the production implications of strategic plans along with a subcommittee (staffed by the ministries) under a chairman appointed by the minister of defense. The minister of defense chaired both the Production and the Service Minister's Committee. A Research and Development Committee consisting of the service R and D chiefs would deal with scientific policy under a chairman appointed by the defense minister. These two appointed chairmen would have no power independent of the minister.

The only interservice organizations to be directly administered by the minister of defense dealt with planning (Combined Operations Headquarters), intelligence (Joint Intelligence Bureau), and staff training (the Imperial Staff College).

[33] Ibid., p. 276.
[34] Ibid., p. 278.
[35] Ibid.

Fig. 6

THE MINISTRY OF DEFENSE, 1963

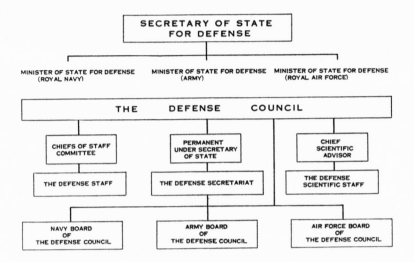

The White Paper defined in some detail the relationship between the minister of defense and the COS. He was in no way to act as a filter for COS strategic advice to the Defense Committee. "It is essential that the Cabinet and Defense Committee should be able to have presented to them directly and personally the advice of the Chiefs of Staff...." [36] But in their corporate capacity, the COS were within the new Ministry, "and the chiefs of staff will meet under the chairmanship of the new Minister whenever he or they may desire." [37] Furthermore, the minister would formulate resource allocations only after such consultation.

Finally, the Ministry itself would consist of the minister, the Secretariat, the chairmen of the R and D and the Joint War Production Boards, and the COS. The Secretariat, as in the past, was to be headed by a chief staff officer, while members would be drawn from both the civil service and the military. The Ministry numbered 300 strong.

Contemporary British Defense Organization

The British Ministry of Defense and its subordinate agencies underwent modification and refinement in 1958 and again in 1963. The most recent changes, announced in July, 1963, were not to be implemented

[36] *Ibid.*, p. 280.
[37] *Ibid.*

until April, 1964.[38] Although a complete analysis of these latest revisions must await their implementation and a period of trial and adjustment, there is an unmistakable trend toward tighter central direction.

In 1957, Prime Minister Harold Macmillan gave his minister of defense "authority to give decisions on all matters of policy affecting the size, shape, organization and disposition of the Armed Forces, their equipment and supply . . . and their pay and conditions of service." [39] The following July, these changes were formally incorporated in a White Paper explicitly setting forth increased authority for the minister of defense.[40] At the same time, the prime minister authorized a chairman for the Chiefs of Staff Committee who was to also act as the chief professional advisor to the minister of defense. The 1958 White Paper changed his title to chief of the defense staff and specified that he was to tender his own advice to the minister along with that of the Chiefs of Staff Committee in the event of disagreement. Together, these changes strengthened the position of the minister of defense, but did not alter the basic character of the committee structure within the Ministry.

In March, 1963, amid one of the most serious and far-reaching debates over the future of British foreign and military policy since World War II,[41] the Macmillan government announced plans to absorb the three service ministries into a reconstituted Ministry of Defense. The defense minister was redesignated secretary of state for defense and the first lord of the admiralty along with the secretaries of state for war and air were abolished in favor of three ministers of state for defense. Furthermore, all statutory authority vested in the service ministries was transferred to the secretary of state for defense.

Although the Chiefs of Staff Committee remained unchanged, the three service staffs were designated the defense staff—to be housed in the same building. The defense staff is responsible to the Chiefs of Staff Committee.

The White Paper replaced the Cabinet Defense Committee by a Committee on Defense and Overseas Policy on which only the secretary of state for defense, not the three ministers of state, would sit by right.

[38] "Central Organization for Defense" (White Paper, Cmd. 2097, 1963).
[39] Quoted in a lecture over BBC by Professor Norman Gibbs, "Drawing The Line on Defense," November, 1960, mimeograph copy.
[40] "Central Organization for Defense" (White Paper, Cmd. 476, 1958).
[41] For a British perspective on the strategic dilemma which followed in the wake of the Nassau Agreement and the breakdown of negotiations over entry into the Common Market, see Anthony Verrier, "Defense and Politics After Nassau," *The Political Quarterly*, XXXIV, No. 3 (July–Sept, 1963), 269–78.

The Chiefs of Staff Committee continued to be collectively responsible to the government for professional advice on strategy and military operations as well as on the military implications of defense policy. However, the chairman was inserted in the chain of command to combat units.

These changes were heralded as introducing one of the most important constitutional revisions in recent years,[42] however, examination of institutional procedures prescribed in the White Paper suggest such a characterization to be rather exaggerated. The ministers of state are still responsible to Parliament for the execution of "policy on behalf of the Secretary of State in respect of a designated Service as Ministers of State for Defense (Royal Navy), (Army), and (Royal Air Force)." [43] Major defense policy is the responsibility of a Defense Council, chaired by the secretary of state for defense. And management of the three services is delegated to three service boards, chaired by the secretary of state or an appropriate minister of state in his behalf. In short, the basic committee structure and operating style of bringing those responsible for policy execution into policy formulating processes has remained untouched.

The organization and operating procedures of the Defense Staff is far from clear in the White Paper, but it appears that the major change involves a new name and a new building.[44] Since the service staffs are not to be combined, their characteristic mode of operation—negotiation and bargaining—is likely to continue, less publicly perhaps.

The 1963 changes created an enormous bureaucracy by British standards and invited the secretary of state for defense to "run" the services instead of being a "rethinking Minister." [45] They created conditions which would permit the chief advisors to the secretary, the chief of defense staff, the chief scientific advisor, and the permanent secretary, to exercise enormous behind-the-scenes power. Whether these top officials will attempt to administer the entire new Ministry remains to be seen.

Final appraisal of these most recent changes, of course, must be suspended until the new Ministry is operative, however, a tentative evaluation suggests a continuation of the trend to seek closer co-ordination and more effective central direction through a more tightly knit committee structure.

[42] *The Times* (London), March 4, 1963.
[43] "Central Organization for Defense" (White Paper, Cmd. 2097, 1963), p. 3.
[44] *Ibid.*, p. 6.
[45] Editorial, *The Economist*, CCVIII, No. 6256 (July 20, 1963), 237.

NEGOTIATION AND POLICY-MAKING

In terms of both administrative description and actual operation, the key to the British defense system lies in the "two-hat" concept. Although armed with formidable powers, the minister of defense lacks anything resembling an executive staff. Furthermore, the services and the COS have the right of appeal from his decisions. How could such an apparently weak officer be expected to control the three services?

The answer is the British approach to defense policy-making. The minister of defense is not expected to *make* or *decide* policy himself, although he possesses the legal authority to do so. He is the chairman of a number of interdepartmental committees. His control is that of any chairman. But he acts on behalf of the prime minister. Much of his influence depends upon the confidence and backing which the prime minister gives him. In his role as agent of the top executive, the minister is not expected to be able to settle all difficulties. In major issues, those on which the individual service ministers feel it necessary to appeal to the prime minister, the prime minister intervenes directly.[46] The next major source of the minister's power comes from his ability to find common ground among conflicting service positions, and patiently build a program out of those points of agreement. His ability to negotiate agreement gives him his greatest power.

There is no ground whatsoever for assuming that the services in Britain are any more "unified" than in the United States. As a matter of fact, interservice rivalry in Britain has had a long and distinguished history. As early as 1909, air power enthusiasts showed as much zeal as the U.S. Army Air Corps was to show during the 1920's. During World War I, the Air Ministry and the Royal Air Force became a reality.[47] Charges, familiar to every American, of COS "logrolling" and "compromise" marked the development of the tri-service system.[48] During the postwar period, military budgets underwent drastic reduction. And no service was modest in asserting its right to a major share.[49]

The response to these circumstances, not the circumstances themselves, marks the difference between the British and the American

[46] Howard, "Central Defense Organization in Great Britain, 1959," p. 68.

[47] Hankey, *Government Control*, p. 54.

[48] Charges even rang out in the midst of the war. See article in London *Times*, April 11, 1942, p. 5, quoted in Johnson, *Defense by Committee*, p. 284. There was also the cry for a single chief of staff to end compromise, "a lowest common denominator between incompatible ideas." *Ibid.*

[49] Sir Leslie Hollis, "Britain's Defense Organization—A Survey," *Brassey's Naval Annual, 1956*, H. G. Thursfield, ed. (New York: The Macmillan Co., 1956) pp. 24–36.

defense environment. In Britain the services were not criticized for failing to take a "national" view of policy and strategy. Instead, their disagreement and rivalry were looked upon as an occasion to scrutinize carefully the relationship of foreign policy to military strategy. Furthermore, many arguments occurred in which the chancellor of the exchequer did not hesitate to present his views on the major questions of military policy.[50] The result was an elaborate ends-means debate about policy, costs, forces, and strategy. From these negotiations emerged a policy understood, accepted, and feasible.

Sir Leslie Hollis, an observer of this process, described the negotiation as a "meshing" of military plans with foreign policy with budgets. Since there was never enough to go around, each service had to be willing to negotiate. But he marked "leadership" by the minister of defense as the "key" to developing a policy acceptable to all.[51]

Lord Hankey, who had served as head of the Secretariat for years had this comment to make about the COS:

> It is sheer nonsense to say that this [the committee system] means delay and passing on responsibility. A good chairman, who must of course be well acquainted with the policy of the War Cabinet, will never tolerate that. He will watch the situation every day, ever on the lookout for a hitch, finding a solution for every difficulty, never allowing matters to stand still.
>
> .   .   .   .
>
> The truth is that the committee system is only pernicious when it is badly run.[52]

Negotiation, not omnipotence, is the hidden secret to committee conduct. The members are expected to wear two hats, not two heads. A service chief who maintains his departmental influence by devotion to departmental causes is not expected to divest himself of his "parochial" views when he serves on the COS. He is there precisely *because* of his service views, not in spite of them. He is not expected to come with a "national" view of defense policy, but rather to "thrash" one out. It is up to the chairman, the minister of defense, to find the points of agreement upon which a national strategy can be pieced together out of the mosaic of service interest and foreign policy requirements. If the process reveals a gap, or a contradiction in foreign policy prem-

[50] Johnson, *Defense by Committee*, p. 258.

[51] During and before the war, the head of the secretariat performed this leadership function in his capacity as chief of staff to the minister of defense. He was a member of the COS but never chairman. In the absence of the minister at COS meetings, it was he who tactfully sought out points of agreement and encouraged negotiation in the case of disagreement. Johnson, *Defense by Committee*, p. 294.

[52] Hankey, *Government Control*, p. 73.

ises, or a question of available resources, the Foreign Office, the chancellor, even the prime minister must be brought in to clarify them. Then as goals are developed in terms of strategic means and budget allocations, agreement can be reached.

This process goes well beyond any notion of mere structure. It involves leadership, influence, negotiating skill, and raw political power. It defies formulation into neat, concise principles, in fact, it violates most of the canons of organizational theory. But it does something more important, it works.

In 1960, Michael Howard, an observer of the system commented:

It is, . . . largely on the tact, efficiency, and self-effacement of the staff of the Ministry of Defense, both civil and military, that the harmonious working of the machine depends. They create an atmosphere and a tradition which enables interservice negotiation to be carried on, not only without bitterness, but with a remarkable measure of friendly co-operation. It is an atmosphere which makes it possible for comparatively junior officers to be entrusted by their Services with considerable discretion in negotiating on sub-committees and which eliminates all but those major differences of principle which can be thrashed out only at Chief of Staff level. The Services, for their part, contribute a tradition of loyalty which makes them unwilling to embarrass even an unpopular Minister. Whatever the internal conflicts may be or have been among those responsible for the Defense of the United Kingdom, all of them, military and civil, politicians and civil servants, present a smooth face to the outside world. That in itself is no mean achievement.[53]

No mean achievement indeed![54]

CID: A MODEL FOR AMERICAN ORGANIZATION?

The extent to which British defense organization influenced U.S. thinking and later organizational development is difficult to determine.

[53] Howard, "Central Defense Organization in Great Britain, 1959," p. 70.
[54] The process of co-ordination by bringing operators into the policy process is by no means confined to the British committee system. The concept underlying this system is described at length by Rensis Likert, "A Motivational Approach to a Modified Theory of Organization and Management" in Haire, *Modern Organizational Theory*, pp. 184–217. He refers to this integration of policy and operations as the "linking-pin function." British organization has been used solely for the purpose of elaborating the concept, its assumptions and its implementation within a specific, empirical, and military context.

There were remarkable similarities between the British reorganization of 1947 and the National Security Act of 1947, but the seeds of the American system were present in wartime defense organization. There can be little question that American leaders deeply admired the British system and were quite aware of its chief structural elements.

Lords Hankey and Ismay, the two directors of the CID Secretariat, who accounted for virtually all the occupancy of that position from its creation through World War II, both shared their knowledge and appreciation for the system with their American associates. As early as the summer of 1943, during a flight from Northern Ireland to Gibraltar, General Ismay explained to General George C. Marshall the workings of the peacetime CID, the War Cabinet, its committees, and its secretariat. This conversation was followed by a personal correspondence between the two, as well as several American officials' conferences with Lord Hankey.[55] In late 1945, and in July, 1946, Secretary of the Navy James Forrestal invited Ismay to Washington. Long talks with the Secretary and other officials convinced them, and especially Forrestal, of the necessity for top-level civilian co-ordination and a full-time secretariat.[56] These provisions, as well as many others, found their way into the Navy plan and eventually into the National Security Act.[57]

Although men such as Ferdinand Eberstadt said the SWNCC was the real prototype for the National Security Council, Ismay and Hankey both indicated that their wartime conversations with various American officials "were the predominant influence in post-war organization of the top planning and common structure of the American Forces." [58]

The Navy plan and the Eberstadt report upon which it was based could be considered a fair translation of the CID and the COS system into American security structure. Since this same observation has been made in reference to American wartime organization, the evidence seems to support either position equally well. In any event the NSC does resemble the Defense Committee (Operations). As with the CID,

[55] Johnson, *Defense by Committee*, p. 318.

[56] As early as 1939, the Navy developed a proposal for the integration of political and military policy remarkably similar to the Eberstadt plan, and Congress considered a proposed Council of National Defense as early as 1911. Smith, "The Search for National Security Planning Machinery, 1900–1947," pp. 11–61, 275–80.

[57] *Ibid.*, p. 319. American notice of the British committee system actually predates the Ismay-Marshall correspondence. In the first decade of the century, Admiral Alfred T. Mahan, the well-known naval strategist, had urged the creation of a body similar to the CID.

[58] *Ibid.*, pp. 319–20.

it incorporates the two-hat concept. Each of its members is head of a major executive department and its chairman is the President. The NSRB might be considered a refinement of the Defense Committee (Supply). And the MMB approaches the policy role of the British Ministry of Supply. The JCS does correspond to the COS committee.

To the extent the Navy plan reflected the British CID system, it also reflected its defects. It lacked an office or agency to insure central control of the services, short of the President.

The experiences upon which American defense architects had to draw for a system of central control range from the War Department reorganization of 1942, through the system of wartime committees, to the British CID. All these experiences had one element in common. They belied the single-dimensional view of authority and policy which characterizes the hierarchial general staff model.

VI

THE NATIONAL SECURITY
ACT OF 1947

The Collins plan and the Navy plan for unification were proposed in October, 1945. During the following year Congress considered, but failed to act on, several bills which sought to incorporate elements of both plans. In February, 1947, a bill was introduced that had the support of the President, Congress, and the military services.[1] And in July, unification became a reality when Congress passed, and the President signed, the National Security Act of 1947.

The National Security Act established three levels or categories of defense organization. The national security machinery consisting of the National Security Council and the National Security Resources Board was placed at the apex.[2] The national military establishment consisting of two levels was below.[3] The first level, headed by the secretary of defense, consisted of four committees: the Joint Chiefs of Staff, the War Council, the Munitions Board, and the Research and Development Board. The second level included the three military

[1] For an account of the negotiation that resulted in the final unification bill see Elias Huzar, *The Purse and the Sword: Control of the Army by Congress through Military Appropriations, 1933–1950* (Ithaca: Cornell University Press, 1950), pp. 297–314; Legere, "Unification of the Armed Forces," pp. 349–61; Stanley, *American Defense*, pp. 76–77; Millis, Mansfield, and Stein, *Arms and the State*, pp. 170–77; and Hammond, *Organizing for Defense*, pp. 220–22.

[2] U.S., Statutes at Large, LXI, 253, Title I.

[3] *Ibid.*, Title II.

departments (Army, Navy, and Air Force), and the unified field commands.[4]

NATIONAL SECURITY MACHINERY

The function of the agencies comprising the national security machinery was to provide integrated policies and procedures for all departments, agencies, and functions of government relating to national security. The act thus provided for both elements of the policy process, ends and means. Policy would be developed in terms of resource capability and resource planning would be related to policy objectives. Two executive committees would conduct this adjustment.

The National Security Council

The National Security Council (NSC) would advise the President on integrating domestic, foreign, and military policies that related to national security. The council was assigned two duties. One was to recommend action on actual and potential United States military power, based on objectives, commitments, and risks. The other was to recommend action on matters of common interest to federal activities concerned with national security.[5]

Its permanent members included the President (chairman), the secretaries of State, Defense, Army, Navy, Air Force, and the chairman of the National Security Resources Board. Its optional members included the secretaries of executive departments, the chairman of the Munitions Board, and the chairman of the Research and Development Board. An executive secretary was provided for but his functions and duties were not specified.

In its concept of operation, the NSC was the issue of a marriage between the British Committee of Imperial Defense and such native American organizations as the SWNCC. Congress viewed the NSC as a means of legalizing and formalizing the instruments of presidential control which had developed randomly during World War II. Further-

---

[4] Drafters of the legislation actually approached the subject with this threefold division in mind. See testimony, U.S., Congress, Senate, Committee on Armed Services, *Hearings, National Defense Establishment, Unification of the Armed Services,* 80th Cong., 1st Sess., 1947, p. 154. Cited hereafter as Senate Committee on Armed Services, *Hearings, 1947.*

[5] U.S., Statutes at Large, LXI, 253, sec. 101.

Fig. 7

NATIONAL DEFENSE ORGANIZATION, 1947

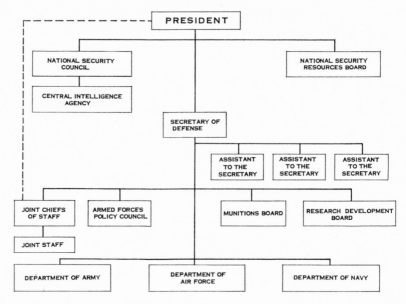

more, political, strategic, and resource factors were represented. Like the agencies of higher control during the recent war, the NSC was composed of operators. Unlike the wartime agencies, however, it was designed as an agency of co-ordination as well as control. It would co-ordinate security policy, not through a staff, but in the British manner of bringing operational executives together in one committee. Decisions would be made and communicated at the same time.

An Agency of Control

The drafters of the act unquestionably conceived of the NSC not simply as an executive device but also as a bridge between Congress and the administration. Indeed, in early drafts, the act authorized the President to appoint, for example, members of the Armed Services Committee to the NSC.[6] This arrangement was implemented by a

---

[6] During House hearings, the following exchange took place between Representative J. Caleb Boggs (R-Del) and Secretary of Navy James Forrestal: "MR. BOGGS: How far can the President go? SECRETARY FORRESTAL: Well, it was designed to make it possible for him to designate, for example, the chairman of the Armed Services Committee of the House, and the comparable committee in the Senate..." U.S.,

provision that the NSC could include, as optional members, "such other members as the President may designate." This provision was deleted from the final draft seemingly because Congress was more concerned with the possibility that the President might designate a person not subject to senatorial confirmation than with the possible impact of this provision on the doctrine of separation of power. As passed, the act restricted optional NSC membership to specified members of the executive branch.

This proposal to include members of Congress on the NSC was significant. If a President chose to include members of Congress on the NSC, the traditional role of congressional committees as critics of administration proposals would be somewhat compromised. But at the same time, presidential independence from Congress would also be compromised. In theory, this arrangement should produce a "unity" between the administration and Congress on national security policy. Criticism would take place within the calm and objective atmosphere of a cabinet room. Members of the administration would not have to make successive trips to the "Hill" to defend policy and programs. The NSC would replace congressional committees as the focal point of interservice rivalry. Although for some, such outcomes seem to justify the limits which this arrangement would place on both presidential and congressional independence and power, there is little possibility that such an arrangement would work, let alone be wanted. In the case of a party split between Congress and the President, the arrangement would fail. Even if one party controlled both branches, neither the President nor the congressional members of the NSC could bring the kind of sanctions to bear on one another, in case of a breached agreement, which are available to the prime minister or a member of Parliament. In the British sense of the term, the NSC could never become a "war cabinet."

However, in the sense that President Roosevelt used the various wartime agencies, the NSC could be a war cabinet.[7] The NSC had all the characteristics which made wartime agencies effective tools of presidential control. Information came directly from an agency with operating responsibility. It was not filtered through a staff. Competing viewpoints were assured by the kinds of agencies represented. Although NSC

Congress, House, Committee on Expenditures in the Executive Departments, *Hearings on the National Security Act of 1947*, 80th Cong., 1st Sess., 1947, p. 11. See also *ibid.*, p. 175.

[7] See Secretary of War Henry L. Stimson's views on the possibilities and need for a war cabinet in this sense, Stimson and Bundy, *On Active Service*, pp. 562–63.

would take primary responsibility for informing the President, it would not be his only source of information. Indeed, competition between NSC and other informal sources of information would help the President develop a broad and realistic appraisal of policy alternatives —a major step in the process of translating NSC policy into national policy.[8]

One must be careful not to view the NSC as a substitute for presidential choice or as a blurring of presidential responsibility. The NSC was not intended to be, nor could it be, a staff agency in the way the proponents of the general staff system view a staff agency. The NSC can not be an extension of the President's personality. It is an instrument to make him aware of the need for decision, and an instrument devised to bring to him alternative solutions as well as problems.[9] In order to exploit this instrument fully, the President might have to pit one member of the NSC against another. But regardless of the President's use of the NSC, he must *use* it and not consider himself "as one man in a group with a collective reputation, conscious of a common problem, trying to resolve it...." [10] The NSC is an instrument of presidential control, not a substitute for it.

Because of the contrasting operation of the British and American political systems, the NSC and the British War Cabinet, as instruments of control, must operate in different ways. However, they both seek to capitalize on similar characteristics. Whereas members of the CID or the War Cabinet were agents of both legislative and executive control, the NSC is composed of executive officials and thereby is only an agency of executive control.

An Agency of Co-ordination

In addition to preserving the elements of presidential control which characterized the operation of wartime agencies, the act sought to promote interagency co-ordination. It did this by providing for automatic registering of "spill-over effects" which might accompany any presidential decision in national security policy. No matter how many channels of control or information the President might choose to use in exercising control and gaining information, the NSC would be

[8] For a comparison of the possibilities of framing national policy within the orbit of a cabinet agency such as the NSC, see an affirmative view by Neustadt, *Presidential Power*, pp. 108–23, and a negative view by Hammond, *Organizing for Defense*, pp. 363–65.

[9] House Committee on Armed Services, *Hearings, 1947*, p. 17.

[10] Neustadt, *Presidential Power*, p. 119.

the one agency where the directors of all national security operating agencies might be allowed to: (1) find out what decisions have been made; (2) bring up unanticipated consequences of past or pending decisions which affect their department; and (3) press for decision where they think decision is necessary.[11]

This process provides a very definite and operational content for the term "co-ordination." The hierarchical general staff concept of organization seeks to eliminate poorly defined allocations of function, unclear delegation of responsibility, and overlapping and duplication of effort. It is possible that these "evils," to some extent at least, are inevitable. When they do exist they can be used as an occasion for co-ordination. If, for example, security policy is viewed as a responsibility shared by both the national military establishment and the State Department, disputes about the proper conduct of security policy are sure to arise. These disputes become the ingredients of control by the President. But even presidential decision does not guarantee equal understanding by either agency of the final resolution of the dispute. An agency such as NSC provides the mechanism where the "principle" upon which decision has been based (so often vague or ambiguous) can be interpreted in terms of specific issues or items of implementation. Co-ordination becomes a process of spelling out respective departmental responsibilities in terms of the contribution which they are to make to policy.[12]

The NSC is based upon the "two-hat" concept. For the means-end adjustment to take place, operators, those concerned with means, must understand how they are expected to act. This can be determined with some clarity if they have an opportunity to express their views about what should be done. The NSC was intended to be the point where policy and administration were linked at the highest level.

The National Security Resources Board

The National Security Resources Board would advise the President regarding the co-ordination of military, industrial, and civilian mobilization. The President would appoint its chairman and the act permitted the President to determine which executive departments would be represented on the board.[13]

[11] See testimony of Admiral Forrest Sherman, House Committee on Expenditures, *Hearings, 1947*, p. 175.
[12] See testimony by Admiral Forrest Sherman, *ibid.*, pp. 165–66.
[13] U.S., Statutes at Large, LXI, 253, sec. 103.

The National Security Resources Board was to provide the machinery through which manpower, resources, and productive potential could be geared to support foreign and military policy. Its peacetime functions would involve providing a continuing review and maintaining an up-to-date blueprint or balance sheet of resources and productive capacity.[14] In wartime it would be the agency through which the commander-in-chief could develop an optimum allocation of resources and production between civilian and military requirements. It would control and allocate critical materials. It would insure the harmony of military plans and material capacity.

Because of the vital nature of its functions, the board was directly responsible to the President. The concept of its operation, as in the case of the NSC, was that persons having the responsibility to implement policy should participate in policy formulation. Their participation would take on added meaning because the chairman of the board had no independent decision-making authority. He was "first among equals." However, so long as he enjoyed the confidence of the President and had ready access to the President, he would have real authority. In this way, the act sought to provide a device of delegation for the President without impinging on presidential prerogative.

There was a great similarity between the United States national security machinery and the British Committee of Imperial Defense system. As indicated in Chapter VI, the Committee of Imperial Defense operated through two major subcommittees, Operations and Supply. The National Security Council and the National Security Resources Board resembled these committees. In each case the concept was the same. The agencies responsible for operations were tied together at the top by committees. Policy-making was centralized; operations were decentralized. Although all agencies participated in policy formulation, decision-making was tied to political responsibility.

The major point of deviation between the Committee of Imperial Defense subcommittees and the Council-Board arrangement was the nature of the presidential system rather than the concept of its operation. Whereas decisions of the British Committee of Imperial Defense in peacetime become, by definition, government policy, such could never be the case in a system of divided power. In peacetime, Council-Board activity must be confined to policy formulation. Once the President endorsed a policy, it, of course, became only administration policy.

In wartime, based on past delegation of power to the President, there

[14] House Committee on Government Expenditures, *Hearings, 1947*, pp. 23, 372.

was every reason to expect that Council-Board policy, if approved by the President, would be government policy.

Another significant deviation from the British model was the lack of a strong executive secretariat to perform the crucial functions of follow-up and policy monitoring. Those who participated in the Committee of Imperial Defense activities invariably singled out the secretariat as the most important agency of the entire structure. The secretary and staff provided by section 101 (c) of the National Security Act fell far short of their British counterparts. The complete absence of any prescription of duties constituted not only a major variance from the British system, but also an error in organizational planning. No provision was made for follow-up on National Security Council decisions. Each department was on its own. This oversight has had a profound impact on the effectiveness of the council's usefulness.[15]

THE NATIONAL MILITARY ESTABLISHMENT, OPERATING LEVEL

The operating level of the establishment consisted of the three military departments of Air, Army, and Navy. The act provided for the separation of the Air Force from the Army. It was left to presidential discretion whether these military departments should be considered cabinet level. The act also provided for the establishment of "unified commands in strategic areas." [16] The Joint Chiefs of Staff were authorized to create these commands, but no stipulations about the chain of command were included.

After the summer of 1946, the matter of service roles and missions became a major issue of unification. Congress opposed various merger plans precisely because the director of the merged forces would assign roles and missions to the services. But the alternative to merging the services, the Navy plan, did not solve the problem either. The Navy plan, by preserving the military departments as separate and independent agencies, would have defeated a major objective of unification, namely, elimination of needless duplication.

[15] The need for these functions was eventually recognized, however, and President Eisenhower attempted to provide for them by formalizing the National Security Planning Board and the Operations Coordinating Board in 1953. For details see Robert Cutler, "The Development of National Security Policy," *Foreign Affairs*, XXXIV, No. 3 (April, 1956), 441–58.

[16] U.S., Statutes at Large, LXI, 253, sec. 211.

The roles and missions issue was not simply a matter of administrative centralization or decentralization. It was a problem of legislative-executive relations. If Congress permitted any executive officer to reallocate or restrict service roles and missions, it would be delegating him some of its own prerogatives. But if Congress did not allow an executive officer to consolidate or reassign service functions, its prerogatives would be preserved, but existing duplication would be perpetuated.

Congress sought to resolve its dilemma in two ways. First, it wrote a preamble to the National Security Act providing for the continued existence of three services (including naval aviation and the Marine Corps—for a total of five services) and their "assigned functions." More specifically, sections 205 through 208 of the act outlined minimum functions for each service. Second, it agreed to the promulgation of an executive order, endorsed by the services, which allocated functions in greater detail. The proposed executive order was discussed at length during the 1947 hearings and a copy of it can be found there.[17]

The various stages of the service functions controversy have no bearing on the topic of this study. What does have a bearing is that any statutory determination of service roles and missions constitutes a direct limit on both the power of the secretary of defense and the power of the President. And this limitation will be considered in greater detail in the subsequent discussion of the secretary of defense.

CONTROL AND POLICY CO-ORDINATION WITHIN THE NATIONAL MILITARY ESTABLISHMENT

The National Security Act continued the process which characterized the wartime agencies of interservice co-ordination and the War Department reorganization of 1942. It delegated staff functions to the services through a series of interservice committees. It followed the proposals of the Eberstadt report with respect to the division of functions among committees, and recommended four committees: the Research and Development Board, Munitions Board, Joint Chiefs of Staff, and War Council.

The Research and Development Board

The Research and Development Board (RDB) was composed of a chairman and two representatives from each military department. Its

---

[17] Senate Committee on Armed Services, *Hearings, 1947*, pp. 3–5.

function was to advise the secretary of defense on scientific research and to assist him in assuring adequate provision for research and development on scientific problems relating to national security.[18]

Board membership consisted of representatives of the three services. Indeed, service membership was the qualification for board membership. To develop sound policy, policy makers must be informed on the subject, aware of the limitations and capabilities of their respective service, familiar with the problems of research and development, and authorized to speak for their service. These are the prerequisites for those who are to make the ends-means adjustment that is the policy process.

The link between policy and operations was direct, not filtered through a staff agency. The operators were making the policy. The act provided that the board would perform its duties under "the direction" of the secretary. This provision gave board decisions legal status as military establishment policy. And board decisions would become policy *in fact* because those who were to implement policy had shared in its determination, thereby developing a commitment to it.

The arrangement created by the board had significant consequences for the services themselves. Instead of trying to reduce them to "doers," the act sought a method for them to be both "planners" and "doers." While this system brought about co-ordination, it also gave each service a commitment to over-all policy in a way not possible in a general staff system. It also provided a built-in emphasis on *program* as opposed to management.[19]

The chairman of the board was the representative of the secretary of defense. His function was to seek a solution to disagreement. He would resolve disagreement, not by fiat, but by carefully searching out points of agreement and building on them. He would supervise the work of the committee secretariat in setting up board agenda, gathering from the service departments factual data necessary to facilitate board action.

On behalf of the board, the chairman, along with the secretariat would perform the important task of policy follow-up. When non-compliance or problems occurred, he would bring these to the board for consideration.

Significantly, the chairman had no authority, other than the prerogatives of a chairman, in his own right. He was the agent of the secretary. This means that in case of serious board disagreement, it is

[18] U.S., Statutes at Large, LXI, 253, sec. 213.
[19] See *supra*, Chapter III, pp. 43–44.

the secretary who must resolve it, not the chairman. And whatever power the chairman exercised would have to come from the secretary.[20]

The board was not intended to be a planning agency. It was to negotiate and decide. It had neither the time nor the facilities to perform the detailed process of plans development. Plans were to be made within the respective services. The job of the board was to integrate, modify, or reject plans.

The RDB made the services participate in the policy process. They negotiated a common policy and the secretary of defense gave it authoritative approval. The services themselves became the agents of the secretary in enforcing the policy within their own agencies.

Finally, provision that the secretary use the board as his tool for handling research and development gave him a means of delegating much of his responsibility. And delegation would free the secretary of a great burden in time and energy. However, his freedom would not be purchased by a loss of control.

The Munitions Board

The same analysis which applied to the Research and Development Board applies to the Munitions Board. Again the concept of the board as a bridge between operations and top management was implemented. The Senate report on the bill clearly indicated the board was intended as a means through which the secretary would exercise his authority. It stated: "In time of peace and in time of war, he [the secretary of defense] would delegate to the chairman of the Board such power of decision, coordination, and control as he considered necessary." [21]

As in the case of the Research and Development Board, this body consisted of a chairman and representatives of the three service departments. In this case, the service representatives were to be the undersecretary or an assistant secretary.

The board was to advise the secretary on matters of military production, procurement, and distribution. It would recommend programs in procurement and allocate procurement responsibility so as to contribute to greater efficiency and economy of operation. Similar to the

---

[20] The framers of the act considered the chairman as an agent for the secretary. See U.S., Congress, Senate, Committee on Armed Services, *National Security Act of 1947*, 80th Cong., 1st Sess., Sen. R. No. 239, to accompany S. 758, 1947, p. 14. Cited hereafter as Senate Committee on Armed Services, *Report, 1947.*

[21] *Ibid.*

Research and Development Board, the duties of the Munitions Board were to be carried out under the direction of the secretary. The board was not a centralized purchasing and contracting agency, but rather a policy-integrating staff. The services were to put its policies into effect.

The Joint Chiefs of Staff

The chief of staff Army, chief of naval operations, chief of staff Air Force, and the chief of staff to the commander-in-chief (if one existed) would constitute the Joint Chiefs of Staff.[22] Its function was to act as principal military advisor to the President and the secretary of defense. It was to prepare strategic plans and to provide for the strategic direction of all military forces. In addition, the JCS would develop joint logistic plans and assign logistic responsibilities to the various services. It would also establish unified commands in strategic areas.

An interesting aspect of the hearings on the National Security Act of 1947 was the treatment received by the JCS. Although earlier in hearings on the Collins plan for merger, the JCS had been criticized as an agency unable to make decisions, such appraisals were absent in 1947. A statement found in the Senate report on the bill sums up the general attitude prevailing throughout the 1947 hearings: "The bill contemplates the continuance of the Joint Chiefs of Staff with duties substantially as at present, and permits functioning in accordance with procedures developed by war experience." [23] This statement must be considered in light of the origin of the JCS. It came into being without the benefit of a charter, mandate of any kind, or stipulation of duties. And in some respects its operation was a mystery. Secretary of War Patterson, in response to a question about the ability of the Joint Chiefs to enforce its decisions said:

... no one knows today the authority of the Joint Chiefs of Staff. No one knows the boundaries of it. That agency, the Joint Chiefs of Staff, has never been set up by Congress, by act of Congress. . . . Right today, I do not think anyone can say what matters belong to the two Secretaries . . . and what matters belong in the domain of the Joint Chiefs of Staff. . . . There are no rules or provisions that I know of for their activity.[24]

[22] U.S., Statutes at Large, LXI, 253, sec. 211.
[23] Senate Committee on Armed Services, *Report, 1947*, p. 13.
[24] House Committee on Expenditures, *Hearings, 1947*, p. 20.

Professor Samuel Huntington, distinguished student of defense organization, has said that the National Security Act of 1947, when it provided for the JCS did not begin with a *tabula rasa* or blank tablet on which to draw an ideal system. The JCS was an existing fact. "Born to power in wartime and antedating all other central defense institutions by six years, the Joint Chiefs experienced great difficulty in adjusting to a purely professional [non-political] role." [25]

These statements reflect the development, traced in Chapter V, by which the JCS moved from questions of strategy to foreign policy. Nothing stood between it and the President. During the 1947 hearings, Secretary of War Patterson was asked what happened when the JCS failed to reach agreement? He answered that "there was no executive short of the President himself with power to stop the prolonged debate and make the required decision." [26] In response to queries as to how this would be avoided under the proposed legislation, witnesses responded that the secretary of defense would resolve disagreement, act as a "catalytic agent" for the Joint Chiefs, and that "he should have authority under the President to do the things that the President could himself do, with his powers now, if he had full time to devote to the task." [27] Crucial to the operation of the national military establishment would be the relationship of the secretary to the JCS. This relationship will be considered in the subsequent discussion of the authority of the secretary.

The 1947 act made a significant change in the status of the JCS. The Joint Staff was to be an independent unit working directly under the JCS.[28] This status differed from wartime practice and contrasted with the British system. Although the Joint Staff was composed of officers from each service, the direct tie between service planning and JCS planning was severed.[29] And if the secretary of defense did not sit with the JCS, all direct contact between the JCS as a corporate group and other parts of the military establishment would be lost.

In the concept of its operation, the JCS embodied the same characteristics as the Research and Development Board and the Munitions Board. It brought the representatives of the services together to integrate policy. In the case of the JCS, the policy—strategy and logistics— was the most important of all. It was also the most explosive and po-

[25] Huntington, *The Soldier*, p. 430.
[26] Senate Committee on Armed Services, *Hearings, 1947*, p. 60.
[27] Testimony of Admiral Forrest Sherman, *ibid.*, p. 170. See also testimony of Secretary Patterson, House Committee on Expenditures, *Hearings, 1947*, p. 348.
[28] Senate Committee on Armed Services, *Report, 1947*, p. 14.
[29] Cline, *Washington Command Post*, p. 361.

litically significant of all defense policy issues. Strategic and logistic planning requires decisions as to what functions will be performed by which services—that is, roles and missions. Furthermore, since questions of roles and missions spill over into every other phase of the top planning process, failure to settle the problem in the JCS would impair the operations of these other agencies.

The nature of the issues to be handled in the JCS meetings explains the absence of a chairman. Only the secretary of defense or the President could deal with disagreements which might arise in the area of strategy and logistics.

The War Council

The War Council included the secretary of defense (chairman), the secretaries of Army, Navy, and Air Force, the chiefs of staff Army, Navy, and Air Force. The act specified that the secretary of defense should have "power of decision" over the council.[30] The function of the council was to advise the secretary on broad armed forces policy matters. The act specified no duties.

The War Council seems to have been an outgrowth of the War Department War Council established by the National Defense Act of 1920.[31] Of all the agencies in the new structure, the War Council received the least (and the vaguest) consideration during the 1947 hearings. This agency probably was to bridge the gap between civilian secretaries and the chiefs of staff which characterized the wartime operation of the War and Navy departments. The exact purpose, need, or nature of this link was left unspecified. Admiral Nimitz said the War Council was simply a tie between the "civilian" and the "military" within the structure.[32] Secretary of War Patterson viewed it similarly.[33] Ferdinand Eberstadt suggested a similar function when he said that through this agency, "the civilian Secretaries can be kept closely in touch with strategic plans and military operations." [34]

The key to understanding the War Council lies in the history of the relationship between the civilian secretaries and the chiefs of staff considered earlier. In order to preclude the possibility that the

[30] U.S., Statutes at Large, LXI, 253, sec. 210.
[31] This consisted of the secretary of war, the undersecretary, and the chief of staff. Senate Committee on Armed Services, *Hearings, 1947*, p. 55.
[32] House Committee on Expenditures, *Hearings, 1947*, p. 349.
[33] See Admiral Nimitz's testimony, Senate Committee on Armed Services, *Hearings, 1947*, p. 55. Similar statements were made by Admiral Forrest Sherman, *ibid.*, p. 201.
[34] *Ibid.*, p. 671.

service secretaries again might be isolated by any direct relationship which might develop between the JCS and the secretary of defense, all of them would be brought together on the War Council.

THE SECRETARY OF DEFENSE

The act specified that the secretary of defense be a civilian, and that he should be the "principal assistant to the President in all matters relating to national security." [35]

His duties were: (1) to establish general policies and programs for the national military establishment; (2) to exercise general direction, authority, and control over the establishment; (3) to eliminate unnecessary duplication or overlap in procurement, supply, transportation, storage, health, and research; and (4) to supervise and co-ordinate budget matters of the component activities, including formulation of budget estimates for the establishment.

This list of responsibilities and powers was followed by a list of *caveats*. The powers of the secretary were not to be construed so as to prevent free access of the service secretaries to the President. The service departments would be administered as individual executive departments by their respective secretaries. The act stated: "All powers and duties relating to such departments not specifically conferred upon the Secretary of Defense by this Act shall be retained by each of their respective Secretaries." [36]

The secretary was authorized to appoint not more than three special civilian assistants, and an unspecified number of military assistants and aides (not to constitute a military staff, however).[37]

The role which the secretary of defense was to play was made remarkably clear in the hearings. Consider the following excerpts from the testimony:

SENATOR TYDINGS. Do you know of any better way that we can unify these services and at the same time protect the three services against what might be called top discrimination from the Secretary of National Defense, than the way we tried it, the way we attempted to do it in this bill?

What are other alternatives, if any? Let us put it that way?

ADMIRAL SHERMAN. This thing has been talked over rather extensively, and I think that the agreement that was finally reached be-

[35] U.S., Statutes at Large, LXI, 253, sec. 202.
[36] *Ibid.*
[37] U.S., Statutes at Large, LXI, 253, sec. 203.

tween the Secretary of the Navy and Mr. Symington, who was acting Secretary of War at that time, was to have a Secretary of National Defense whose powers, to describe him loosely, would be powers of the President, powers now belonging to the President, which would be exercised by this official, under the direction of the President, but with full time in which to do it. And that has been my concept throughout; that this Secretary of National Defense was, in effect, a deputy to the President who, under the direction of the President, and with these safeguards would carry on the work which the President does not have time to do adequately under peacetime conditions.

SENATOR TYDINGS. Was it assumed that if you did not have this top man over the three Departments, so to speak, the unification would not be complete?

ADMIRAL SHERMAN. Well, we felt that we would not have anyone who could terminate disagreements, who could, when a controversy over a particular question developed, bring about the end of the controversy.

And when three Departments are concerned, we have to have someone who will resolve differences so that they will not drag on and build.[38]

.   .   .   .

SECRETARY FORRESTAL. The Secretary of National Defense has very wide and very sweeping authority. . . .

.   .   .   .

The bill is drafted to remain within the framework of our institutions and our traditions. The Secretary of National Defense has power to set policies and make decisions. It is my expectation that the organization will be administered along the lines of expert top management by the Secretary of National Defense, who will exercise overall direction but will not go down into the departments themselves and deal with their functions, daily operations and administration—and my support for the bill is based on that expectation.[39]

When some witnesses suggested that the provision of a *single* secretary of defense constituted the most "feasible" step by which "there may be eventually realized" an organization to meet our needs, and when others expressed fear that the act might be the first step in a process of centralization, the implications of this were immediately noticed

[38] Senate Committee on Armed Services, *Hearings, 1947*, p. 212.
[39] House Committee on Government Expenditures, *Hearings, 1947*, p. 100.

and rejected.[40] The secretary was not to "run" the three service departments.

The secretary of defense was to be a broad or general policy maker, not an administrative manager. Free from the details of routine operations, he would be a deputy to the President in formulating and declaring top policy. Furthermore, he would arbitrate conflicting departmental positions with real authority to make decisions in the name of the President and with the promise of presidential backing. Although the act clearly intended the secretary to share presidential power, only the President could make this possible. Legislation could not force this. The authority which the secretary was intended to exercise was presidential authority, and, as it happens, presidential authority of the most absolute nature. In short, the secretary's authority was *political*, not administrative.

The restricting clause that all powers and duties not conferred upon the secretary were retained by the respective service secretaries has to be understood in two contexts. The first context involved executive-congressional relations. What was denied to the secretary was denied to the President as well. Congress was referring to its own prerogatives over service roles and missions.[41] This issue was brought up and directly considered during the testimony of Mr. Ferdinand Eberstadt. In fact, he suggested the inclusion of the "reserve powers" clause. In considering how the act could be worded to prevent the secretary from interpreting his powers as permission to change or merge the services, or abolish their functions, Eberstadt suggested that "the administrative autonomy of the departments can best be preserved if the bill provides that all powers not conferred upon the new secretary are reserved to, and remain with the several departments." [42] Congress was putting the secretary on notice that it did not intend to abdicate its right to pass on service roles and missions.

The other context, which will be considered in the next chapter, refers to the role which the secretary was to play. He was not to "run" the individual service departments.[43]

[40] See testimony by General Dwight D. Eisenhower, House Committee on Expenditures, *Hearings, 1947*, pp. 272–73; and by General A. A. Vandergrift, *ibid.*, p. 240.
[41] See dialogue between Admiral G. F. Brogan and Representative J. F. Wilson (D-Tex) in House Committte on Expenditures, *Hearings, 1947*, pp. 692–93; the statement of Representative J. W. Wadsworth (R-N.Y.) in *ibid.*, pp. 248–49; the dialogue between Admiral W. F. Halsey and Senator Leverett Saltonstall (R-Mass) in Senate Committee on Armed Services, *Hearings, 1947*, pp. 584–85.
[42] Senate Committee on Armed Services, *Hearings, 1947*, p. 673.
[43] Senate Committee on Armed Services, *Report, 1947*, pp. 5, 11.

The Matter of Legal Authority

Witnesses, although clear about the role of the secretary, found difficulty in describing the legal authority which he should have. For example, in testifying for the bill, Secretary Patterson suggested that the phrase "general authority," be clarified by a description of the service secretaries' role:

> I might say that I agree with the statement by Secretary Forrestal that the direction referred to here, the direction of the Secretary of National Defense, is general direction, and not detailed direction. I think that this is clearly shown by the structure of the sentence which says, "shall be administered as individual units by the respective secretaries, under the direction of the Secretary of National Defense." [44]

The difficulty evidenced here by Secretary Patterson is typical of the problem encountered by most witnesses, the Congress, and even the original drafters of the bill, to articulate the powers needed by the secretary to implement his responsibility over the defense establishment. That the role was more readily stated than the legal authority necessary to realize the role is clearly evidenced by this later statement of Secretary Patterson:

> From this brief outline of the bill, it will be seen that the heart of it is the creation of a single establishment, the National Defense Establishment, to be made up of the Departments of Army, Navy, and Air Force and to be directed by a Secretary of National Defense, with broad power to establish policies and programs for all agencies in the Establishment, to exercise direction, authority and control over them, and to set up the budget estimates of the Establishment on a unified basis. The Secretary, as I see it, is to be an executive but not an administrator.
>
> I have in mind a distinction between these two terms. It may not be in everyone's mind in the same way, but as I see it, the Secretary of National Defense is to be responsible for over-all programs and for comprehensive over-all planning but is not to attend to details or matters of administration. [45]

One can only sympathize with the framers of the act who had to translate terms like "over-all, general policy-maker, and executive" into

[44] *Ibid.*, p. 54.
[45] *Ibid.*, p. 56.

legal terms of authority. Sufficient power had to be provided, but care had to be taken to prevent the secretary from construing his power as warrant to delve into the details of administration. Admiral Sherman identified this dilemma very clearly:

> It seems obvious that effective supervision requires *decisive* authority for use when needed.
>
> .   .   .   .
>
> ...whatever official is to exercise the top management should be freed from the mass of minutiae which not only would absorb his time, but would necessitate the creation of a very large executive office, a very large personnel, which would be really the reverse of what we are trying to accomplish; which is to let each one of the three services have a department in which the detail work will be done, and *control at the top level only questions of policy* and matters which require a decision as between the departments on the lower level.[46] [Italics added.]

As the congressional committees listened to these descriptions of the role of the secretary, a device for translating this role into law began to emerge for them. If the secretary was to be responsible for *general* policy, he should have *general* authority, *general* control, and *general* direction over the establishment. To prevent any loose interpretation of these powers which might construe *general* as a mandate to centralize the departments,[47] a device, borrowed from the Federal Constitution, was made to buttress the already included provision that the service departments "shall be separately administered." This device, the reserve powers concept of the Tenth Amendment, was added to the bill.[48]

In addition to these two qualifying clauses, the act contained a preamble which stipulated the intent of Congress to provide for "authoritative coordination and unified direction" of the military departments "but not to merge them."

Regardless of the intent of the drafters of the act or of Congress, the National Security Act only established the general organizational structure, the allocation of responsibility, and the legal authority. How the system would operate depended as much upon the way the secretary of defense sought to use his authority, and how he viewed his role, as upon the various provisions of the law.

[46] *Ibid.*, p. 200.
[47] Some felt sure this was precisely what would happen. See testimony of General A. A. Vandergrift, Senate Committee on Armed Services, *Hearings, 1947*, p. 240.
[48] See *supra*, p. 104.

VII

POLICY AND POLITICS

The National Security Act provided only a skeletal organizational structure, a framework. The operation of the national security system would depend upon the view which the various participants took of their role, and the uses they made of their tools of control. And these would depend largely on their understanding of the policy process.

As indicated in Chapters II and III, some see the policy process as a downward flow. Premises, values, or goals are inserted at the top, and through a process of analysis and administration, actions emerge at the bottom. One former army chief of staff described it as follows:

> The statesman, the senior civilian authority, says to the soldier (and by "soldier" I mean the professional military man—the Army, the Navy, and the Air Force as represented in the persons of the Chiefs of Staff): "This is our national policy. This is what we wish to accomplish, or would like to do. What Military means are required to support it?"
>
> The soldier studies this problem in detail.
>
> "Very well," he says to the statesman, "here is what your policy will require in men and funds, in ships and planes."
>
> . . . .
>
> If the objective the statesman wishes to achieve is a costly one, that is not the soldier's business. If it is greater than the political leaders wish to support . . . that is not his business.[1]

[1] Matthew B. Ridgway, *Soldier: The Memoirs of Matthew B. Ridgway* (New York: Harper and Bros., 1956), pp. 271–72. Such views are not peculiar to the military. For a similar view expressed by a congressman see Warner R. Schilling, "The

Means and ends in policy are separate and distinct. Policy is separate from administration. The statesman merely has to tell the soldier what he wants, and the soldier analyzes the problem and comes up with a set of means to accomplish the job. It is that simple.

Attractive as this view of the policy process may be, especially to the soldier, it is unreal.[2] Policy or goals somehow have a way of failing to provide a guide by which the soldier can compare alternative means. In fact, goals (or ends of policy) take on their meaning only by what the soldier recommends.[3] The question is not whether this is good or bad, but can it be otherwise?

The Nature of Defense Goals

In the context of national defense, issues (as the example illustrates) resolve themselves into the question of what allocations of resources should be made to which services for what weapons systems? Or, one might say: how much is enough?[4] Such questions are inherently unanswerable. How are they to be put to operational tests? In the absence of such tests, the relationship of a particular allocation of resources (means) to a desired level of defense (ends) is a matter of judgment, not mechanical analysis.

Any particular allocation of resources can be considered as the creation of a series of subgoals. The relationship between these subgoals and the goal is simply postulated. It is hoped (judgment) these subgoals will add up to the goal. These subgoals, in turn, may or may not be capable of operational tests.[5] But the real substance of policy-making is the selection of the subgoals.[6]

If the policy process is not a puzzle to which there is one and only one right answer, as some like to think, what is it? Some guide for action is needed? This very statement—that there must be some guide for action—provides an important hint to the policy process. Whatever

---

Politics of National Defense: Fiscal 1950," Warren R. Schilling, Paul Y. Hammond, and Glenn H. Snyder, *Strategy, Politics, and Defense Budgets* (New York: Columbia University Press, 1962), pp. 133–34.

[2] See Janowitz, *The Professional Soldier*, p. 272.

[3] March and Simon, *Organizations*, p. 156. In fact, the military has seldom refused to consider matters of "what" as well as "how." See Cline, *Washington Command Post*, for a survey of military involvement in foreign policy during World War II, pp. 313–32.

[4] Millis, Mansfield, and Stein, *Arms and the State*, p. 18.

[5] See Hitch and McKean, *Economics of Defense*, pp. 159–81.

[6] See *supra*, Chapter III, pp. 47–48.

the ends, a choice must be made in terms of operational means, to guide the actions of the military. The need for operational means can be illustrated by referring to a recent criticism of the NSC.

The NSC spends most of its time readying papers that mean all things to all men.[7]
Papers which do not affect the course of governmental action are not policy; they are mere statements of aspirations. NSC papers are policy only if they result in action.[8]

If, then, statements of ends are not automatically translatable into action, why does not the NSC back up its statement of ends with detailed statements of means (plans) which will be guides to action?

But neither the President nor the NSC . . . can make the detailed plans necessary to give effect to the basic strategy decisions. Planning of this sort requires the knowledge and experience of the expert and also the resources and the environment of the department with the main responsibility for the operations being planned.[9]

This comment reveals the policy process in a different perspective. Means and ends cannot be separated. If policy is to be something more than a pious declaration of aspirations, it has to be spelled out in terms of means (plans) which can serve as guides to action. And only those engaged in operations have sufficient knowledge of these means. The soldier, then, cannot disregard questions of "what," because these questions are answerable only in terms of "how."

The statesman's task does not end with a declaration of goals and the soldier's task is more than providing the means in terms of men, funds, ships, and planes. Each task shades off into the other; both the soldier and the statesman must participate in policy-making.[10]

[7] Henry M. Jackson, "To Forge a Strategy for Survival," *Public Administration Review*, XIX, No. 3 (Summer, 1959), 160.
[8] U.S., Congress, Senate, Committee on Government Operations, *Organizing for National Security, The National Security Council*, 86th Cong., 2d Sess., 1960, p. 6. Cited hereafter as Senate Committee on Government Operations, *The NSC*, 1960.
[9] Jackson, "To Forge a Strategy for Survival," p. 159.
[10] As obvious as this may be, soldiers continue to criticize statesmen for failing to provide a "defined and accepted national objective toward which strategy can be oriented." Archie J. Knight and Allen F. Herzberg, "A Proposal for the Next Step in Defense Reorganization," *Air University Quarterly Review*, XII, No. 2 (Summer, 1960), 60. And the statesmen accuse the soldiers of being unable to agree upon means. See Millis, Mansfield, and Stein, *Arms and the State*, p. 402; and Janowitz, *The Professional Soldier*, pp. 271, 355.

Senator Jackson, chairman of a Senate subcommittee investigating national security organization, observed:

The true goal of "completed staff work" is not to spare the President the necessity of choice. It is to make his choices more meaningful by defining the essential issue which he alone must decide and by sharpening the precise positions on the opposing sides.[11]

These words should be engraved on the door of every staff room, everywhere, especially on the doors of the JCS and the NSC. The purpose of planning is to clarify alternatives, not cloud them. To be clear, alternatives have to be spelled out in terms of the action they involve. Policy, planning, and decision must result in a guide for behavior.

Policy is controlled at the top only when those at the top select the subgoals—the means which translate aspirations into operations. Since the statesman has charge of the aspirations and the soldier has charge of the means, both must share in the policy process. Neither can delegate his role to the other. Delegation really means abdication.

POLICY AND DECENTRALIZATION

The policy process produces a set of subgoals which in turn become the operational goals for the organization. This point, when goals become operational, is the only dividing line that can be made in the policy process. Once goals attain an operational level, authority and responsibility can be delegated without abdication. For example, once a decision to build a super-carrier is reached, the authority and responsibility for letting contracts, designing the details, training the crews, developing the tactics for its use, and so on, can be delegated to the Navy. The means the Navy uses in carrying out this responsibility are subject to certain operational tests, cost analysis, for example. But there is no way to arrive at operational tests of whether the super-carrier should be built. This decision cannot be deduced from the proposition that part of our national policy is to defend our sea lanes.[12]

[11] Senate Committee on Government Operations, *The NSC*, 1960, p. 8.

[12] The distinction between operational and non-operational goals is not a mutually exclusive proposition. It is rather a continuum. It is convenient to speak of the two ends of the continuum. March and Simon, *Organizations*, p. 156. Even the construction of a super-carrier is not a puzzle to which there is only one right answer to each problem. Choices will have to be made on the basis of judgment as well as fact. So the ends-means process applies at lower as well as higher levels of the policy process.

The dividing line between less operational and more operational goals provides a general guide for top executives. They can delegate responsibility for the latter, but not the former. The choice of subgoals will determine what the lower echelons will do. The choice of subgoals adds up to control.

The Matter of Control

If policy is the process of adjusting plans and objectives (means and ends)—the process of translating aspirations into operational subgoals —whoever controls the selection of subgoals exercises policy control. The National Security Act sought to adapt defense organization to this reality. The National Security Council and the Joint Chiefs of Staff were crucial to the operation of the system. The operators, those who would have to implement policy, were brought together on these committees to translate aspirations into actions. If used for this purpose, these committees would tie control to responsibility. Each committee consisted of individuals who could be expected to have the greatest awareness of how specific means might serve as limits or instruments of policy. Each committee consisted of individuals who could determine the feasibility of means.

The role played by the President in choosing subgoals would be the real center of policy-making and policy control in the NSC. The role played by the secretary of defense in choosing subgoals in the JCS would be the very heart of his policy control.

The committee process has very valuable side effects. The operators, the members of the NSC, for example, by sharing in the policy process, would understand it as actions they are expected to perform. The service secretaries, for example could force clarification of policy in terms of specific capabilities expected of their departments. The NSC could be both a decision-making and a communication device.[13]

The JCS could perform the same function at lower levels. Once strategy objectives were developed as capabilities expected of the services, the JCS could translate these objectives into requirements. At this point very specific alternatives would have to be considered and decided upon.

A committee of equals cannot be expected to select among alternatives when disagreement exists over the relation of alternatives to the

[13] For a discussion of the problems of communication and decision, see Leo B. Moore, "Too Much Management, Too Little Change," *Harvard Business Review*, XXIV, No. 1 (Jan.–Feb., 1956), 41–48.

goal. Each member has an absolute veto over the others. In case of disagreement nothing discourages them from "logrolling" and agreeing the best solution is the sum of their respective requests. The role of the secretary of defense is to force a selection of alternatives.

The President's ability to end debate in the NSC and to reach a decision may be more obvious than the ability of the secretary of defense to do this for the JCS. But in each case the ability stems from the same factor—power. On the JCS, however, the secretary is not the only person with power. In previous chapters (I and II), the power sources of the army bureaus were discussed. These same sources would work for the services against the secretary of defense. They might be summed up as consisting of four elements: status, expertise, public relations, and Congress.[14] What are the power sources of the secretary that would be sufficient to offset those of the services?

The Secretary's Power Sources

The secretary's legal authority is his most obvious source of power. The National Security Act gave him three important elements of power. He could recommend promotion or dismissal of subordinates.[15] Because he was "principal assistant to the President in matters of national security," his recommendations could be considered to carry substantial weight. The second important element of the secretary's power was his control over the departmental budget. The act authorized him to "supervise and coordinate the preparation" of individual agency budgets; "formulate and determine the budget estimates for submittal to the Bureau of the Budget"; and "supervise" the spending of appropriations. Finally the act gave him "general direction, authority, and control" over all agencies in the national military establishment.

Although these elements of legal authority are important, their real significance is not in what they stipulated. The most significant aspect of legal authority is its endowing of power with legitimacy. And the power available to the secretary is considerable.

---

[14] For additional discussion of these power sources see Elias Huzar, *The Purse and the Sword: Control of the Army by Congress through Military Appropriations, 1933–1950* (Ithaca: Cornell University Press, 1950), pp. 74ff; James M. Gavin, *War and Peace in the Space Age* (New York: Harper and Bros., 1958), pp. 255–56; Douglass Cater, *The Fourth Branch of Government* (Boston: Houghton Mifflin Co., 1959), pp. 6–11; and Janowitz, *The Professional Soldier*, pp. 372–401.

[15] For discussion of the significance of this power see Wallace, *Federal Departmentalization*, p. 37; Ginzberg and Reilly, *Effecting Change*, p. 208; and Pfiffner and Sherwood, *Administrative Organization*, p. 335.

More than two decades ago a student of administration observed that authority depends upon acceptance.[16] Authority can be measured only by the willingness of subordinates to accept it. Authority is of no value without obedience.[17] Authority is a license for, rather than a cause of, power.

The ability of the secretary to elicit obedience might be regarded as political in nature. It operates in the following manner. When there is conflict in an organization, the executive immediately above those in conflict has the opportunity to resolve the disagreement. The significance of conflict cannot be understated. Indeed, conflict may be a key source of power. "When an organization is operating" smoothly "questions may rarely come to the executive for decision, or, if they do come, only one point of view may be presented to him." [18] It would be foolhardy for the executive to substitute his own point of view for the recommendation—the crystallization of thinking—of the operators below him. In a smooth running organization "the different points of view will have been submerged, or some overruled, in the complex administrative process below him." [19]

If the National Security Act had really achieved "unity" among the services, as some hoped it would, or if the secretary had to work with a single chief of staff instead of the JCS, he would have had practically no influence or control over the military. He would have been presented with an agreed set of recommendations and he would not have had knowledge of the conflicts or disagreements submerged in the process. In other words, he would have been given no opportunity to control by helping frame the final agreement.

If, then, conflict and disagreement are the opportunities for the secretary to use power, why can he expect the services to accept his solutions to disagreement? What is to prevent the services from appealing over him to the President and Congress? In fact, the act itself guarantees the services this right. Section 202 provides:

Nothing herein contained shall prevent the Secretary of the Army, the Secretary of the Navy, or the Secretary of the Air Force from presenting to the President or to the Director of Budget, after first so informing the Secretary of Defense, any report or

[16] Chester I. Bernard, *The Functions of the Executive* (Cambridge: Harvard University Press, 1938), pp. 92–94.
[17] See *supra*, Chapter III, p. 45.
[18] Simon, Smithburg, and Thompson, *Public Administration*, p. 167.
[19] *Ibid.*

recommendation relating to his department which he may deem necessary.[20]

And the availability of congressmen to hear the views of individual servicemen during committee hearings (or at cocktail parties) is legendary.

THE NATURE OF POLITICAL POWER

To observe that the military uses political channels is to note the obvious. Policy is a political process and the power sources of the secretary, indeed of the entire executive branch, are political. An instance taken from the early history of the national military establishment will serve to illustrate the nature of this process.

The services rarely hope to gain a sympathetic ear by appealing over the secretary to the President. One of the greatest sources of service disagreement involves the allocation of a limited defense budget. The President is usually the author of budgetary ceilings and he expects his secretary of defense to get the services to accept them. In April, 1949, Secretary of Defense Louis Johnson proceeded to do precisely this. He cancelled construction of the Navy's super-carrier, the U.S.S. United States. Congress had already approved the funds for this carrier. Secretary Johnson further reduced the Navy's budgetary claims by decreasing the number of large carriers in commission from eight to four, and the number of authorized carrier air groups from fourteen to six.

If it had any friends in Congress, the Navy could be expected to enlist their enthusiastic support against the secretary in this decision. It had, and it did! A full-blown investigation by the House Armed Services Committee resulted. However, the position of the secretary was far from weak.[21] He had gained the approval of both the Air Force and the Army chief of staff. Furthermore, he had the backing of the President. This alliance was sufficient to defeat the Navy and its allies.[22]

---

[20] U.S., Statutes at Large, LXI, 253.

[21] A good narrative of the events leading up to the congressional investigation can be found in Millis, Mansfield, and Stein, Arms and the State, pp. 234–81; and Hammond, "Super Carriers and B-36 Bombers," American Civil-Military Decisions, ed. Stein, pp. 467–564. The best testimony to the secretary's power is found in the final report of the committee. U.S., Congress, House Committee on Armed Services, Unification and Strategy, A Report of Investigation, 81st Cong., 2d Sess., 1950. See also, Huzar, The Purse and the Sword, pp. 192–94.

[22] Ibid., 495, 497, 500, 501, 514–15 and 554; and the testimony of Louis C. Johnson in U.S., Congress, House, Committee on Armed Services, Hearings, to Convert the National Military Establishment into an Executive Department of Government, 81st Cong., 1st Sess., 1949, pp. 2710–11.

Interestingly, no one contested the legal authority of the secretary to make the decision. In fact, the Armed Services Committee, in its report, conceded it. What was challenged was his power. But, in spite of widespread popular and congressional support, the Navy lost.

The key to the secretary's victory in 1949 lay in his allies: the Air Force, the Army, and the President. Moreover, each of them had allies in Congress to enlist in support of the secretary. The allies the secretary can win and keep give him power. And the way to form firm political alliances is to find common interests and build on them.[23]

Events behind the 1949 incident illustrate the process through which the secretary can translate disagreement into power to make his decisions stand. Involved in the question of the 1949–1950 budget was the universal military training plan of the Army and the 70-group Air Force. This was the beginning of the great debate over balanced, limited war forces versus massive retaliation via air power. Congressional studies (the Finletter report)[24] had encouraged the advocates of air power, and Congress accepted the view that "massive expansion of the Air Force could serve as a substitute for the unpopular universal training system." [25] The Navy would gain no matter how the debate was resolved because its ships represented limited war capability and its super-carrier represented strategic air power potential.[26]

When James Forrestal, the first secretary of defense, assumed office in September, 1947, the 1948–49 budget was virtually an accomplished fact. The issue of air power versus universal military training would have to be settled in the 1949–50 budget.[27] The fiscal 1949 budget approved the Air Force's 70-groups, but the actual allocation of funds was inadequate for the air force program. The Secretary used a proposed supplemental budget as an opportunity to determine the allocation of the fiscal 1950 budget. He asked the JCS what adoption of a 70-group Air Force would require in additional army and navy allocations to keep the defense structure in "balance." Thus, the Secretary sought to establish "a rational and logical method by which the joint chiefs of staff will participate in, and share responsibility" for these allocations.

The implications of the Secretary's approach are highly important.

[23] Neustadt, *Presidential Power*, pp. 18–19, and Janowitz, *The Professional Soldier*, p. 320.

[24] For findings of Finletter Commission and its report see Millis, Mansfield, and Stein, *Arms and the State*, pp. 203–7.

[25] Walter Millis, ed., *The Forrestal Diaries* (New York: Viking Press, 1951), p. 378.

[26] See Janowitz, *The Professional Soldier*, pp. 277, 319.

[27] Letter to Hanson W. Baldwin, 16 June 1948, quoted in Millis, *The Forrestal Diaries*, p. 449.

To determine the requirements for a "balanced" military force while allowing the Air Force to expand to 70-groups, the JCS would first have to determine the degree to which the defense program should be committed to the doctrine of strategic air power. The Secretary actually tried to get the JCS to provide the political premises for its allocation decision.[28] The response of the JCS was classic. It started off with the disclaimer: "Based solely on military considerations. . . ." It simply recommended the sum total of what each service wanted.[29]

Power Must Be Understood

The secretary's view of the policy process is precisely the one considered at the beginning of this chapter. The secretary tried to tell the JCS: "Here is what we wish to accomplish—a balanced force with a 70-group Air Force. What military means are required to support it?" Balance had no meaning aside from the budget levels recommended by the JCS. Therefore, it is not at all surprising that the JCS merely recommended increasing the army and navy appropriations in proportion to the increase for the Air Force. It is a committee of equals. Each member has an absolute veto over the others. It was an all or nothing proposition for the JCS.

When the JCS "logrolled" the allocation of the 1950 budget, the secretary's view of the policy process became critical. It would determine what, if any, role he would play. His view is evident from his subsequent actions. First he sought to appoint General O. M. Bradley as his "principal military advisor." When General Bradley declined, he appointed a board under General McNarney to scale down the service requests. He abdicated his role in the policy process because he saw the question of "how" (the allocation among the services) as separate from the question "what" (a balanced force).[30]

The nature of the policy process is clearly revealed in this sequence of events. The policy of a 70-group Air Force, along with a balance among the services, had absolutely no meaning aside from the actual allocation of funds to the services. This allocation was in no sense a

[28] See testimony of James Forrestal, U.S., Congress, Senate, Committee on Armed Services, *Hearings, National Security Act Amendments of 1949*, 81st Cong., 1st Sess., 1949, p. 7; and Hammond, "Super Carriers and B-36 Bombers," *American Civil-Military Decisions*, ed. Stein, p. 471.

[29] Millis, *The Forrestal Diaries*, p. 214. See also Millis, Mansfield, and Stein, *Arms and the State*, pp. 215–16.

[30] Warren R. Schilling has prepared a brilliant analysis of the roles played by Forrestal, Truman and the Congress in *Strategy, Politics, and Defense*, pp. 5–166.

mechanical or administrative procedure to be deduced from the policy aspiration. It was *the* policy.

If such a policy question is thought too important for the JCS, it is certainly too important for a military advisor or an *ad hoc* board. If the secretary considered this issue too important for him to make, he certainly should have referred it to the NSC and not down to the services. The decision of the secretary to abdicate his role in the budgetary decisions of 1949–50 had consequences beyond the budget itself. His abdication cost him his power.

The President wanted a program within his budget ceiling. The Air Force wanted its 70-group program. The Army did not want to jeopardize its UMT program. And the Navy wanted its super-carrier. More important, each of these groups had its backers in public and in Congress. The secretary could expect support from these groups only to the extent that he could support all or part of their competing claims. To get support he had to search exhaustively for points of agreement. He had to raise the implications of the claims of the several services with Congress and the President and to explore the jungle of conflicting interest in search of a value, long- or short-range, on which all or most could agree.[31] Then the secretary, *with the assistance of the JCS*, would have to translate these *agreements* into budget levels. The *agreements* would be both his guide and his power base, because from agreements he gains allies. And without allies he is powerless.

This episode demonstrates that the power and control of the secretary are virtually independent of his legal authority. What authority could the secretary have been given to prevent the partisans from contesting any decision he might have made? The only authority that meant anything was his ability to persuade, cajole, threaten, find points of agreement, and build alliances. This kind of authority he had to develop; no one could give it to him.[32]

The secretary did not need to expect a congressional investigation on every decision. Most issues would not generate that much interest. Most issues would have more elements of agreement than disagreement. Certainly the military would be reluctant to jeopardize its own power sources by carrying its allies down in too many public defeats. In most

[31] This analysis of political bargaining was suggested by Lindblom, "Bargaining," RAND, RM–1434–RC, esp. pp. 23–25.
[32] As Samuel P. Huntington put it: "It [military policy] is the result of politics not logic . . . ." *The Common Defense: Strategic Programs in National Politics* (New York: Cambridge University Press, 1961), p. 2.

cases, the secretary could use his bargaining power to resolve dispute within the confines of the Pentagon.

Care should be taken not to place a sinister connotation on the idea of political or bargaining power. If the future does hold uncertainties, and if, therefore, defense policy is not a puzzle to which there is one and only one right answer, there is no alternative other than forcing those charged with responsibility for defense to find the points on which they can agree or to clarify the points on which they disagree. In the words of Professor Warner R. Schilling:

> The size and composition of the armed forces are issues on which the blood, treasure, and freedom of society turn in increasing and fateful degree. Yet the determination of these forces is inescapably tied to questions of value and questions of fact for which there are no definitive answers.... They must be resolved through the exercise of power in the political arena.[33]

Congress, the President, the Secretary of Defense, the military departments—each shares in the responsibility; each has a role to play. If any player wishes to abdicate his role, others will only be glad to usurp it.

THE NATIONAL SECURITY ACT AND THE POLICY PROCESS

The National Security Act provided the framework in which the ends-means analysis of the policy process could operate and could be controlled. If disputes about budget levels are resolved in the JCS under the direction of the secretary, the other interservice boards can operate. But if disputes are permitted to deadlock in the JCS, they will spill over into all other areas of interservice contact.

Crucial to the entire defense policy process is that the secretary of defense see his task for what it really is. His authority and control is in his ability to find agreement and to make and preserve alliances. Through his alliances, he can supervise interservice negotiation through to defense policy. In the terminology of Sir Leslie Hollis, an observer of the British defense system, the secretary must "mesh" the gears of strategy, budgets, and foreign policy.[34]

[33] "The Politics of Defense Policy: Fiscal 1950," in Schilling, Hammond, and Snyder, *Strategy, Politics, and Defense*, p. 214.
[34] See *supra*, Chapter V, p. 84.

The fate of a secretary who forgets his alliances is congressional opposition (not to mention service opposition). In 1957, after Senate friends of Secretary of Defense Charles Wilson had fought to restore House cuts in the military budget, Wilson announced that he would cut the Army by 100,000 men and

> a portion of the Senate increase would be saved. That announcement not only made the senators look silly—and forced the Senate conferees to drop their base for bargaining—it also seriously hampered the Senate advocates of foreign aid on which debate had just begun. Nine months later, Wilson's letter still caused scathing comment on the Senate floor, and there were no defenders in the chamber.[35]

Alliances are the secretary's base of power and disagreement is his occasion for control. He needs both. Most of his external alliances, especially those with Congress must flow through the President, but alliances within the department depend upon his ability to find and foster common interest.

In addition to allowing someone to stand between himself and the JCS, or in losing his alliances, one other danger threatens the power of the secretary of defense. He can waste his power by dissipating his time on detail.

In order that the secretary avoid this temptation to abdicate control in favor of becoming an administrative manager, lost in the detail of working out a uniform code of military justice, or developing a common catalogue for the services, the National Security Act enjoined him from getting involved in the administration of the individual services. It specified that the three military departments

> shall be administered as individual executive departments by their respective Secretaries and all powers and duties relating to such departments not specifically conferred upon the Secretary of Defense by this Act shall be retained by each of their respective Secretaries.[36]

The secretary was to delegate detail. He could never delegate his "authority, direction, and control." These he could only abdicate. But if he was to "direct and control," he could not allow his time to be absorbed by minutiae. The act ordered him to do what the British had

---

[35] Neustadt, *Presidential Power*, pp. 74–75.
[36] U.S., Statutes at Large, LXI, 253.

learned by experience, what Marshall had been forced to do in 1942 —clear the detail out of his office.

This dilemma of top executives is not limited to the national military establishment or even to government. It is the same one faced by all executives. Few, however, have ever had so much to lose. If the top executive prefers to behave like a shop superintendent or a section chief, and insists on immersing himself in routine matters, the organization will usually adapt itself to him. A major problem in all organizations is to get top executives to act like executives and stop being shop superintendents.[37]

The only way for the secretary of defense to have the time to consider adequately and deal forcefully with the budgetary crisis confronting him immediately after World War II was to delegate as much responsibility for current operations as possible. The details of how the Air Force was organizing its air groups were much less important than how many it should be authorized.

The purpose of having three separately administered services and the interservice boards was to permit delegation of routine to lower echelons.[38]

The National Security Act must be viewed as a milestone in the history of defense legislation. It is probably the only time that Congress placed so much power in the hands of an administrator. Furthermore, the act must be considered as a lonely landmark in the history of civil-military relations. For the first time, a civilian secretary was placed in a position from which he could really control the military—a relationship from which both the military and the secretary stood to gain. If the concept underlying the act was complex and misunderstood, it was because of the realities to which it was adjusted. The source of the early conflicts is not to be found in narrow service parochialism, nor in organizational structure, nor in the foibles and weaknesses of the

[37] Discussions of this problem can be found in Ginzberg and Reilly, *Effecting Change*, pp. 1ff; Wallace, *Federal Departmentalization*, pp. 76–78; and Pfiffner and Sherwood, *Administrative Organization*, pp. 198–201.

[38] The concept of policy and control embodied in the act has numerous counterparts in other organizations. The best explanation of the concept is to be found in Peter F. Drucker's *Concept of the Corporation* (New York: The John Day Co., 1946), esp. pp. 73–75; and his *The New Society: The Anatomy of Industrial Order* (New York: Harper and Bros., 1950), Chapter 30. Pfiffner and Sherwood describe various applications of the concept in private businesses, *Administrative Organization*, pp. 91–93. They also describe methods of decentralization within two churches which place a high premium on policy (dogma) control, pp. 92–93. Kaufman, *The Forest Ranger*, pp. 190–91, describes an application of this concept within a hierarchical structure.

humans involved. The source of the conflicts was the profound and awful nature of the problems faced.[39]

The vision that interpreted the act was less than the vision which created it. Students of organization were unable to understand why the act was based on *"negotiation* among service representatives rather than on *decision* by independent authority in the Office of the Secretary of Defense." [40] Within the military itself, there was a

> rapid growth of the indoor sport of debating the authority of the Secretary of Defense. . . . The ramifications . . . of the term "Establishment" versus "Department" were explored with gusto. The phrase "general direction, authority and control" contracted or expanded depending upon who was trying to prove what. . . . Some practitioners of the art found that by concentrating one's gaze fixedly upon . . . the proviso that the Services should be administered as individual Executive Departments, a good part . . . of the remaining . . . structure gradually faded away.[41]

A student of organization recently judged the secretary "a strange and pathetic figure, an executive responsible for over half, by any measure, of the executive branch, yet, in comparison with lesser executives, the power given him to act and the authority given him to decide were confusing and doubtful." [42]

Look as they would for the traditional regalia of executive control, no one could find it. There was no general staff, no chief of staff, no merged service. There were just the simple, unadorned tools of control: four committees and enormous bargaining power. There was *real* authority, yet few recognized it. But then, before authority can be recognized, one must know of what it consists.

[39] For an elaboration of this point see Schilling, "The Politics of National Defense: Fiscal 1950," in Schilling, Hammond, and Snyder, *Strategy, Politics, and Defense,* pp. 214–66.
[40] Stanley, *American Defense,* p. 78.
[41] *Ibid.,* p. 85.
[42] Hammond, *Organizing for Defense,* p. 226.

PART III

RETURN TO ORTHODOXY

VIII

THE 1949 AMENDMENTS
TO THE
NATIONAL SECURITY ACT

UNIFICATION IN ACTION

Limited defense budgets and interservice conflict characterized the first two years of unification, 1947–49. Army demands for universal military training, Air Force insistence on a 70-group program, and Navy requests for a super-carrier force could not be accommodated within the restricted budgets allocated to the defense establishment. Service competition, especially between the Air Force and the Navy, largely centered on the question of atomic weapons. Should the Air Force have exclusive or only primary responsibility for nuclear weapons? What role, if any, should the Army play in the use of nuclear weapons?

Answers to these questions depended upon the roles and missions of the services. For example, if the role of the Navy was to protect sea lanes, it would have little need for nuclear devices. If its role was to launch carrier planes against an enemy territory, then it would require atomic weapons. Since most military leaders thought nuclear devices would be the most important weapons in future wars, whichever service controlled them would become dominant and could expect the largest share of defense budgets.[1]

[1] Details of the nuclear weapons controversy can be found in Hammond, *Organizing for Defense*, pp. 237–38; Millis, Mansfield, and Stein, *Arms and the State*, pp. 210–11; Millis, ed., *The Forrestal Diaries*, pp. 396–412; Henry A. Kissinger, *Nuclear*

Secretary of Defense James Forrestal recognized the relationship of service roles and missions to the problem of budgetary allocations. He realized that the issue of service missions had to be settled before the joint chiefs could be expected to agree on a defense budget. Since Forrestal was determined that the JCS share responsibility for the 1949 budget, he called a meeting at Key West, Florida, to consider the question of roles and missions. The product of this meeting, the Key West Agreement, failed completely as a basis for service agreement. In fact, the services disagreed about correct interpretation even before publication.[2]

As in any attempt to state policy separate from the specific means of implementation, the Key West Agreement did not contain clear criteria for choosing one particular set of means over another. The agreement could not substitute for a final choice or negotiation among specific service proposals. And in spite of the agreement, the JCS, a committee of equals, could not do more than endorse the proposals of each individual service.

In his first annual report to Congress, the secretary of defense pointed to the inability of the JCS to agree upon a program within budgetary ceilings. He proposed the appointment of a chairman for the JCS as an amendment to the National Security Act—an expedient that he had previously attempted when he appointed the McNarney Board and when he relied on General Gruenther—that a chairman be appointed to the JCS. He also recommended strengthening the statutory authority of the secretary by removal of the word "general" from his authority, direction, and control. He further suggested the removal of the service secretaries from the National Security Council, and an increase in the size of the Joint Staff. And finally he recommended the appointment of an undersecretary to act as his *alter ego*.[3]

Shortly after the secretary's report, the Hoover Commission task force on National Security Organization submitted its report to Congress.[4] The report said the defense policy process was operating improperly. Relatively junior officers were making assumptions in their planning that involved matters of highest defense policy—"matters which should

---

Weapons and Foreign Policy (New York: Harper and Bros., 1957), p. 27; and Thomas K. Finletter, *Power and Policy: U.S. Foreign Policy and Military Power in the Hydrogen Age* (New York: Harcourt, Brace and Co., 1954), *passim*.

[2] Hammond, *Organizing for Defense*, p. 238.

[3] National Military Establishment, *Report of the Secretary, 1948*, pp. 3–4.

[4] The Commission on Organization of the Executive Branch of the Government, headed by Herbert Hoover, submitted its report to Congress in January, 1949. The Task Force on National Security Organization submitted its report separately as Appendix G. It is hereafter cited as Hoover Commission, *Task Force Report*.

be decided by no one less than the President acting on the advice of the National Security Council." [5]

The Hoover Commission report cited the history of the 70-group Air Force as an example of the making of national policy by a service program. National policy, said the report, should determine service programs. The organization, the report emphasized, was adequate, but it was not properly used. The difficulty was in expediting decision among the joint chiefs and in securing "from them soundly unified and integrated plans and programs and clear, prompt advice." [6] Although the secretary had ample authority over the Joint Chiefs, he lacked means for "expediting their business and resolving basic differences among them...." [7]

The recommendations of the Hoover Commission task force closely resembled those of Secretary Forrestal. It recommended deleting the word "general" from the secretary's statutory authority, sharpening the secretary's budgetary control, eliminating the provisions to permit appeals by the service secretaries directly to the President, and removing the "reserved powers" clause. These changes would "clarify and strengthen" the secretary's authority.

In regard to disagreement on the JCS, the task force suggested allowing the secretary to appoint a chief staff officer or a principal military assistant who "should sit with the Joint Chiefs of Staff, but without membership, and be responsible ... for presenting and interpreting the Secretary's point of view, and for bringing 'split decisions' ... to the attention of the Secretary...." [8]

The task force also recommended a chairman for the JCS, preferably selected from among the members of the JCS. The chairman would preside, handle agenda, and help to expedite business, but he would not have authority or precedence over his fellow chiefs. Most task force recommendations became presidential proposals for defense reorganization submitted to Congress on March 3, 1949.

PROPOSED AMENDMENTS TO THE NATIONAL SECURITY ACT

Defense Comptroller

None of the Hoover Commission task force recommendations to give the secretary better control over departmental budgets were included in

[5] *Ibid.*, p. 38.
[6] *Ibid.*, p. 53.
[7] *Ibid.*, pp. 11–12.
[8] *Ibid.*, p. 13.

the President's reorganization recommendations or in the early draft
of the 1949 reorganization bill (the Tydings bill). During testimony on
the Tydings bill, Ferdinand Eberstadt, chairman of the task force, suggested the Senate consider adding fiscal provisions to the Tydings bill.
He said there would be "no substantial advances" in economy or efficiency until budget procedures and fiscal policies were "overhauled
from top to bottom." [9] The Senate committee asked Mr. Eberstadt to
frame such an amendment. This amendment eventually became Title
IV of the 1949 reorganization act.

Title IV created the position of the defense comptroller. He was given
authority over all defense agencies in budget estimates, accounting,
audit, and statistical reporting, subject to the "authority and direction"
of the secretary of defense.[10]

Although both the Senate and House armed services committees
accepted Title IV without change, the comptroller's authority caused
much controversy. In a letter to the Senate Armed Services Committee,
the Bureau of the Budget objected to this provision. The major flaw,
of the 1947 act, the letter said, had been the assignment of statutory
functions to subordinate agencies in the defense establishment. The
letter cited the statement of the Hoover Commission report on general
management in the executive branch that "the line of authority from
department heads through subordinates is often abridged by individual
authorities granted to bureau or division heads. . . ." [11] This practice
must stop, if department heads are to be made "fully responsible" for
the conduct of their departments. The Budget Bureau concluded by
repeating the Hoover Commission stipulation that each department
head should have full "administrative authority" to organize his department and to "control" its administration.

The President and Secretary of Defense Louis Johnson repeated this
request. Independent statutory authority for subordinates departed
from "the principles of management" and violated the control of top
management by establishing "an inflexible unit beyond the reach of
the department head." [12]

[9] *Ibid.*, p. 57.
[10] For a full explanation of the duties of the controller see the testimony of Ferdinand Eberstadt in U.S., Congress, Senate, Committee on Armed Services, *Hearings,
National Security Act of 1949*, 81st Cong., 1st Sess., 1949, pp. 196–201. Cited hereafter
as *1949 Hearings*.
[11] *Ibid.*, p. 206.
[12] U.S., Congress, House, Committee on Armed Services, *Hearings on H.R. 5632 to
Reorganize Fiscal Management in the National Military Establishment: To Promote
Economy and Efficiency, and Other Purposes*, 81st Cong., 1st Sess., 1949, p. 2648. Hereafter cited, House Committee on Armed Services, *Hearings on Fiscal Management,
1949*.

The major change made by Title IV in the concept of the 1947 act was neither raised nor considered. In the 1947 act, all legal authority in the defense establishment was shared by the services and the secretary of defense. Provisions regarding the performance of specified functions by various boards forced the secretary to delegate functions to the services because they manned these boards. As staff agencies of the secretary, the boards were subject to the secretary's superior authority. And the board system brought the services into the policy process.

Title IV introduced the comptroller, a third person, into the policy process. He, rather than the services, shared the secretary's authority. In effect, the controller came between the service departments and the secretary. The comptroller's intrusion into defense policy-making violated the "two-hat" concept of the board system. As the Bureau of the Budget pointed out, it also violated the hierarchical general staff concept of centralizing authority in the department head.

Board Chairmen

According to the Hoover Commission's concept of department management, statutory responsibility for the Munitions Board and the Research and Development Board constituted a limitation on the authority of the secretary. The Tydings bill proposed to overcome this limitation by changing the status of board chairmen. The secretary of defense could assign decisional authority to board chairmen. Both the Hoover Commission task force and Secretary Forrestal had justified this change on the grounds of efficiency and economy. The final wording of the act provided:

> The Board shall be composed of a chairman, who shall be the head thereof and who shall, subject to the authority of the Secretary of Defense and in respect to such matters authorized by him, have the power of decision upon matters falling within the jurisdiction of the Board. . . .[13]

The Senate report clarified the purpose of this particular choice of words. The secretary of defense may prescribe the performance of the board's functions by the chairman himself.

The result of this provision was to change the board from a group of service representatives sharing in the policy process to a group of advisors for the board chairmen. It was the chairmen, not the services, who would share authority with the secretary. The boards were changed

[13] U.S., Statutes at Large, LXIII, 109, sec. 8.

from a committee of operators assisting in policy integration into a group of advisors without authority. And the chairman became a staff officer for the secretary.[14]

Behind the decision to change the boards into elements of a General Staff for the secretary was the same issue which resulted in a change in the JCS (to be considered subsequently). The boards could not operate because the JCS could not agree upon the premises needed by the boards for their work. In particular, the Research and Development Board needed policy premises from the JCS. It could not make missile assignments to the services because the JCS could not allocate service missile responsibilities. Consequently, every time the board considered a missile research and development project, a contest developed among the services. The solution evolved by the board was to permit each service to undertake whatever research studies it wanted. And the first service to develop a suitable weapon would acquire the mission that went with it.[15]

When the budgetary ceiling of 1949 was imposed, the contest among the services reached a critical point. Since no guidelines about missions were forthcoming from the JCS, the board appointed a subcommittee of six officers to determine how to meet service requests within financial limitations. The result was similar to the solution developed by the JCS about budgetary allocations. Service requirements were not questioned and the "budgetary pie" was cut as equally as possible.

When Louis Johnson became secretary of defense in 1949, he divided the missile question into two parts. The Research and Development Board was to confine itself to research allocations, while the JCS would assign operational control. The JCS promptly delegated its portion of the task to a subcommittee which promptly split on the issue. The deadlock once again proved the inability of committees of equals to reach decisions in the absence of clear policy premises or superior authority.

The 1949 amendments tried to solve the committee problem by giving board chairmen statutory authorization to determine the allocation of research and development projects. The idea seems to have been: get a decision, even in the absence of decisional premises.

[14] U.S., Congress, Senate, Committee on Armed Services, *Report on the National Security Act Amendments of 1949*, 81st Cong., 1st Sess., S.R. No. 366, 1949, sec. 7. See also Senate Committee on Armed Services, *1949 Hearings*, p. 283.

[15] Murray Green, "The First Secretary of the Air Force and Unification" (Ph.D. dissertation, Dept. of Political Science, American University, 1959), Chapter IV, pp. 46ff.

Chairman of the JCS

The Hoover Commission found much to criticize in the operation of the JCS. The chiefs were too remote from other parts of the defense establishment and they were "too detached from the vitally important political, economic, and scientific factors that must enter into all valid strategic plans." [16] The chiefs, as individuals, were influenced too much by considerations of "service particularism and aggrandizement." Their departmental duties prevented them from giving the "time and thought" required by JCS duties. And because of these factors they were unable, as a group, to handle service conflict and rivalry. But the most important source of its problems was the absence of criteria upon which to base decisions.[17]

In order to offset these difficulties, the task force suggested that the secretary appoint a chairman from among the members of the JCS who would be responsible for expediting its business and keeping its docket current. Furthermore, the secretary should appoint a principal military advisor or chief staff officer. This officer was not to become an intermediary military authority able to override the advice of the JCS or to relieve it of its legal responsibilities.

The Tydings bill combined the two recommendations of the task force. It established the chairman as a fourth member of the JCS. He, instead of the JCS, was to be the "principal military adviser to the President and the Secretary of Defense." [18] Presumably this would have satisfied Secretary Forrestal's request that the chairman secure agreement among the Joint Chiefs. Failing this, he must be able to "identify the basis of the difference" and have the right to submit his own recommendations to the secretary.[19]

Once again the purpose was to get decisions made. In the words of Secretary of the Air Force Stuart Symington:

I would say that the important thing to do in the Joint Chiefs of Staff is to get a decision. I believe most of the troubles we have had and the obvious problem of not having the services operate properly under the previous bill has been because of lack of decision in the Joint Chiefs of Staff.[20]

[16] Hoover Commission, *Task Force Report*, p. 66.
[17] Hoover Commission, *Task Force Report*, p. 67.
[18] Senate Committee on Armed Services, *Report No. 366*, p. 8.
[19] *Ibid.*, p. 10.
[20] Senate Committee on Armed Services, *1949 Hearings*, p. 95.

The Tydings bill provided for the assignment to the secretary of defense personally of all responsibilities previously distributed among the service boards and the JCS. He was free to delegate these responsibilities to the service boards as he saw fit. He could delegate the responsibility to the chairmen, in the case of the munitions and research and development boards. And although the proposed bill did not authorize him to delegate the functions of the JCS to its chairman, it did not deny him this right.

Members of the JCS were the first to object to this arrangement. Admiral Louis Denfeld testified:

> The way the section now reads in the proposed legislation, the Secretary of Defense could have the Joint Chiefs of Staff do these seven functions or he could give them to anybody else he wanted, and we think they are proper functions of the Joint Chiefs of Staff and they are functions we now perform.[21]

In response to a question by Senator Tydings, General Bradley clearly expressed the feelings of the JCS:

> SENATOR TYDINGS. As I see this thing here, you gentlemen are recommending that the responsibility of training and preparing strategic plans shall be that of the Joint Chiefs of Staff and not the Secretary of National Defense per se. As the law comes before us, it gives him the responsibility of doing it and you the assisting responsibility. What you want is the direct responsibility of running the war under his supervision.
> GENERAL BRADLEY. If we are going to be held responsible, we would like to know it.[22]

The same question, of course, is germane for the other service boards, but nobody raised it. If the chairman was given decisional authority, would he or the board be responsible for his decisions?

The version of the Tydings bill adopted by the Senate omitted provisions for assigning JCS responsibility to the secretary. But it made the chairman, not the JCS, the principal military advisor of the President and the secretary.

The role of the JCS chairman came under severe criticism during House hearings. Much time was spent considering the precedence and rank of the chairman, his relation to the secretary, and the value of having a chairman at all. Some feared establishment of a chairman was

[21] *Ibid.*, p. 115.
[22] *Ibid.*

a step in the direction of a single chief of staff. Insight into the validity of this fear can be gained from the following exchange:

> MR. BROOKS. I would like to address one question to the Joint Chiefs of Staff. But I would like to ask the Joint Chiefs of Staff if this amendment now meets the situation and if everybody on the Joint Chiefs of Staff is happy about the amendment as presently drawn.
> ADMIRAL DENFELD. It is entirely satisfactory to me.
> MR. BROOKS. Is it all right with you General Vandenberg?
> GENERAL VANDENBERG. I think it is as good a compromise as we could get at this time, sir. It doesn't go nearly as far, as I expressed before, as I believe it should.
> MR. BROOKS. How far do you think it should go?
> GENERAL VANDENBERG. I think I am on the record, sir, for a Chief of Staff.
>
> . . . .
>
> GENERAL VANDENBERG. I don't think, though, at this time that the time is ripe for that. I think, therefore, that this is a good amendment because it goes, I think, about as far as we can get.
> THE CHAIRMAN. And goes a step in the right direction, from your viewpoint?
> GENERAL VANDENBERG. That is right, sir.[23]

Representative Carl Vinson, the committee chairman, warned the committee about the two points of concern to him and, as it later turned out, of concern to Congress in every subsequent reorganization proposal:

> When I started out studying this bill I had two objectives in mind. One was to keep the Congress from being pushed out of the picture. . . . And the other was to fix it so that there would be no Chief of Staff just around the corner. But the committee seems to have drifted to the thought that we should have a Chief of Staff.
>
> . . . .
>
> Now . . . in actual application I haven't fooled myself. I know what is going to happen.[24]

[23] U.S., Congress, House, Committee on Armed Services, *Hearings on S. 1843, To Convert the National Military Establishment into an Executive Department of Government, to be Known as the Department of Defense*, 81st Cong., 1st Sess., 1949, p. 2914. Hereafter cited as House Committee on Armed Services, *Hearings on Department of Defense, 1949.*
[24] *Ibid.*, p. 2915.

In his testimony, Secretary Forrestal left little doubt about the role he intended for the chairman to play. It was the same role he had tried to get the McNarney Committee, and later General Gruenther, to perform. He must be able to "identify the basis of the differences of opinion," and he must submit "his recommendations" as to the proper decision.[25]

Secretary Forrestal was articulating one of the most common myths of the organization folklore. There is a single, consistent plan to accomplish every policy goal. If the joint chiefs could not develop such a plan, someone who could had to be placed between them and the secretary. Forrestal gave no indication that he might sit with the JCS and attempt to resolve their conflicting views or negotiate an acceptable solution.

Secretary Forrestal went on to state his feeling of an inherent conflict in the relationship between the two roles the services chiefs had to perform. Their roles as head of a service and as advisors to the secretary were incompatible. The incompatibility could only be offset by having a chairman make a separate recommendation when they failed to agree.

The addition of a chairman who made his own recommendations, of course, would destroy the value of the JCS. If the Joint Chiefs were not forced to negotiate an agreement, they could not be held responsible for the final decision. The chairman, not the JCS, would make the final recommendation to the secretary.[26] Who would be responsible? It would not be the JCS, for they could not agree. It would not be the chairman, for he had no authority to implement decisions.

Ferdinand Eberstadt uncovered the core of the problem:

> As contemplated in the amendment, the "principal military adviser" would carry no responsibility for carrying out his own advice, nor any authority for doing so. If his advice proves wrong and results in disaster, he can point the finger of responsibility at any or all of the three services and charge them with deficiencies of execution. They, in turn, in case of failure, can lay the blame on the chairman's advice. There would seem to be serious dangers in such severance of advisory power from the responsibility and authority to carry out the advice.[27]

In its final form, the reorganization act of 1949 made the chairman a

[25] Senate Committee on Armed Forces, *1949 Hearings*, p. 10.
[26] For elaboration of this point refer to Schilling, Hammond, and Snyder, *Strategy, Politics, and Defense*, pp. 174–75.
[27] House Committee on Armed Services, *Hearings on the Department of Defense, 1949*, p. 2734.

non-voting member of the JCS. He would preside at its meetings, but the JCS, *not* the chairman, would be the principal military advisor to the President and the secretary. And the JCS, *not* the secretary, was assigned the duties of strategy, logistics, and training.

In view of these "watered down" provisions, the creation of the office of chairman would have little significance aside from the previous experience of the JCS and the congressional testimony which cast him in the role of an alternative source of military advice.

The attack on the "two-hat" concept was unmistakable. Although defeated in the case of the JCS, the other service boards lost their "two-hat" character. They were transformed into staffs for the board chairman. And the chairman became the advisor to the secretary. While retaining their committee appearance, the Munitions Board and Research and Development Board were transformed into general staff agencies.

Authority of the Secretary of Defense

Although there was some disagreement among the recommendations of the Hoover Commission, the presidential message, the first report of the secretary, and the Tydings bill, there was complete agreement on one point. The secretary of defense needed more authority. And of all the proposed changes in the National Security Act, Congress seemed least convinced of the need for this change. Its misgivings were deepened when Ferdinand Eberstadt, chairman of the Hoover Commission task force, denied the need for further grants of authority to the secretary. Before the House Armed Services Committee, he emphatically stated that he knew of no time when the secretary's authority was ever challenged. In his testimony before the Senate committee, he remarked that he had observed the secretary, with commendable courage, make a decision going to the "heart of this Military Establishment," and while he had observed criticism of the decision, no one raised any question as to the secretary's authority.

This view was not shared by the man who made the decision in question. After justifying his decision in the matter of the aircraft carrier, Secretary Louis Johnson insisted that he did not have enough authority: "I think the authority is not there. I am convinced it is not. I ask for it on the same basis which my predecessor and all these other people have asked for it." [28]

The Secretary's statement caused some dismay among committee

[28] *Ibid.*, pp. 2794–95.

members. They had difficulty understanding how the Secretary could do something, justify it, and then say he had insufficient authority to do it. After prolonged questioning, the committee began to penetrate the apparent ambiguity of the Secretary's statements:

> MR. SHORT. You perhaps have practical authority, if you wanted to exercise it, by running to the President every day. But what you want is statutory authority.
> SECRETARY JOHNSON. That is right.
> MR. SHORT. And the difference is between practical and statutory authority.
> SECRETARY JOHNSON. That is right.[29]

The Secretary seemingly said that his real power exceeded his legal authority! This was a commendable display of candor before a congressional committee, but it demonstrated real confusion on the part of the Secretary. Taken literally, the remarks of the Secretary constituted a request that he be given, by statute, those aspects of presidential authority relating to national defense. One committee member, Mr. Cole, picked up this inference immediately:

> Reverting to the Chairman's apprehensions that this bill forecloses the Congress from exercising its constitutional responsibility. ... I am wondering if that same apprehension might not exist with respect to the constitutional obligations of the Commander in Chief.[30]

Subsequent testimony clearly indicated that the Secretary had no intention of impinging on the prerogatives of the President, but the matter raised an extremely important issue. The National Security Act had made the secretary of defense the principal assistant to the President in national security matters, and gave him "general direction, authority, and control" over the military establishment. Therefore the secretary's real power source was his ability to gain presidential support for his decisions and actions. Although the Secretary and other defense reformers were aware of this, it did not square with their concept of legal authority. The secretary, according to organization folklore, should be able to compel obedience without seeking presidential support.

An exchange between the Secretary and Carl Vinson, Chairman of the House Armed Services Committee, confirms this interpretation. The

[29] *Ibid.*, p. 2704.
[30] *Ibid.*

discussion involved the authority of the Secretary to take necessary steps to eliminate wasteful duplication:

THE CHAIRMAN. But you have plenty of authority right now to eliminate duplication, and you stated you were going to run the Department.

. . . .

SECRETARY JOHNSON. You have to clear the line of authority so I can work this thing out, sir, or the language of the 1947 Act is inadequate and insufficient.

THE CHAIRMAN. Mr. Secretary, how could it be any more positive from Congress, without specifically saying that you can consolidate and you should consolidate this or that named institution. . . .

. . . .

SECRETARY JOHNSON. All I am asking you to do, sir, is to clarify the law, so that some lawyer in one department doesn't say to me, "You can't do it."

THE CHAIRMAN. You are developing the point you couldn't do it. I was pointing out that the statute today gives you positive instructions, if you reach the decision there is duplication.

SECRETARY JOHNSON. Well, accepting your version, which I don't agree with, then I am asking you, sir, to clarify the law so there is no question that I have the right to do that.[31]

The word used by the Secretary—"clarify"—involved the same problem raised by the earlier distinction between "practical" and "legal" authority. The Secretary admitted he could eliminate duplication. But he insisted that he lacked legal authority, or at least his authority was not clear.

Chairman Vinson then offered to change the wording of the provision about eliminating duplication to make the Secretary's mandate more positive. At this point the Secretary removed all doubt as to what he was after. He said: "what I am pointing out is; you leave these executive departments under the old language, which I seek to change. . . . I am convinced now, since you and I agree on the objectives, you are going to take out the confusing line of command. . . ." [32] A few moments later the Secretary added, "if you just get the word 'general' out then I could agree with the legal interpretation the chairman made awhile ago." [33]

The Secretary's intent was now clear. He could only have sufficient

[31] *Ibid.*, pp. 2698–99.
[32] *Ibid.*, p. 2700.
[33] *Ibid.*

authority when he was the head of an executive department with a clear chain of command to his subordinates, the services. He was equating his authority with his hierarchical position. The defense establishment must be transformed into an executive department, pyramidal in configuration, with the secretary at the apex. Then, and only then, would the prescription of organization folklore be fulfilled. Then, and only then, would the secretary's authority be sufficient.

There is a corollary that normally accompanies this view of authority. The man who sits at the apex of the pyramid must really run his department. He must be an administrative manager. It should come as no surprise, then, to find Herbert Hoover testifying that the major deficiency of the National Security Act was the "lack of a center point of clear *administrative* authority." [34] [Italics added.]

While advocating more "authority" for the secretary, he explained that:

> Increase in power, as recommended here, is power to administer by civilians and it is quite a different thing from power to make policies or power to the military arm. That power is proposed by the committee to be conferred on the Secretary of Defense— the power to *administer*. The policies are to be made by the Congress and the various committees set up under the act and by the President. That proposed here is not a dangerous form of power.[35] [Italics added.]

These words are familiar. They describe the major assumption of the hierarchical general staff system. Policy and administration are separate. The policy process is a downward flow. Goals are inserted at the top by Congress and the President. The secretary of defense will merely administer them. Interservice disputes have resulted simply because the secretary has not been given sufficient administrative control. Disputes can be avoided by the simple expedient of centralization under an administrative manager.

Most witnesses agreed with this analysis. Secretary of the Air Force Stuart Symington testified that:

> From the very beginning of hearings on the proposal to unify the armed services, the Air Force has favored centralization and clear definition of authority and responsibility for the positions of the Secretary of Defense and the head of the Joint Chiefs of Staff. ... Therefore, the Air Force recommends against the addition

[34] Senate Committee on Armed Services, *1949 Hearings*, p. 128.
[35] *Ibid.*, p. 134.

of any qualifying language which would water down the authority and responsibility of the men at the top so as to make them co-ordinators instead of administrators.[36]

The equation of centralization with authority was constant and un-questioned. Unquestioned, that is, except by Congress.

Committee members had misgivings about this neat arrangement by which policy would be put in at the top of a structure and action would come out at the bottom. Their experience with the executive suggested otherwise. They felt policy implementation might not be as obvious as witnesses assured them it was. Senator Styles Bridges, for example, evidenced a certain frustration when he said:

> I wish there were some way that it were possible to distinguish between an administrator and a person who is in a policy-making position, or executive. . . . While I agree with you, sir, that the ad-ministration has to be headed up in one individual, I want, in some way, to maintain the integrity of thought and judgment in a great crisis here, if such should arise, so that we can get a combination of views, if the safety and security of my country is at stake, rather than perhaps the judgment of one man who I can conceive might be appointed here to a post who would be absolutely unsound.[37]

But worries like those of Senator Bridges did not seem to bother most witnesses. For example, Robert P. Patterson, former secretary of war, be-gan his testimony by saying that the principles of sound organization are simple. "One of the basic principles is comprehensive control by the man at the head of the agency." [38] He went on to say that in the armed forces a complicated system of boards will "break down everytime." The chain of command from "top to bottom must run in sure, straight lines. Simplicity of organization is indispensable." [39] Duplication, empire building, and interservice rivalry, he continued, were inevitable so long as three separate service departments existed. At this point, Senator Bridges interrupted to ask, if this was so, why did these things still exist within individual service departments.

> Is there anything hopeful in the steps that have been taken within individual departments that leads you to believe that consolidation of authority . . . would accomplish any of these things?

[36] Ibid., pp. 135–36.
[37] Ibid., p. 151.
[38] Ibid., p. 145.
[39] Ibid., p. 146.

Mr. Patterson replied:

> It is a vice that exists in the Departments; that is true. Good control at the top will keep it in check, but it is an unending struggle, I will admit that fast enough, because from the point of view of the man who is doing this empire building, from his point of view, it is generally the right thing to do.[40]

Only one witness did not agree that organization was simple and subject to common-sense solutions. Ferdinand Eberstadt pointed out that the proposed amendments would merge the services and "redistribute them as military departments, leaving behind a vague and undefined residium of authority in the newly created Executive Department of Defense. . . ." [41] He felt merger would aggravate rather than clarify the authority of the secretary.

Organization can only facilitate, not automatically assure, sound policy. He continued:

> From shattered illusions that mere passage of a unification act would produce a military utopia, there has sprung an equally illusory belief that present shortcomings will immediately disappear if only more and more authority is conferred on the Secretary of Defense, and more and more functions put into his office, and more and more people added to his staff. . . . I suggest that great care be exercised lest the Office of the Secretary of Defense, instead of being a small and efficient unit which determines the policies of the Military Establishment and controls and directs the departments, feeding on its own growth, becomes a separate empire.[42]

After hearing all the arguments, Congress decided to give the secretary of defense most of the provisions he requested. Representative Carl Vinson reflected the attitude of many congressmen, however, when he observed:

> As I have said all along, my observation in life has been when people don't get things run like they want to run them they lay it on lack of authority. When I can't get things done up here like I want to do I say "I don't have enough jurisdiction." That is true with any executive. When he is not getting things off like he wants he says "The reason I can't do this, I haven't enough authority." I think the Secretary could accomplish everything he wants to accom-

[40] *Ibid.*, p. 151.
[41] *Ibid.*, p. 50.
[42] *Ibid.*, p. 49.

plish under the present law. But he doesn't think so. So I think it is the duty of the Congress to strengthen his hand and give him what he thinks he needs, because he is charged with the responsibility.[43]

Provisions of the 1949 Act

On August 22, 1949, the President signed the provisions of the reorganization into law. They did not include all proposals desired by reformers, but they did much to substitute the hierarchical general staff system for the decentralized concept of the 1947 act.

The Munitions Board and the Research and Development Board were transformed into staff agencies under the control of their chairmen. The secretary was given a deputy secretary and three assistant secretaries. The word "general" was removed along with the "reserved powers" provision. And a non-voting chairman was added to the JCS.

The National Military Establishment was converted into a single executive department and the service secretaries were removed from the National Security Council. These changes denied the services a direct role in defense policy-making. They were merely semi-autonomous administrative subdivisions of the new executive department. All these provisions were in keeping with the hierarchical general staff concept of organization.

LEGISLATIVE-EXECUTIVE RELATIONS

The debate over the powers of the secretary and how to clarify them involved more than concepts of administration. After some resistance, Congress decided to create the kind of organization the secretary wanted, but it did not intend to lose its own prerogatives in the process. Congress might well agree with Mr. Hoover's statement about policy-making being the prerogative of the President and Congress, but it also realized its own need for access to the services to make its policy function meaningful. It needed to hear of disagreement and controversy. Disagreement means alternatives. Without examining and judging alternatives, Congress could not control.

Congress took its constitutional mandate to provide for the common

[43] House Committee on Armed Services, *Hearings on the Department of Defense, 1949*, p. 2920.

defense very seriously.[44] If the secretary successfully eliminated inter-service rivalry and secured agreement within the department, Congress would be reduced to accepting whatever the secretary recommended. Congress refused to be limited to this course for two reasons. First, the appropriation (or the withholding) of funds is control in name only. At best, it is negative and, at worst, it is partisan harassment. Second, policy can be put to no valid test beyond the agreement of those charged with the responsibility for executing it.[45] Congress wanted to be sure that those with the knowledge of military operations had an opportunity to express their views in the making of defense policy. And Congress must be credited with a much more sophisticated view of the policy process than most of the "expert" witnesses testifying before it.

Congress wrote the final act in such a way as to guarantee the continued existence of the service departments. The act stipulated that the secretary could not use his authority as department head to eliminate the services. It required separate administration of the services under the secretary's direction, authority, and control. Although the President might not want to hear service views on the National Security Council, Congress did want their views. Therefore, the act included a provision guaranteeing the right of the services to make reports, on their own initiative, to both Congress and the President.

These provisions, of course, frustrated the very purpose of the reorganization. A challenge of the secretary's authority has meaning only in that it might be followed by an appeal to the President or Congress. Furthermore, the only sure way for the secretary to prevent such challenges was to destroy or alter the organizational identity of subordinate units which constantly disagreed with his policy. As was the case in the prewar Army, unmanageable subordinate units were to be centralized or destroyed rather than controlled.

[44] See the statements of Representatives Short, Vinson, and Van Zant in *ibid.*, pp. 2822, 2686, and 3801, respectively.

[45] In its report on the B-36 hearings, the House Armed Services Committee said: "The concern of the committee, in this labyrinth, is therefore not whether or not this or that strategic doctrine is the sound one; for neither the committee nor the services themselves can ever know, short of war. The committee interest is directed to the more basic question; is there adequate insurance in the Department of Defense that each highly specialized service view will be adequately considered?" U.S., Congress, House, Committee on Armed Services, *Unification and Strategy: A Report of Investigation*, 81st Cong., 1st Sess., 1950, p. 36. Cited thereafter as House Committee on Armed Services, *B-36 Report.*

ORGANIZATIONAL CONCEPTS

The 1949 amendments to the National Security Act must be considered a victory for the hierarchical general staff concept of organization and control. The service committees were changed from devices for linking policy and operations into general staff agencies for the secretary of defense. Only the JCS retained its "two-hat" character, but it was threatened by the establishment of a chairman. In practice the chairman was to grow into an alternative to, rather than a part of, the JCS.[46]

The services lost their formal role in the policy process by removal of service secretaries from the National Security Council and the imposition of a staff between them and the secretary. Although the façade of a committee system was retained, the direct contact so important for its successful operation was lost. The assistant secretaries, the board chairmen, and the chairman of the JCS displaced the service secretaries and the joint chiefs as the primary advisors of the secretary of defense.

Since the view of policy-making held by the reorganizers of 1949 would have reduced congressional contact to one point—the secretary of defense—Congress could not permit full implementation of the hierarchical concept. As noted previously, congressional concern centered upon the issue of executive-legislative relations. Nevertheless, the measures taken to assure continued congressional access to the services, prevented the complete revision of departmental policy machinery. Service integrity was preserved by requiring their separate administration. And so long as service integrity was preserved, the JCS could function as a responsible element of the policy process. Whether the JCS would be used was another matter. But if service integrity was destroyed, the JCS would simply become another element of a general staff, not responsible for implementing the advice it gave.

It is difficult to understand why, after less than two years' experience with the committee concept, the defense establishment and Congress scrapped the system. Apparently they knew what they were doing. Secretary Forrestal had said:

> What I call the philosophy of the act is essentially different under this concept than it is under the act of 1947. . . . One is based on the idea of coordination. The other is the present bill, and is based on the concept of straight line authority.[47]

[46] See Hammond, *Organizing for Defense*, p. 353; and *infra*, Chapter X, pp. 169–70.
[47] Senate Committee on Armed Services, *1949 Hearings*, p. 19.

In one of its reports, the House Armed Services Committee remarked:

The concept of this new law, as contrasted to the federation concept of the original Unification Act, was one of centralized, clearly defined civilian authority in one executive department.... The new law changed the synonym of unification from "coordination" of the armed forces to "centralization" under the Secretary of Defense.[48]

In regard to various members of the executive departments, it is possible to develop a plausible explanation for their views. Most of the men involved grew up at the time policy was considered separate from administration. They believed control meant hierarchical control and a general staff. Their image of an executive was straight out of the myths of organization folklore. He must "run" his department.[49]

Members of the Hoover Commission task force provided a good example of these attitudes. When they noted junior officers making assumptions involving major policy issues, or when they saw the Air Force 70-group program actually reversing their own notions of the policy process,[50] they sought to make the policy process conform to their preconceptions of what it should be instead of questioning their own assumptions. The task force reported: "Presently, national policy is not emanating, clearly and firmly, from above and descending effectively through the chain of agencies for translation into an efficient and economical military establishment measured against our national needs." [51] Policy, if inserted at the top, would naturally flow down!

The behavior of Secretary Louis Johnson is extremely difficult to understand. He was the first secretary of defense to use his potential power fully. He seemed quite aware of the need for presidential support and allies. But apparently these needs did not conform to his idea of an executive. He *ought to be able* to make decisions, and they *ought to be carried out*—automatically. He failed to understand why his decision in the matter of the super-carrier succeeded. It succeeded not because he had made it, but because he had enough allies in Congress to support him.

Finally, why did Congress accept the reversal of a concept it had insisted upon two years earlier? Congress also seemed to accept the

[48] House Committee on Armed Services, *B–36 Report*, p. 3.
[49] Norton E. Long attributes these attitudes to the tendency to use the individual as a model for organization. See his discussion in "The Administrative Organization as a Political System," *Concepts and Issues*, Mailick and Van Ness, eds., pp. 110–21.
[50] Hoover Commission, *Task Force Report*, pp. 37–38.
[51] *Ibid.*, p. 52.

policy-administration dichotomy regarding the nature of the policy process within an administrative department. For example, Senator Bridges agreed that one man must head an administrative department and control the administrative process.[52] Senator Hunt compared the secretary of defense to a field general.[53] However, Congress realized that complete centralization would strangle the policy process. And it felt an agency as large as the defense establishment could not be run by one man at the top.[54]

But despite doubts it may have had, Congress decided to accept the requests of the defense reformers up to the point where congressional participation in defense policy would be impaired.[55] As it happened, this was also the point beyond which service participation in policy-making would be eliminated.

The timing of the B–36 hearings may have affected the outcome in 1949, but this is difficult to prove. The Senate considered presidential reorganization proposals first. The reorganization bill passed by the Senate conformed quite closely to presidential requests. During hearings in the House, the B–36 controversy came up and the House Armed Services Committee decided to postpone reorganization hearings pending the outcome of the new investigation. The House later passed Title IV (comptroller and fiscal procedure provisions) of the Senate bill, but other parts of the reorganization act were decided in conference committee. Although the House did get many of its views incorporated into the final bill, some members considered the House's influence was substantially reduced in the process.[56] Whether this was the case must be left to conjecture.

The real victim of the 1949 changes in the National Security Act was the secretary of defense. He was weakened. The role of the secretary as agent of presidential control was rejected for the role of an administrative manager. The chairmen of the JCS and of the service boards, not the secretary, fell heirs to the power derived from resolving disagreement.

The secretary, in effect, had asked Congress to relieve him of the burden of policy control. To be sure, he thought he was only asking for relief from the constant "din" of "petty interservice squabbles."

[52] Senate Committee on Armed Services, *1949 Hearings*, p. 136.

[53] *Ibid.*, p. 23.

[54] See the exchange between Representatives Hardy and Vinson in House Committee on Armed Services, *Hearings on Department of Defense, 1949*, p. 2809.

[55] See Representative Vinson's statement in *ibid.*, p. 2920.

[56] House Committee on Armed Services, *Hearings on Fiscal Management, 1949*, pp. 2676–77.

But when the executive branch, or any part of it, abdicates its role in policy-making as it did in 1949, Congress is usually quick to take up the slack. A columnist observed that unification became a joke when the service secretaries constantly appealed over the heads of the secretary of defense and the President.[57] Indeed, it did, but the columnist's statement was slightly inaccurate. He should have said unification became a joke when the secretary of defense decided to abdicate his role in the policy process.

[57] Hanson Baldwin, *New York Times*, April 15, 1948, p. 1.

IX

DEFENSE REORGANIZATION
OF 1953

DEPARTMENT OF DEFENSE, 1949–53

The principal effect of the 1949 changes in the National Security Act was to increase vastly the functions of the secretary's staff. Although the individual service secretaries still retained statutory obligation to administer their military departments, their removal from the National Security Council and their loss of cabinet status focused operating responsibility at Defense Department rather than service department level.[1] The Munitions Board and the Research and Development Board no longer provided a means of service access to the secretary of defense. The chairmen of these boards, not the boards themselves, were the advisors to the secretary. Of all service agencies, only the JCS maintained a direct involvement in departmental policy-making.

Downgrading the Services

As the secretary of defense came to rely on his assistant secretaries and board chairmen rather than the service departments for advice, the services and especially the civilian secretaries began to lose their role in departmental policy-making. What was more, the reduced role

[1] U.S., Congress, House, Committee on Government Operations, *Hearings on Reorganization Plan No. 6 of 1953: Department of Defense*, 83d Cong., 1st Sess., 1953, pp. 110–11, cited hereafter as House Committee on Government Operations, *Hearings on Plan 6;* and Finletter, *Power and Policy*, p. 259.

147

of the service secretaries produced a situation similar to that characterizing the operation of the War and Navy Departments during World War II. As individuals, the Joint Chiefs were responsible to their service secretaries. Collectively, the Joint Chiefs constituted the military advisors of the secretary of defense. And since the Joint Chiefs were the only service department representatives with a statutory role in the departmental policy process, they became the *spokesmen* for the services. The service secretaries, as was the case with Stimson and Knox, were bypassed.

Changing Role of the JCS

Between 1947 and 1949, the Secretary of Defense had tried with little success, to get the JCS to agree upon force levels and budget allocations within the ceilings fixed by the President.[2] The Secretary did not intrude himself into JCS deliberations because he viewed its work as military in character. In the absence of guidance from the Secretary, the JCS at first could not arrive at a budget within the prescribed ceiling; and when it did, as in fiscal year 1950, it divided authorized funds almost equally among the services.[3] As a committee of equals, each with an absolute veto over the other, the JCS could hardly do otherwise.

With the start of the Korean conflict in June, 1950, budgetary ceilings were removed, but JCS operations did not change. Although service force levels were increased, they were increased almost equally for each service. The JCS was left free, indeed it was expected, to arrive at decisions without the benefit of policy guidance.[4] That is to say, questions of military means were separated from, or even allowed to determine, policy ends.

During the first year of the Korean conflict, the only change in JCS operation was external—removal of budget ceilings. Its stature grew, however, because it directed military operations and, in the process, it had direct access to the President.[5]

The position of the JCS at the department level, its relative isola-

[2] See *supra*, Chapter VIII, pp. 125–26.

[3] In fiscal year 1950, the Army and Navy received $4.4 billion and the Air Force received $5.4 billion.

[4] For a description of the JCS and its procedure during these years, see Finletter, *Power and Policy*, pp. 260–67.

[5] For JCS operation in directing the Korean conflict see Millis, Mansfield, and Stein, *Arms and the State*, pp. 281ff; and Schilling, Hammond, and Snyder, *Strategy, Politics, and Defense*, pp. 351–59.

tion from civilian interference, its prominence in directing military operations—all these conspired to reduce the position of the service secretaries and the service departments. And this development was soon to cause serious difficulties.

The Stretch-Out

The program of service expansion recommended by the JCS during 1950 and 1951 involved enormous defense budgets for the following three or four years. As early as 1951, members of Congress began to call for expansion of nuclear weapons programs as a means of achieving "peace power at bearable cost." [6] In the fall of 1951, Robert Lovett, the fourth secretary of defense, asked the JCS to "stretch-out" the pace for achieving projected force levels. And once again, budget ceilings began to enter the JCS decision process.

The situation in the fall of 1951 was not unlike the one that precipitated the B–36 investigation two years earlier. Not only did the JCS have to keep its recommendations within budget ceilings, it had to face the question of nuclear weapons and service roles. Once again the JCS failed to reach agreement.[7]

As in 1949, the Secretary of Defense did not attempt to intervene in JCS deliberations or break its deadlock by forcing service negotiation. But neither did he try what Forrestal had tried earlier. He did not turn the deadlocked question over to another military board or a military advisor.[8] He handed the question to the civilian service secretaries.

Lovett's decision demonstrated some realization that force levels were "political" as well as "military" problems. But the service secretaries were no better equipped than the JCS to measure force levels against policy goals. In fact, after 1949 when they were removed from the National Security Council, the service secretaries were more isolated from high level policy agencies than the JCS. What was more, they lacked the professional knowledge and experience of the JCS. In all probability they would have to accept the counsel of their individual military chiefs in deciding budgetary and force level questions. Because of these considerations, shifting the problem to the service secretaries represented no important change and certainly no improvement.

[6] Millis, Mansfield, and Stein, *Arms and the State*, p. 354.
[7] *Ibid.*, p. 352.
[8] For a description of the Budget Advisory Committee subsequently created see Huntington, *The Common Defense*, pp. 227–28.

In other respects, Lovett's decision represented a major shift in approaching the explosive issue of force levels and service roles. Since the service secretaries were political appointees, they might be more subject to domination by the secretary of defense than the JCS, especially if the secretary used the chairman of the JCS to support his own proposed solutions to service disagreements. If this was what the Secretary intended, it raised some serious questions about the resulting policy. Could the decisions of the service secretaries in these circumstances be considered responsible? Could civilian secretaries be expected to possess sufficient knowledge of weapons, strategy, and force levels to make sound decisions? And what role would the JCS play?

Sufficient evidence is not available to determine whether Secretary Lovett was trying to place force levels and service roles questions where they would be more easily subject to his control. However, it is clear that he did view the service secretaries and the chairman of the JCS as an alternative source of military advice.[9] And it is clear that he did not try to tie the solution of these "military" questions to the "political" goals they were supposed to support. Instead of trying to promote the analysis of "means" in terms of "ends," thereby establishing a basis of service negotiation, Lovett merely handed the isolated consideration of "means" over to the civilian service secretaries. Against these background developments a new administration came to power and promised to take a "new look" at defense policy.

REORGANIZATION PLAN NO. 6 OF 1953

The Rockefeller Committee

During his campaign for the presidency in September, 1952, Dwight D. Eisenhower promised "security with solvency." [10] Shortly after his election, the President directed his secretary of defense, Charles E. Wilson, to appoint a committee under the direction of Nelson A. Rockefeller to examine defense organization. The committee drew up

[9] House Committee on Government Operations, *Hearings on Plan 6*, p. 117.

[10] Glenn H. Snyder provides a detailed analysis of the series of military decisions made by the Eisenhower administration which are collectively called the "New Look" in "The 'New Look' of 1953," *Strategy, Politics, and Defense*, Schilling, Hammond, and Snyder, pp. 383–524. A collection of documents, speeches, newspaper clippings, and journal reports on the "New Look" has been compiled by W. Barton Leach in *The New Look* (Maxwell AFB, Ala.: Air Command and Staff College, Air University, 1954).

a reorganization plan for the Pentagon which eventually became Presidential Reorganization Plan No. 6. of 1953.[11]

The Rockefeller plan stressed the need for strengthened civilian control, improved strategic planning, and effectiveness with economy. These three points of emphasis became the three major parts of the President's reorganization proposals.[12]

Strengthened Civilian Control

The President recommended clarification of the authority of the secretary of defense and exercise of control through the three civilian service secretaries. In order to bring the service secretaries into the chain of command, a provision of the Key West Agreement of 1948 had to be changed. The agreement had provided that the JCS (not the secretary of defense) designate one of its members as executive agent for each unified military command. Orders to these commands (for example, forces in Korea) proceeded from the secretary of defense, through the JCS, to the unified command. Service secretaries were completely by-passed. The President said this practice led to "considerable confusion and misunderstanding"[13] about the relationship of the JCS to the secretary and the relationship of the individual service chiefs to their service secretaries.

The President directed the secretary of defense to revise the Key West Agreement and to designate a military department as executive agent for each unified command. This arrangement would provide a clear and unmistakable "channel of responsibility and authority" from the President, through the secretary of defense, and a service secretary to a unified commander.[14]

The reason for appointing a service department rather than a JCS member as executive agent for unified commands was discussed during the hearings on the reorganization plan held by the House Committee on Government Operations. Nelson E. Rockefeller argued that the

---

[11] The reorganization of 1953, unlike the 1949 reorganization, was submitted under a special device provided by Congress in 1949. Instead of requiring legislation, this device (the Reorganization Act of 1949) permitted presidential reorganization proposals to become effective after a specified time providing neither House of Congress passed a disapproving resolution.

[12] The President's proposals were sent to Congress along with an explanatory message on April 30, 1953. U.S., President, *Message Accompanying Reorganization Plan No. 6 of 1953, Relating to the Department of Defense*, 83d Cong., 1st Sess., H.D., 136, 1953. Cited hereafter as *President's Reorganization Message, 1953*.

[13] *Ibid.*, p. 3.

[14] *Ibid.*

basic issue was whether the secretary of defense was going to exercise real control over the entire department. If he was to control it, he had to have a clear channel of control running to all agencies within the department.[15] The practice of allowing the JCS to designate one of its members as executive agent for unified commands both prevented clear channels of control and diminished civilian control. For effective civilian control, orders must pass through the civilian secretaries, not the JCS.

On the other hand, the secretary of defense could authorize the service chief of the designated military department to "act for that department" in strategic direction, operational control, and conduct of combat. Therefore, under the new arrangement as well as the old one, the same individual acted as executive agent for unified commands. The only difference was that the service chief acted on behalf of the service department instead of the JCS under the new arrangement. Behind this apparently minor "tinkering" with command channels a very important issue was at stake. And this issue can be understood only in terms of the evolving role of the JCS itself.

During the Korean War, the JCS dealt directly with the President in implementing United Nations' directives. So long as budget ceilings were removed, nothing marred the smooth operation of the system, but the service secretaries were fading into the background. Once budget ceilings were reintroduced, the JCS, while maintaining its pre-eminent position in directing the war, deadlocked in its attempt to solve the problem of reduced budgetary allocations. Any attempt by the secretary to force JCS decisions as Secretary Johnson had done in 1949 seemed much less likely to succeed. The JCS had indirectly challenged the ability of the secretary of defense to control it. And because of JCS prestige, the secretary of defense did not have as strong a bargaining position as Louis Johnson had had in similar circumstances in 1949. The position of the JCS as director of combat operations in Korea gained it a position of dominance, or so the Secretary thought.

The changes in command line, therefore, merely formalized the undermining of the JCS begun by Secretary Lovett. The reconstituted command lines clearly sought to reduce the role and the political power of the JCS.[16] And this is what the President really meant when he spoke of establishing firm civilian control and a single channel of command.

[15] House Committee on Government Operations, *Hearings on Plan 6*, p. 152.
[16] See the testimony of Admiral Charles M. Cooke in *ibid.*, pp. 129–30.

Improved Strategic Planning

Removal of the JCS from the command channel was the first step in accomplishing the next major objective of the President's reorganization plan. The JCS was a planning not a command agency, said the President. As the principal military advisors of the secretary of defense, the Joint Chiefs were to formulate plans to "cope with the challenge of any enemy." [17] As military chiefs of their respective services, they were responsible to their service secretaries for the efficiency and combat readiness of their services. They were "staff" and not "line" officers. They were to plan and advise, not command. Command responsibility resided with the civilian secretaries. This arrangement, said the President, meant effective civilian control.

The President's analysis of the function of the JCS stood in sharp contrast to the concept of the original National Security Act. The 1947 act had provided for no such dichotomy between line and staff. As military commanders and subordinates of the secretary of defense, the Joint Chiefs commanded their service forces. Because they were service commanders, they were qualified to act as military advisors of the secretary. As military chiefs of their service departments, the Joint Chiefs had intimate involvement and understanding of the requirements of military operations. And this very knowledge of operations qualified them to advise the secretary.

In 1953, the command responsibility of the JCS was considered a disability. Involvement in the operational requirements of their services made the Joint Chiefs service partisans, unable to take a "national" view of defense problems. In order for the Joint Chiefs to "rise above the particular views of their respective services and provide the Secretary of Defense with advice which is based on the broadest conception of national interest," [18] they must be relieved of all command and serve only as an advisory staff.

Some members of the Rockefeller Committee had recommended the termination of the "two-hat" role of the JCS.[19] They approached the planning process in terms of the hierarchical general staff model of organization. The only way the Joint Chiefs could cease being mere

[17] *President's Reorganization Message, 1953,* p. 5.
[18] U.S., Congress, Senate, Committee on Armed Services, *Report of the Rockefeller Committee: Department of Defense Organization,* 83d Cong., 1st Sess., 1953 (Committee Reprint), p. 4. Cited hereafter as *Rockefeller Committee Report.*
[19] Robert A. Lovett, Vannevar Bush, and General Omar N. Bradley disagreed with this and other specific recommendations, *ibid.,* p. 5.

representatives of service interest was to sever completely their relationship with the services. As staff for the secretary, by definition, the JCS would stop giving "parochial" advice and start giving "national" advice.[20]

Other members of the commission, and Rockefeller himself, felt operational and planning responsibility should not be entirely separate.[21] And because of the divergent views of its members, the commission faced a dilemma. On the one hand, as service commanders, the JCS were representatives of service interest. On the other, as staff officers without command, they would be in danger of making plans in a vacuum.[22]

This formulation of the planning problem and its solution were not unique. The commission recommended the same solution that the Hoover Commission had recommended for the interservice boards four years earlier. The operation of the JCS would be improved by strengthening the position of the chairman. Strengthening the chairman would bring about a reorientation of the JCS and its subordinate staff structure. Its role as staff for the secretary would be emphasized. The role of the individual chiefs, as service representatives would be de-emphasized, not ended.

The President's reorganization plan provided for the chairman's approval of the appointment and tenure of individuals assigned to the Joint Staff. And the management of the Joint Staff and its director was to be transferred from the JCS to the chairman. The purpose of these changes, said the President, was to "relieve the Joint Chiefs of Staff, as a body, of a large amount of administrative detail. . . ." [23]

In addition to these changes requiring modification of the National Security Act, the President said he would direct the chairman of the JCS to seek the fullest "collaboration" between the JCS and other staff agencies in the Defense Department. Furthermore, "competent civilian scientists and engineers" should be invited to participate in the strategic planning of the JCS.[24] In sum, all efforts would be made so that the JCS would "reach an agreement on what is right and best to do in the national interest. . . ." [25]

[20] Various interpretations of the Bush, Lovett, and Bradley proposals can be found in Hammond, *Organizing for Defense*, pp. 257–59; and Millis, Mansfield, and Stein, *Arms and the State*, pp. 369–71.
[21] See the testimony of Nelson Rockefeller and Undersecretary of Defense Roger Kyes, House Committee on Government Operations, *Hearings on Plan 6*, pp. 171–75.
[22] This is the way Rockefeller and Kyes formulated the issue. See *ibid.*
[23] *President's Reorganization Message*, p. 6.
[24] *Ibid.*
[25] *Rockefeller Committee Report*, p. 6.

During hearings, a number of witnesses testified that provisions relating to the chairman of the JCS, when placed in the perspective of actual JCS operation and the reorganization of 1949, indicated the chairman was actually becoming an alternative source of military advice for the secretary.[26] These witnesses pointed out that the chairman had no responsibility for the conduct of military operations, and, therefore, could not be held accountable for any advice he gave. They asked, if the secretary wanted advice from persons with operational responsibility, why build up the stature and position of the chairman as spokesman for the military? The answer, of course, was to be found in the developments of the three previous years. And the full meaning of building the stature of the chairman can be understood only by referring to these developments.

Secretary of Defense Lovett found his hierarchical position and legal authority insufficient to control the decisions of the JCS. Instead of attempting to use his political power (as Secretary Louis Johnson had done on at least one occasion), he sought to place major decisions, such as force levels and budgets, with the service secretaries, subordinates he could more easily control. This approach to the problem raised a serious question of legality. The National Security Act specifically provided that the JCS (not the civilian secretaries) would "review . . . major material and personnel requirements of military forces. . . ." [27]— that is, force levels.

Congress strenuously opposed the 1949 attempts to make the chairman, rather than the JCS, the principal military advisor to the secretary, or to transfer the function of the JCS to the secretary himself. The only other way the JCS could be made subject to the hierarchical authority of the secretary was to change its function. The JCS must be made a staff to the secretary, rather than a body of service chiefs. The surest way to do this would be to sever their service ties. Why the final recommendations of the Rockefeller Commission fell short of this proposal is hard to determine. But, the Commission merely recommended elimination of the JCS command functions.

Mere removal of command authority was not enough, however. Even if the JCS was a staff agency for the secretary, what was to prevent it from offering three separate service-oriented recommendations on all questions? The answer seemed to lie in transforming the chairman

[26] See the testimony of Robert W. Johnson, Ferdinand Eberstadt, and Admiral Charles Cooke, House Committee on Government Operations, *Hearings on Plan 6*, pp. 48–65, 77–103, and 128 respectively; Schilling, Hammond, and Snyder, *Strategy, Politics, and Defense*, pp. 491, 518–20.

[27] U.S., Statutes at Large, LXI, 253, sec. 211.

from merely a presiding officer into an alternative source of military advice. But, elevation of the chairman had to be accomplished in such a way as to preserve the integrity of the JCS. Mr. Rockefeller felt he had determined a way of simultaneously accomplishing all these objectives.

During his testimony, Rockefeller recalled the statement made by Herbert Hoover in his 1949 recommendations that:

> All statutory authority now vested in the service departments or their subsidiary units be granted directly to the Secretary of Defense, subject to the authority of the President, and with further authority to delegate them as he sees fit and wise.[28]

If this had been done, Mr. Rockefeller pointed out, the statutory authority of all boards, including the JCS, would have been given to the secretary. And the secretary would have been able to do "just what this reorganization plan recommends, which is to correct the administrative weaknesses of the Joint Chiefs." [29] He went on to say that the proposed changes in the role of the chairman were purely *administrative*.

Members of the House Committee then asked Mr. Rockefeller what administrative weaknesses would be overcome by having the chairman direct the Joint Staff. He pointed out that in the previous year 1,700 items had come to the JCS for consideration. They ranged from matters involving the United Nations to determining service responsibility for maintaining paved roads in France that were damaged by United States military traffic. The reason for the strengthened position was to *control the flow* of this deluge of business and make sure only the "major items of national importance" came to the JCS.[30] The expression "major items of national importance" was crucial to the significance of these changes. Would questions of force levels and budget allocations be among these "major items?" Only subsequent operation of the system would tell, but the delegation of these questions to the service secretaries in 1951, plus the emphasis in 1953 on the "strategic planning" role of the JCS, suggested the probable course of future events.

Although the question of force levels never appeared in either the Rockefeller Commission Report or the hearings, the report did raise the equally difficult questions of research and development and the

---

[28] House Committee on Government Operations, *Hearings on Plan 6*, p. 152.
[29] *Ibid.*, p. 153.
[30] *Ibid.*, p. 156.

integration of new weapons systems into established programs. It recommended that the Joint Strategic Survey Committee, the committee to which the JCS had earlier delegated research and development questions,[31] "be the agency to work out the integration of new weapons into established weapons systems. . . ." [32] This committee, although not part of the Joint Staff, was subordinate to the JCS. Presumably this would be one of the subordinate committees referred to by the President when he said: "The proposed changes will relieve the Joint Chiefs of Staff, as a body, of a large amount of administrative detail involved in the management of its subordinate committee and staff structure." [33]

Notwithstanding statements about the "purely administrative" nature of these changes, the control over the Joint Staff and other subordinate JCS agencies given to the chairman had profound policy consequences. Whereas in 1949 the chairman was the presiding officer of the JCS, after 1953 he controlled the planning structure of the JCS system. In view of Secretary Lovett's attempts to by-pass the JCS, the JCS changes of 1953 probably ratified existing practices rather than instituted new ones. But after 1953, the chairman, not the JCS, became the spokesman for the military.

Efficiency with Economy

In his reorganization message, the President noted economy could be attained "only by decentralization of operations, under flexible and effective direction and control from the center." [34] The President went on to say that central control was impossible because some functions were "rigidly assigned by law to unwilling boards. . . ." [35] He wanted the boards eliminated, their functions given to the secretary, and six additional assistant secretaries appointed.[36]

The reorganization of 1949 had already substantially changed the Research and Development Board and the Munitions Board. Although maintaining the appearance of committees, they were in fact only advisory staffs for their chairmen. The boards in no way approached the concept of a committee used in the British Defense Committee

[31] See *supra*, Chapter VIII, p. 130.
[32] *Rockefeller Committee Report*, p. 8.
[33] *President's Reorganization Message*, p. 6.
[34] *Ibid.*, p. 3.
[35] *Ibid.*
[36] This would make a total of nine assistant secretaries.

system. Therefore, the President was merely pointing to the obvious: a committee does not make a good general staff agency. As the President said, committees are slow and clumsy.

The Rockefeller Committee had said the major weakness of the Defense Department was the difficulty in obtaining "complete, accurate, and understandable information on which to base decision." [37] The committee might well have added "non-conflicting" to its list of requirements. Service boards, intended as devices to bring operating levels into the policy process, simply did not serve as sources of a single recommendation.

In his testimony before the House Committee, Deputy Secretary of Defense Roger Kyes assured the committee members that these boards were not the "good, hard hitting organizations" capable of really doing "a job for this country." [38] He said committees simply couldn't operate. Constructive and destructive ideas just swirled around and around, and there was no way to pin down responsibility, continued the Deputy Secretary. He seemed to think staff agencies *had* to operate. He underscored the impossibility of expecting a committee to operate by relating the excessively long time it took the Munitions Board to write and publish a manual standardizing industrial security requirements for the three services.

Advocates of the committee system, the British, for example, would completely agree with Secretary Kyes about committees being ineffective operating devices. But they would point out that committees are not supposed to operate. If, for example, a security manual had to be standardized, the committee could approve or order the modification of manuals prepared by the service departments. It could not be expected to write one. It has more important duties.

Kyes' explanation of the role of service boards explained an apparent contradiction in the President's message. The President had begun his comments by stressing the need for nine assistant secretaries of defense, and operational decentralization. Kyes made it clear who the operators were to be and how decentralization was to take place. Operations were "decentralized" horizontally at the top. Each of the nine assistant secretaries would be assigned separate areas of responsibility. (Note the similarity of the President's message and the recommendations of the War Department's Simpson Board in 1945.)[39] Decentralization is the process of parceling out operating responsibility to staff officers at department level.

[37] *Rockefeller Committee Report*, p. 11.
[38] House Committee on Government Operations, *Hearings on Plan 6*, p. 34.
[39] See *supra*, Chapter II, pp. 31–32.

One might wonder what these provisions would do to the service secretaries, who the President described as the "principal agents for the management and direction of the entire defense enterprise." [40] Indeed, a member of the House Committee asked Nelson Rockefeller this question. Mr. Rockefeller answered that once these various staff agencies have made their recommendations to the secretary of defense (and the President, or both), the secretary (or President) would translate the recommendations into operating instructions for the service departments. The service departments would carry out the instructions. Mr. Rockefeller made no pretense about the participation of the service secretaries in the policy-making process. They were "doers."

The practice of parceling out responsibility and authority to various levels of an organization consisting of a horizontal staff and a vertical line requires a fiction. In order to preserve unity of command and hierarchical configuration, subordinates must report to only one superior and all lines of authority must converge on one man at the top. But at the same time, staff officers are to have real responsibility for their assigned functional areas. And in order to implement their responsibility they must have authority.

To whom do service secretaries report? The secretary of defense only? The secretary and the nine assistant secretaries? Who is really responsible for various aspects of operations? Just the service secretaries? Or do the assistant secretaries share responsibility with the service secretaries? Organization folklore solves this dilemma by its myth that staffs never exercise authority. They merely supervise or co-ordinate.[41] Mindful of this, the President said:

> Without imposing themselves into the direct lines of responsibility and authority between the Secretary of Defense and the Secretaries of the three military departments, the Assistant Secretaries of Defense will provide the Secretary with a continuing review of the Programs of the Defense Establishment and *help him institute major improvements in their execution.* They will be charged with *establishing systems* within their assigned fields for obtaining complete and accurate information to support recommendations to the Secretary. The Assistant Secretaries will make frequent inspection visits to our far flung installations and check for the Secretary the effectiveness and efficiency of operations in their assigned fields.[42] [Italics added.]

[40] House Committee on Government Operations, *Hearings on Plan 6*, p. 148.
[41] See *supra*, Chapter III, p. 40.
[42] *President's Reorganization Message*, pp. 5–6.

The inconsistencies of such statements seemingly do not bother advocates of the hierarchical general staff system, and they did not bother the reorganization advocates in 1953.

THE MEANING OF THE 1953 CHANGES

Assistant Secretaries of Defense

As in the case of the JCS changes, the addition of six more assistant secretaries and the elimination of the service boards ratified existing practice rather than instituted a new one. Indeed, the 1949 changes began the practice of substituting staff assistants for service policy boards. At that time the three assistants to the secretary were changed into assistant secretaries. Later, prior to the 1953 amendments, a fourth assistant was created for manpower and personnel.[43] The additional assistants recommended by the President simply continued the trend.

The President explained the position of the assistant secretaries by appealing to the myths of the hierarchical general staff system. They would usurp the "legal authority" of neither the secretary of defense nor the service secretaries. Both the President and the Rockefeller Committee had stipulated that the assistant secretaries would not be in the direct line of administrative authority. What more was necessary? By definition, they had no authority.

When authority is considered solely in terms of legal stipulations as it was in 1953, the lack of consideration to the complete contradiction between the "authority" of the assistant secretaries and that of the service secretaries is not surprising. The contradiction was not considered because the folklore of organization covers this contradiction with the myth that staffs do not exercise authority. But, if assistant secretaries were responsible for manpower and personnel, finance and budget, supply and logistics, properties and installations, health and medicine, did the service secretaries also have responsibility for these functions? If the assistant secretaries had the real responsibility, then the department would be centralized. If the service secretaries had the real authority, then the department would be decentralized. If they both had responsibility, then the department would be in a state of confusion.[44]

---

[43] House Committee on Government Operations, *Hearings on Plan 6*, p. 167.
[44] For a contemporary analysis of the significance of adding six assistant secretaries in terms of the service departments, see Eugene S. Duffield, "Organizing for Defense," *Harvard Business Review*, XXI, No. 5 (Sept.–Oct., 1953), 29–42.

A law of conservation of authority might be developed out of the confusion produced by assigning the authority to both the service secretaries and the assistant secretaries. If assistant secretaries have authority in functional areas, then the service secretaries do not. If the service secretaries have this authority, then the assistant secretaries do not. If they share authority, then each has less than full authority. But in all the alternatives except the first, centralization results. The only difference between the last two alternatives is in degree. But in either of these two cases, the authority of the service secretaries was diminished after 1953.

The JCS

After 1953, the services were in the process of becoming administrative subdivisions of the Department of Defense—unruly and at times insubordinate subdivisions, but subdivisions nonetheless. The "legalized" submerging of the services had implications for the operation of the JCS not apparent from merely considering the statutory changes involving the chairman. The JCS became an anachronism left over from an entirely different concept of organization. Its base of power was no longer three autonomous service departments, but three subordinate agencies within a centralized department. The JCS did not meet as the military heads of operating departments, but as a military staff whose advice was to be heeded at the discretion of the secretary. When these changes in its status are added to its loss of control over its own subordinate staff structure, it is clear that the JCS at best constituted a collective tenth assistant secretary of defense, or at worst, the advisors to its chairman who was the tenth assistant secretary of defense.

In terms of hierarchy and organization, the JCS had completely lost the position it held in 1947. Any resemblance between the American Defense Department and the British Ministry of Defense was completely gone by 1953. Defense policy in the United States was now reestablished in the classic mold. Policy aspirations were to be inserted at the top of a centralized organization and action was supposed to emerge at the bottom. The fact that the policy process never operated this way did not cause defense reformers to re-examine their organizational premises. Instead, it fortified their determination to make policy conform to their preconceptions of what it should be.[45] For example, if

[45] This practice is by no means peculiar to government. Amitai Etzioni observes that consultants working with one universal model, for example the Weberian model,

the Joint Chiefs failed to reach agreement, it was because they were parochial in their views.[46] They were parochial because the services were not sufficiently centralized. It never occurred to anyone that legal authority and hierarchical position might not be sufficient for the secretary of defense to control the JCS.

AUTHORITY OF THE SECRETARY OF DEFENSE

As in 1949, the first and foremost objective of the 1953 reorganization was to "clarify" the authority of the secretary of defense. And every change called for sought to place the secretary at the top of an organizational pyramid. Of the four specific organizational changes urged by the Rockefeller Committee, all dealt with lines of hierarchy (chairman of the JCS, Joint Staff, assistant secretaries, chain of command to unified commands). Rearranging the boxes and shifting the lines on an organizational chart would give the secretary the authority he needed.

The Hensel Study

The emphasis on redrawing organizational charts is rather strange in view of one study in the Rockefeller report. This study, an analysis of the legal authority of the secretary of defense, was made by H. Struve Hensel (legal counsel to the secretary of defense). It started with the words: "In our opinion, the Secretary of Defense now has by statute full and complete authority, subject only to the President and certain specific restrictions . . . over the Department of Defense, all its agencies, subdivisions, and personnel." The six restrictions contained the limitations noted in the previous chapter against merging the services or altering statutory roles and missions of the services. They also included prohibitions against a single chief of staff and denial of service access to Congress.[47]

---

have a tendency to recommend changes designed to bring the organization in line with the model. "Since the general models as a rule include some specific statements which appear as universals, the consequences may be regrettable." *A Comparative Analysis of Complex Organizations* (New York: The Free Press of Glencoe, 1961), pp. xii–xiv.

[46] See remarks by President Eisenhower, in Robert J. Donovan, *Eisenhower: The Inside Story* (New York: Harper and Bros., 1956), p. 330.

[47] See *supra*, Chapter VIII, p. 141. The six limitations were: (1) The secretary could not exercise his authority so as to change the statutory combatant functions

The secretary's statutory authority, the report continued, was superior to any other in the department and all other authorities assigned by Congress to subordinate units must be exercised in consonance with the secretary's will. There were no separate preserves within the department, immune from secretarial authority. "Congressional intent," said the study, "is clear and unmistakable. Nothing more is necessary." [48] This last statement is obviously wrong. Something more was necessary. The secretary had to *use* his authority.

The limits on the secretary listed in the report contain a clue to secretarial authority that everyone missed. Every one of these limits dealt with the preservation of the three armed services as separate entities. Throughout the hearings on defense organization from 1944 to 1953, it was difficult to tell whether Congress was more concerned with preserving its own prerogatives or with preserving combatant organizations that had proved their value in war. As one reads the lavish praise for the Air Force, Army, Navy, and Marine Corps, an impression is created in favor of the latter alternative. However, whatever Congress' motive, the clue for secretarial authority was obvious. No matter what the organization of the Defense Department, the secretary is going to have to share his authority with Congress. His effective authority must be political, not hierarchical.

The Hensel report exhausted all the adjectives possible for use in describing the omnipotent and universal legal authority of the secretary over the department. But no matter how great this power might be, or no matter how completely the secretary might succeed in centralizing the department, so long as one person disagreeing with a decision managed to gain a hearing in Congress, the secretary's authority would be challenged. But who was really challenging the secretary? His subordinates or Congress? What meaning did interservice rivalry really have aside from the partisans' ability to appeal their case to Congress?

Politics and Authority

The problem of authority was never a legal one; it was always political. Attempts to increase the secretary's authority were actually

---

of the services; (2) he could not change combatant functions indirectly by reassigning personnel and withholding funds; (3) he could not merge the three services; (4) he could not create a single military commander or a general staff; (5) he must submit department reorganization plans to the Congress; and (6) he could not deny service secretaries or JCS members access to the Congress or the President.

[48] *Rockefeller Committee Report*, p. 18.

efforts to prevent disagreement which might precipitate congressional intervention. Both Secretary Lovett's move to take deadlocked issues away from the JCS and the centralization of 1953 were attempts to submerge the level of disagreement.

This kind of a solution to policy disagreement makes two very questionable assumptions. The first is that defense problems are puzzles to which there is only one right answer. If this is so, then disagreements with the "one right answer" are parochial and unworthy assertions of service self-interest. The second assumption is that determination of the "one right answer" by the Defense Department and the executive is sufficient to make national policy.

Just as the executive branch must develop sufficient public and congressional support for other aspects of its program, so it must develop sufficient public and congressional support for its defense policy. The real authority of the secretary of defense depended upon his ability to galvanize presidential, congressional, and public support for his decisions. If a service could present a convincing case against the secretary's decision, Congress felt the secretary might not have the "one right answer" after all. Even if there was "one right answer," it could never become national policy until Congress was convinced.

The fatal flaw in the 1953 reorganization was its encouragement to the secretary to think he could make defense policy by virtue of his legal authority alone.

Hierarchy and Authority

After 1953, the Defense Department closely resembled the ideal model of a hierarchical general staff organization. The secretary of defense was at the top of the pyramid. Reporting to him were nine assistant secretaries who were assigned functional responsibilities. Unified commands and the service departments were beneath all these staff agencies. The flow of authority and responsibility was vertical and everything—communications, information, command, and authority—converged on the office of the secretary. Finally, the reformers considered the secretary in a position to "run" the department.

The JCS was the only box on the organizational chart detracting from this model bureaucracy. It just did not seem to fit (as indeed it did not fit) the pattern. But, on the other hand, its chairman did fit the pattern. Despite the absence of statutory authorization, the secretary could ignore the JCS if the chairman could in fact fill the role of his chief military advisor. As in the case of the Munitions Board and the Research and Development Board after 1949, the conflicting and confused counsel of the JCS would not be seriously harmful if the secretary could rely on the chairman.

A bitter and explosive issue, civil-military relations, seethed behind this apparently minor contradiction in an otherwise model hierarchy. Many members of the armed forces had long advocated a single chief of staff, but he was to be something more than just another assistant secretary of defense. In the Collins plan of 1945, for example, the chief of staff was to be an "executive" for the secretary. In the history of the War Department before World War II, the chief of staff was the channel through which the secretary reached (or, in actuality, tried to reach) all components of the Army. The chief of staff should have hierarchical status second only to the secretary himself. Nine civilians should not be equal to him.

In many respects the 1949 changes resembled the Collins plan. There were only three assistant secretaries. And the Joint Chiefs of Staff was the primary source of contact between the secretary and the services. Then a change occurred. After 1951, Secretary Lovett began to turn to the civilian service secretaries for counsel. Except for its role in directing the Korean War, the JCS began to play a smaller part within the department in terms of either administration or policy-making. Then in 1953, the JCS was removed from the chain of command to even the combat commands. What was more, six additional assistant secretaries appeared on the scene at the same time the JCS chairman was being strengthened. Not only was the JCS eased into a "purely planning" role, but also even the chairman was only one of ten voices demanding the attention of the secretary.

Then there was the matter of the service departments themselves. Although in his message, the President referred to them as the "principal agents" of the secretary of defense, in the next breath he described the important policy role of the assistant secretaries. The service departments were clearly reduced to operating subdivisions. And as the service departments declined, so did the JCS. The Joint Chiefs no longer represented the agencies that were the major partners in the defense policy process. They merely represented operating divisions which were subordinated in some undetermined degree to the assistant secretaries.

The 1953 reorganization created a General Staff. But it was a General Staff completely unknown to the military. It had its own character. It was a civilian General Staff. Thus another, and more explosive, dimension was added to the problems of defense organization. Whereas the issue had been one of centralization versus decentralization, after 1953 it became one of the services versus the Department of Defense—the military versus the civilians.

166   III: RETURN TO ORTHODOXY

Congressional Opposition

Hearings were held on the 1953 reorganization plan because some members of Congress wanted to introduce a resolution opposing changes affecting the chairman of the JCS. During the hearings, attention of the House Committee on Government Operations centered on the role of the chairman of the JCS. Members expressed concern that he would become too powerful, or that he might challenge civilian control and become a man on horseback.

The committee approved a resolution to delete those parts of the reorganization plan relating to the chairman. And this resolution condemned the proposed changes as "but another step on the road toward control by the military." [49] The resolution was defeated in the House. But the attitude of most congressmen and witnesses was best summarized during the testimony of Admiral William D. Leahy. He said the proposed changes regarding the chairman would create a situation substantially different from the system which had existed during the war; and he showed a general lack of enthusiasm for the reorganization plan. Finally when a congressman asked him why the changes should be approved, he replied: "President Eisenhower wants it; that is all." [50] The chairman of the committee asked Admiral Leahy if that was the only reason. He responded: "That is the only reason I can see." [51] He continued:

He [the President] has been a grand soldier and he has been in it all his life. When people ask me whether I object to this or not, I say, "How can I object to it if the President approves it?" He has more experience in wars than I have had. He is recognized as an expert. So if he wants it why not let him have it? That is my answer to it.

MR. DAWSON. You have given the best reason for it I have heard yet.[52]

Other congressmen seemed to have shared these views. Who would challenge the authority and experience of a man who had spent his life in the military? If this is what the President wants, why not give it to him?

---

[49] U.S., Congress, House, Committee on Government Operations, *Providing for the Taking Effect of Provisions of Reorganization Plan No. 6 of 1953*, 83d Cong., 1st Sess., H.R. 633 to Accompany H.J. Res. 264, 1953, p. 8.
[50] House Committee on Government Operations, *Hearings on Plan 6*, p. 211.
[51] *Ibid.*
[52] *Ibid.*, pp. 224–25.

X

THE REORGANIZATION
OF 1958

THE NEW LOOK

Two rivalries divided the Department of Defense after 1953. The first rivalry, one characterizing the defense establishment since its creation in 1947, was among the three services. The second rivalry, one taking recognizable form only after 1953, was between the services and the Department of Defense. However, between 1953 and 1958, two developments—sharply reduced defense budgets, and centralization of defense policy-making—focused attention on interservice rivalry and all but obscured the service-department rivalry.

Reduced Defense Budgets

Shortly after the new administration took office in 1953, campaign promises of "security with solvency" and a "new look" at defense policy were translated into drastically reduced defense budgets. The outgoing administration had prepared a budget of $40.1 billion for the 1954 fiscal year.[1] The new administration reduced this estimate 15 per cent,

---

[1] This budget was part of the "stretch-out" program begun under Secretary Lovett in 1951. And this program involved the following downward trend in defense spending: fiscal year 1952—$59.9 billion; fiscal year 1953—$48.4 billion; and fiscal year 1954—$40.1 billion. Because the JCS had deadlocked over these budgets, Secretary Lovett had turned force-level problems over to the service secretaries. See *supra*, Chapter IX, p. 149. Glenn H. Snyder provides a good summary of the "new look" in Schilling, Hammond, and Snyder, *Strategy, Politics, and Defense*, pp. 383–524.

to $34 billion. And in the following year the budget ceiling was further reduced another 14 per cent, to $28.8 billion—a 29 per cent cut in defense expenditures in two years.

The budgetary reductions of the new administration coincided with a complete turnover of JCS membership. Some authors on defense policy have dubbed this the "politicalization" of the JCS,[2] an attempt to select military commanders not committed to programs of the previous administration. Indeed one author said the power of the chairman was enhanced precisely because the newly selected chairman agreed with the new President, and he could be expected to vigorously support his policy in the JCS.[3] But whatever the real motives behind the particular selections made in 1953, the new chiefs agreed no more often than their predecessors. The operation of the JCS as a partner in the policy process did change, however.

Before 1953, the JCS had helped determine over-all defense budgets and over-all defense goals. It developed force level requirements and budgetary allocations among the services. Then the secretary of defense or the Budget Bureau, or both, attempted to scale down these recommendations to meet projected fiscal ceilings.[4] Military means, although considered separately from policy ends, at least influenced the final determination of policy.

The process was reversed after 1953. Budget and manpower ceilings were established first by the secretary of defense, at the direction of the President and in consultation with the assistant secretaries and the JCS chairman. Only then was the JCS asked to allocate funds among the services and establish force levels.[5] Furthermore, the JCS was directed to submit unanimously approved recommendations within budgetary ceilings.[6]

An observer of the budgetary process during these years described it as follows: "The budget as finally received by a service is a directed one in every sense. Each service then tailors its requirements to fit the money to be provided. . . ."

General Ridgway, a member of the JCS in 1953 had this to say:

They [force levels] were not based on the freely reached conclu-

---

[2] Millis, Mansfield, and Stein, *Arms and the State*, pp. 377, 403–4; and Schilling, Hammond, and Snyder, *Strategy, Politics, and Defense*, pp. 410–15.

[3] Millis, Mansfield, and Stein, *Arms and the State*, p. 377.

[4] See *supra*, Chapter IX, p. 148, and Finletter, *Power and Policy*, pp. 260–61.

[5] Millis, Mansfield, and Stein, *Arms and the State*, pp. 268, 403; Ridgway, *Soldier*, pp. 287–89; Gavin, *War and Peace*, pp. 166–68; and Huntington, *The Common Defense*, pp. 71–72.

[6] Gavin, *War and Peace*, p. 170.

sions of the Joint Chiefs of Staff. They were squeezed between the framework of arbitrary manpower and fiscal limits, a complete inversion of the normal process.

. . . the efforts of the Secretary of Defense and the chairman of the Joint Chiefs were directed toward securing the unanimous assent of the country's top military men to these preset plans.[7]

These statements describe the actual role of the JCS chairman. In 1953, Congress had opposed his elevation because of its fear the chairman would become an all-powerful spokesman of the military—a man on horseback. In practice, the reverse developed. The chairman became spokesman for the secretary of defense. The chairman, not the secretary, was captive.[8]

In public, and especially before Congress, the split between the JCS and the chairman of the JCS (and the secretary of defense) never became obvious. The members of the JCS found themselves caught between limited budgets and individual service requirements. Since funds for all were insufficient, each service chief tended to view the requirements of his own service as essential for national defense. When a service chief broke ranks before congressional committees, he did so to argue the superior claims of his service against the others. He did not reveal the extent of the split between the services and the Department of Defense.[9] And although Congress and the public might view the services' willingness to break ranks as interservice rivalry, the secretary of defense saw it for what it really was—rejection of the defense budget.[10]

Centralization

The changes of 1953 operated in such a way as to put great pressure on the JCS to accept the chairman's recommendations. The planning and staffing which linked strategic and force level decisions to logistics,

[7] Ridgway, *Soldier*, p. 289.

[8] General Maxwell D. Taylor discusses this role of the chairman at some length in *The Uncertain Trumpet* (New York: Harper and Bros., 1959), pp. 106–11.

[9] For further development of this point see Donald G. Gumz, "The Bureau of the Budget and Defense Fiscal Policy," *United States Naval Institute Proceedings*, LXXXV, No. 4 (April, 1959), 80–89.

[10] In Professor Huntington's words, the civil-military debate was "sublimated and deflected into a controversy among the services." "Interservice Competition and the Political Roles of the Armed Services," *The American Political Science Review*, LV, No. 1 (March, 1961), 40–52.

supply, and operations were still performed in the service departments by service staffs. If the Joint Chiefs disregarded the recommendations of the chairman either because they found his recommendation unacceptable or because they could not agree upon a supporting service strategy, planning in the service departments would become meaningless. And in either case the final budget allocations would reflect the chairman's recommendations, not those of the JCS. Furthermore, the chairman, when acting without the support of the JCS, had neither means nor *responsibility* to develop the logistic plans necessary to implement his strategic or force level recommendations.[11]

There was still another pressure on the JCS to submit to the chairman. If service planning was rendered meaningless by the failure of the JCS to accept its chairman's recommendations, the assistant secretaries of defense constituted the only other source of plans. Although not equipped in either personnel or knowledge for detailed staff work, the assistant secretaries began to develop supplementary lines of authority and communications to those offices in the service departments whose duties were within their assigned functional areas.[12] At least potentially, the assistant secretaries constituted an alternate source of planning. And thus the JCS found itself threatened by a loss of its policy functions if it submitted to the chairman, and loss of both its policy and planning functions if it did not. In the first instance, policy would be centralized; and in the second, both policy and planning would be centralized.[13]

A further source of dissatisfaction for the JCS was that the JCS left itself open to accusations of the worst kind of obstructionism when it resisted the chairman and the entire planning machinery threatened to break down. When it submitted to the chairman, the JCS was forced to assume responsibility for decisions and policy that it had neither made nor approved. Moreover, JCS members had to defend these policies before Congress.

Centralization and the Policy Process

In form, the JCS still consisted of the military chiefs of the three service departments. As service chiefs, each was responsible for the condition of his own service's forces. The position of the service chief was

[11] Further elaboration of this planning problem can be found in Schilling, Hammond, and Snyder, *Strategy, Politics, and Defense*, pp. 381, 491, 518–20.
[12] Stanley, *American Defense*, pp. 126–27.
[13] General Gavin provides examples of this dilemma in his *War and Peace*, pp. 166–69.

still linked to responsibility for individual service departments. On the JCS, however, the service chief had to accept and implement programs bearing no relation to his concept of service need. In effect, the JCS was expected to answer the question of "how" policy was to be implemented, without considering service capability and the extent to which capabilities might influence policy. The JCS was never permitted to get involved in questions of "what" the policy should be. The contradictions of the "how-what" (or means-ends) dichotomy made the dual responsibility of the JCS an impossible burden.

Policy directives to the JCS included both defense policy ends, and budget and manpower ceilings. The JCS insisted budgetary and manpower considerations were means and not ends.[14] Therefore, although the JCS and the secretary agreed that means and ends must be separated, they disagreed over what constituted ends and what constituted means. And because they accepted the means-end dichotomy, each accused the other of not fulfilling his proper responsibility. From the point of view of the JCS, the secretary was constantly getting into the "purely military" problem of dictating force levels. From the point of view of the secretary, the JCS was trying to dictate policy.

Because it consisted of service representatives, the JCS could not become the impartial staff agency which the secretary of defense tried to make it. Individual members could not be made willing partners in a policy which impaired their service's effectiveness. They could not cut the forces or the budgets of their service in the name of the "national interest." Indeed the secretary's program was not in the "national interest." It was merely the arbitrary dictate of a budget-conscious administration. The *real* "national interest," in the eyes of the JCS, depended upon the well-being of their respective services. Apparently no one considered adjusting the two views.

The secretary's view of the nature of policy and the policy process made him unable to play the political and bargaining role demanded for successful operation of the JCS system. He passed presidential policy on down to the JCS. The JCS *should* be able to come up with the best possible allocation among the services to implement that policy. If the JCS could not agree, what recourse did he have other than to accept the advice of the chairman. After all, the chairman was a military man, and these were purely military matters.

In view of the stress of the times, the limited budgets, and the attitudes of the participants, it is amazing that the system operated at all. Because of the pressures generated in the defense establishment, the

[14] See *supra*, Chapter VII, p. 107.

psychological setback of the Russian sputniks in 1957, and the interservice bickering, the President determined to reorganize the Defense Department. In a special message to Congress in April, 1958, the President set forth his analysis of defense problems. He said that separate ground, sea, and air warfare was gone forever. The next war would involve all services in a concentrated effort. Peacetime organization must prepare for this kind of war. Strategic and tactical planning must be unified, and combat forces must be organized into "truly unified" commands. Forces must be equipped with the most efficient weapons science could develop, and they must be "singly led and prepared to fight as one, regardless of service." [15] No longer was there justification for a separate Air Force, Army, and Navy. Modern warfare demanded new services organized on a new basis.

The problem was not with the policy machinery at all, or so the President seemed to say. The problem was with the operational machinery—the services themselves. Or was it? Later in his message the President said that "we must cling no longer to statutory barriers that weaken executive action and civilian authority. We must free ourselves of emotional attachments to service systems of an era that is no more." [16] He continued that "well meaning attempts to protect traditional concepts and prerogatives" not only impaired a "fully effective defense," but also "impaired civilian authority." [17] The President seemed to be saying that some connection existed between having an Army, Navy, and Air Force and having effective civilian control.

There must be "clear command channels" from the secretary of defense to the operational forces, the President continued. The secretary's military staff had to be strengthened to provide him with needed military advice. Research and development functions had to be reorganized and centralized. And finally, "all doubts as to the full authority of the Secretary of Defense" had to be removed. At this point the President returned to the same theme that had dominated previous defense reorganization—policy machinery and the authority of the secretary of defense. And when the President submitted a set of specific reorganization proposals in mid-April, this theme dominated.

The President's emphasis on the extent to which technology was revolutionizing modern warfare was completely sound. Thermonuclear weapons, intercontinental ballistic missiles, nuclear powered submarines

---

[15] U.S., Congress, House, *Message from the President of the United States Transmitting Recommendations Relative to our Entire Defense Establishment*, 85th Cong., 2d Sess., H.D. 366, 1958, p. 1. Cited hereafter as *Message from the President*.
[16] *Ibid.*
[17] *Ibid.*, p. 2.

were invalidating existing military doctrine and strategies at a rapid pace. The resulting changes in military capabilities impacted on national policy and made unprecedented demands on defense decision makers.[18] Just as in the past combat organizations would have to be adjusted to accommodate the unique demands of revolutionary weapons. However, the President extended this relationship to include the organization of those agencies responsible for the creation and support of combat units. At least neither he nor those who supported his proposed changes indicated an awareness of any possible distinction between the two types of organization involved.

TRULY UNIFIED COMBATANT COMMANDS

During the hearings held by the House and Senate armed services committees, testimony centered on the authority of the secretary of defense, not on the demands of modern warfare. In order to create "truly unified" combatant commands, the secretary of defense must have greater freedom in transferring, reassigning, or abolishing the statutory (combatant) functions of the three services. The President asked to have the secretary make such changes as he deemed necessary after notifying the committees on armed services.[19] Although combatant functions would be assigned to unified commands, the President stressed, the three services would continue to provide logistic, training, and manpower support functions.

The proposed system called for a division of responsibility corresponding to the division of functions between the services and the unified commands. Unified commanders would be directly responsible to the secretary of defense for the combat capability of the unified commands. Service secretaries would be responsible to the secretary of defense for manning, administering, and supplying the forces assigned to

[18] An enormous body of literature dealing with the impact of nuclear weapons on strategy began to appear at this time. A representative sample would include: Oskar Morganstern, *The Question of National Defense* (New York: Random House, 1959), Henry A. Kissinger, *The Necessity for Choice* (New York: Harper, 1960), Bernard Brodie, *Strategy in the Missile Age* (Princeton: Princeton University Press, 1959), Herman Kahn, *On Thermonuclear War* (Princeton: Princeton University Press, 1960), Glenn H. Snyder, *Deterrence and Defense* (Princeton: Princeton University Press, 1961), Arthur I. Waskow, *The Limits of Defense* (Garden City: Doubleday, 1962), and J. David Singer, *Deterrence, Arms Control, and Disarmament* (Columbus: Ohio State University Press, 1962).

[19] U.S., Congress, House, Committee on Armed Services, *Communication from the President of the United States Transmitting a Draft of Legislation,* 85th Cong., 2d Sess., 1958, p. 3. Cited hereafter, *President's Draft Legislation.*

unified commands. Whereas in 1953, the chain of command went directly from the secretary of defense to the service secretary to the unified commander for all activities and responsibilities, in 1958 the President proposed setting up a dual command line, one "military," and the other "civilian."

The President pointed out further that some parts of the National Security Act might contain elements of doubt as to the full authority of the unified commanders. For example, in referring to the authority of the air force chief of staff, the act gave him command over certain air force components. If these provisions remained in the law, they would conflict with the authority of the unified commander when air force components were assigned to him.

Finally, the secretary of defense would need help because he was to command the unified commands directly, instead of through the service secretaries. And help would be provided by making certain changes in the JCS system. First, the Joint Staff should be increased in size. Second, the Joint Chiefs should be allowed more time to devote to JCS duties as opposed to service duties. Third, the chairman of the JCS should be allowed greater authority over the Joint Staff.

Congressional Criticism

Members of the armed services committees expressed reservations about the manner for organizing the "truly unified" combatant commands. They did not doubt the necessity to organize operational units into commands tailored to modern needs, but they did question the provisions which purported to bring about modernization.

Congressmen were particularly concerned with the request to allow the secretary greater authority to determine the roles and missions of the services. They recognized the need for permitting the secretary latitude to determine the functions of the new unified commands, but they failed to see why Congress' role should be so restricted. They were particularly concerned because the only way, under the new proposals, for Congress to prevent an action of the secretary would be to pass a law. A law is subject to veto, and Congress can override a veto only by a two-thirds majority vote. Committee members felt congressional supervision which might require affirmative action by a two-thirds vote approached an absence of supervision. In the words of Carl Vinson, the chairman of the House Armed Services Committee, "If service roles and missions were removed from law and made subject to executive determination, little would remain for Congress except to appropriate funds." [20]

Aside from congressional fears about delegation of power for service roles and missions possibly involving an abdication of their constitutional duty to the executive, members of the armed services committees wondered why the secretary needed such untrammeled authority to establish unified commands. In questioning General Omar Bradley, the counsel for the House Armed Services Committee asked, "Which functions did the Secretary contemplate transferring, if the authority was granted?" Bradley replied that he did not know any to be transferred. The counsel then asked, "Why not bring such matters individually to Congress, if that was the case?" Bradley said some of the changes would be so minor that Congress "wouldn't want to bother about them." [21] The counsel then pointed out if it was not a question of winning or losing the next war, and if the changes would probably be minor, why was this power so important to the secretary? And was it necessary to create "truly unified" commands? Bradley answered that in wartime the changes might be "big things." The counsel replied, "If that was the case, perhaps Congress should be consulted." This line of questioning, although quite interesting, got nowhere.[22]

Despite the insistence of witnesses that military requirements demanded more flexibility in the secretary's authority to assign service roles and missions, no illustrations of this need were provided. Gradually committee members began to sense another use to which the power might be put. It occurred to several members of Congress that perhaps the administration wanted the power to change the three services rather than to develop "truly unified" commands. In the House committee, Representative Paul Kilday asked Secretary of Defense McElroy whether this power would allow him to consolidate the combatant functions of all the services into one command. The Secretary replied: "Yes, that could happen. And I suppose you could also organize your support forces into unified commands if you wished to." [23]

Admiral Burke was asked if he thought the support as well as the

[20] U.S., Congress, House, Committee on Armed Services, *Report, Department of Defense Reorganization Act of 1958*, 85th Cong., 2d Sess., H.R. No. 1765, 1958, p. 35. Cited hereafter as House Committee on Armed Services, *Report, 1958*.

[21] U.S., Congress, House, Committee on Armed Services, *Hearings, Reorganization of the Department of Defense*, 85th Cong., 2d Sess., 1958, p. 6515. Cited hereafter as House Committee on Armed Services, *Hearings, 1958*.

[22] *Ibid.*, pp. 6515–16.

[23] *Ibid.*, p. 5999.

combatant functions of the services would be assigned to unified commands, thereby destroying the services. He replied: "I do not see any danger of it, sir, because I do not think that anybody has the intent to do that. But it is possible to do that perhaps." [24]

At another point in his testimony, the Secretary of Defense assured the House committee there was no intention of consolidating the administrative functions of the three services into unified commands. Unified commands would be operational commands concerned with combat. The three services would continue to provide training, administration, and logistic support.[25] The committee then asked the Secretary to define what he meant by combatant functions. His definition did not do much to reassure the committee: "It had to be major or important, it had to be combatant, which means it involves certain participation in combat, and it had to be a function." [26] The Secretary apologized for the inadequacies of this definition by saying that to be more specific would involve forecasting the future and unwisely limiting a subsequent administration.

The armed services committees found the justifications of additional authority for the secretary to alter service roles and missions unconvincing. They were considerably disturbed because in their opinion the proposed changes would involve an unconstitutional delegation of their obligations. Senator Russell was emphatic and rather eloquent on the point:

> I must say I am intrigued with, but not convinced by, the argument that the Congress ought to resolve all its troubles by just delegating all of its powers to the executive branch. . . .
>
> If that argument is good, with respect to the Department of Defense, it is good with respect to any other department. If we do, it is just a confession that the Congress has outlived it usefulness. . . .
>
> I want to give the Secretary any authority that is necessary in this bill. But I cannot accept the basic argument that the Congress, because it might be criticized for the manner of carrying out its constitutional responsibilities, ought to delegate all of them to any executive officer. . . .[27]

---

[24] U.S., Congress, Senate, Committee on Armed Services, *Hearings, Department of Defense Reorganization Act of 1958,* 85th Cong., 2d Sess., 1958, pp. 116–17. Cited hereafter as Senate Committee on Armed Services, *Hearings, 1958.*

[25] House Committee on Armed Services, *Hearings, 1958,* p. 6138.

[26] Senate Committee on Armed Services, *Hearings, 1958,* p. 306.

[27] *Ibid.,* p. 68.

Whatever the true motives of the administration in requesting such a broad grant for power from Congress, the manner in which the request was justified and the lack of restrictions surrounding the proposed authorization antagonized Congress. As might be suspected, Congress, in the final wording of the reorganization bill, insured its participation. It provided for congressional veto of any proposed alteration of combatant functions by the passage of a disapproving resolution in either House.[28]

With respect to the removal of provisions which might impede the full authority of the unified commander over his forces, the second part of the President's proposed implementation of "truly unified" commands, Congress found little to criticize. Accordingly, it agreed to removal of the word "command" from the statutory duties of the service chiefs of staff.

The final element of the President's proposals for creating "truly unified" combatant commands consisted of three points. The Joint Staff was to be increased in size. The chiefs of staff were to delegate some of their service duties to their vice-chiefs (thus gaining more time for JCS duties). And the authority of the JCS chairman over the Joint Staff was to be increased. During hearings, both armed services committees carefully probed the reasons for these changes. In regard to the delegation of service duties to the vice-chiefs, the committees were concerned that a separation of the JCS from the services might result. Witnesses assured the committees that this would not happen. They said the whole purpose was to give the JCS more time for its corporate duties, not to sever its service ties. The committees accepted this explanation and stressed their conviction that the JCS must represent the services.

The committee's reason for maintaining the tie between the JCS and the services is worth considering. Carl Vinson said the JCS system must be dominated "by the responsible chiefs of the military services, who, subject to the civilian authority of the Secretary of Defense, provide the highest strategic planning and direction." [29] And when a plan is developed "those who have themselves made the plan—subject always to final civilian authority—are responsible for carrying it out." [30] Although the chiefs of staff may delegate some of their functions to deputies, they must never be cut off from their services or delegate their service responsibilities. The "salient characteristic of the Joint Chiefs

[28] U.S., Statutes at Large, LXXII, 514, sec. 3.
[29] House Committee on Armed Services, Report, 1958, p. 32.
[30] Ibid.

of Staff concept—unity of responsibility and authority" must be preserved.[31] In sum, Congress viewed the "two-hat" character of the JCS as essential. But in light of later testimony, it was questionable whether the administration shared its view.

Congressmen wanted to know why the Joint Staff had to be increased in size, and especially why the chairman should be given more authority to direct it. Secretary of Defense McElroy replied that since the chain of command to the combat commands did not go through service departments, the Joint Staff would be taking over some planning functions formerly performed by service staffs. More members were needed to do this additional planning. The authority of the chairman to assign duties to the Joint Staff was only intended to take some of the regular burden of supervising the Joint Staff from the JCS which was already overworked.

The armed services committees were particularly concerned about the centralizing effects of these proposals. They raised and questioned the value of taking service departments out of the chain of command. Five years earlier, the same President had asked for insertion of service departments into the command line. What, they asked, necessitated the change in 1958? The administration's answer was that the shift in command took one step out of the chain of command. It would speed up reaction time. Modern war demanded reflex action.

In questioning Secretary McElroy, the House Committee counsel observed that currently the chain of command to unified commands involved three steps: the President, the secretary of defense, and the service department. The new proposal, he argued, did not remove a step. It merely changed a step. Orders would still have to pass through three echelons: the President, the Secretary, and the Joint Staff. Was this not, he said, merely substituting one step for another? The Secretary responded that he did not consider this as another link. It really was just adding another capability to the Joint Staff.[32]

Later, during the testimony of General Nathan Twining, chairman of the JCS, the question of adding a "new capability" to the Joint Staff came up again. He was asked, "If the services were relieved of planning for the unified commands and if these functions were given to the Joint Staff, did not this transform the Joint Staff into a general staff?" He conceded it did as far as operations went.[33]

Congress decided the proposals of the administration came too close

[31] Ibid.
[32] House Committee on Armed Services, Hearings, 1958, p. 6105.
[33] Ibid., p. 6186.

to separating responsibility from authority. It authorized a doubling of the size of the Joint Staff, and permitted the service chiefs to delegate some functions to their vice-chiefs. However, Congress insisted on authorizing the JCS, as well as the chairman, to assign duties to the Joint Staff. And although the chairman was permitted to supervise the work of the Joint Staff and its director, he was to do so in behalf of the JCS. He was not to have authority independent of the JCS.

The Meaning of the Changes in the JCS System

The 1958 changes in the JCS system take on significance when related to events occurring between 1953 and 1958.[34] Because the chairman of the JCS had no way to develop the plans necessary to support his recommendations to the secretary of defense, his increased control over the Joint Staff could be viewed as an attempt to provide him with a staff. By freeing the Joint Chiefs from their service duties, they could be transformed into a group of senior advisors for the chairman. In total effect, the proposals approximated a single chief-of-staff system. All combatant elements of the three services could be organized into unified commands. Unified commands reported directly to the secretary of defense. The chairman, advised by the Joint Chiefs, and supported by the Joint Staff, would provide military advice to the secretary and direct the unified commands in his behalf.

These arrangements could realize the ideal of the hierarchical system. The command line to operating forces would be short and direct. Operating forces would be "co-ordinated" by the Joint Staff under the chairman of the JCS. The Joint Chiefs would simply be a personal staff for the chairman. The secretary would be at the apex of this organizational pyramid. He could be assured of a single recommendation from the JCS because its chairman would resolve disagreement and report only the final compromise to the secretary.

Whatever the ultimate motives behind the proposed changes in the JCS, they did attack the "two-hat" concept on two fronts. First, there was an attempt to sever or at least reduce the ties between the JCS and the services. Having the service chiefs increasingly delegate their service duties to a deputy might eventually cause a reorientation of the JCS. Second, there was an attempt to reduce the services themselves. The services would no longer consist of operational forces (or at least not very many of them). They were to be transformed into support agencies.

[34] See *supra*, pp. 167–69.

As the services became support agencies, the JCS and the Joint Staff would be transformed from being representatives of the combatant forces into an independent operational staff, similar to the prewar army general staff.[35] Instead of a series of committees horizontally linking the three services, the JCS and the Joint Staff would become central planning agencies, giving orders vertically to a series of "truly unified" combatant forces.

The British had said the "cardinal principle" of their defense system was that "it should be the men responsible in the service departments for carrying out the approved policy who are brought together in the central machine to formulate it." [36] The cardinal principle of American defense organizations seems to have been to separate operational responsibility from command authority. For this was precisely what the administration's proposals would have produced.

Congress fought a delaying action against the 1958 proposals. Although yielding on most points, it insisted upon continued JCS direction of the Joint Staff. And it insisted upon the maintenance of a link of responsibility between the JCS and the services. But no provision was made for linking the unified commands to the JCS structure.

SEPARATELY ADMINISTERED SERVICE DEPARTMENTS

The President recommended deletion of the provision of the National Security Act requiring the separate administration of services by their civilian secretaries. He also asked for removal of the section allowing service chiefs and service secretaries to make recommendations directly to Congress. These changes, said the President, would give the secretary of defense authority to develop the utmost economy and efficiency within the department.

Sand in the Gear Box

Members of Congress asked Secretary McElroy what these provisions had to do with decreased "reaction time" and a streamlined chain of command. He replied that these provisions in the present law conflicted with the authority of the secretary. Carl Vinson of the House Armed Services Committee pressed the point. The provisions, he said, had nothing whatsoever to do with unified commands. The Secretary replied

[35] See *supra*, Chapter I, p. 17.
[36] *White Paper on Defense, 1946*, p. 275.

that he needed additional authority to make the "decentralized" unified command system operate properly.

Congressmen questioned a procession of witnesses from the Defense Department about the relationship between unified commands and the provision requiring separate administration of the three service departments. Witnesses admitted the secretary's authority had never been successfully challenged. They admitted he had overriding authority. But they insisted he still did not have adequate authority.[37] At one point, in exasperation, Representative Vinson demanded that General Bradley suggest "to the committee any English word [sic] that carries more authority than 'direction, authority and control'!" [38]

Secretary McElroy argued that the phrase "separately administered" was not a direct legal limit to his authority, but "sand in the gear box." [39] He could decide and get results, but the phrase lent itself "to the interpretation that the Secretaries of the military departments in some manner stand between . . . the Secretary of Defense and the . . . military services. . . ." [40] Furthermore, said the Secretary, this phrase impeded the "proper delegation of authority and the free exchange of information" between the assistant secretaries of defense and the assistant secretaries and other subordinates within the military departments.[41]

These remarks of the Secretary made no pretense at defending the fiction (which had been defended in 1953) that the assistant secretaries of defense would not "intrude" themselves into the line of authority between the secretary of defense and the service secretaries.[42] The department was experiencing the same problem characterizing all hierarchical general staff systems. Conflict was developing between line and staff.[43] If the conflict was resolved in favor of the service secretaries, the department would be decentralized. If the conflict was resolved in favor of the assistant secretaries, centralization would result. Conflict between line and staff, if it is to be resolved, must result in the subordination of one or the other.

Secretary McElroy left no doubt as to how he thought the conflict should be settled. He said that service autonomy and the phrase "sepa-

---

[37] See the testimony of General Thomas D. White and Mr. Coolidge in House Committee on Armed Services, *Hearings, 1958*, pp. 6471 and 5987, respectively. See also the testimony of Secretary of Defense McElroy and Admiral Radford in Senate Committee on Armed Services, *Hearings, 1958*, pp. 638 and 419, respectively.
[38] House Committee on Armed Services, *Hearings, 1958*, pp. 64–74.
[39] *Ibid.*, p. 5987.
[40] *Ibid.*
[41] Senate Committee on Armed Services, *Hearings, 1958*, pp. 10–11.
[42] See *supra*, Chapter IX, p. 159.
[43] *supra*, Chapter III, pp. 39–41.

rately administered" might have had some meaning between 1947 and 1949. But after 1949, the phrase became an "unnecessary and confusing anachronism. Separately administered," said the Secretary, "beclouds the respective responsibilities of those to whom the Secretary . . . has delegated the responsibility for carrying out certain objectives. . . ."— the assistant secretaries of defense.[44]

The reason that "separately administered" beclouded the authority of the assistant secretaries was that it allowed the service secretaries to resist their intervention into department operations. Service secretaries could claim a statutory duty to administer their individual departments. But the problem would arise only if the assistant secretaries involved themselves directly in the administration of the services. The assistant secretaries were so involving themselves; and this was made clear during the testimony of administration witnesses.[45] Assistant secretaries were issuing directives on such topics as garbage disposal on service posts and soil conservation (jargon for landscaping).

The assistant secretaries were in fact usurping operating functions. And the Secretary was asking for removal of any parts of the National Security Act which might be interpreted as a denial of their "legal right" to do so. When he was asked if he wanted the assistant secretaries to have legal authority to give orders in their own name, Secretary McElroy replied negatively. He said he merely wanted to strengthen the ability of the assistant secretaries "to work out coordinated direction in the department." [46] He went on to say that he needed "lieutenants" to work out in free discussion how to establish co-ordinate positions among the services. In effect, the Secretary expected the assistant secretaries to resolve service disagreement, develop programs, and supervise their execution.

Furthermore, if the assistant secretaries were to have program responsibility, they had to be able to deal directly with subordinate parts of the services. Under present arrangements, the Secretary continued, orders must flow from a section within a subdivision of an assistant secretary's office, up through the various levels to the secretary of defense, and then back down to the appropriate subsection of a service department. Secretary McElroy wanted the subordinate within the assistant secretary's office to proceed directly to the appropriate subordi-

[44] House Committee on Armed Services, *Hearings, 1958*, p. 6787.
[45] See *ibid.*, pp. 6079, 6514, 6778–82; and Senate Committee on Armed Services, *Hearings, 1958*, pp. 13–16, 309–10, 410–19.
[46] Senate Committee on Armed Services, *Hearings, 1958*, p. 17.

nate in a service department. If any appeal was necessary it should be settled between the assistant secretary and the service secretary.[47]

These comments reflect both the degree of centralization which had already taken place and the problems accompanying centralization. When the channels of communication become too long or overburdened, they are often bypassed and short-circuited. Staff officers will deal directly with subordinate line officers.[48] And apparently this was true in the Department of Defense. The assistant secretaries and their subordinates were bypassing the chain of command and the service secretaries. They were going directly to subordinate service agencies. The remarkable development in 1958 was the Secretary's insistence on legalizing the process. The Secretary wanted the assistant secretaries to issue orders to operating agencies. As mentioned earlier, issuance of orders by the staff even violates the myths of the hierarchical general staff concept of staff-line relations. Staff should "co-ordinate" not "command."

Secretary McElroy saw the authority of the assistant secretaries as intimately involved in his own authority. If his authority was to be effective, he must be able to delegate it to his assistant secretaries. And, by the way, this was what the Secretary meant by decentralization: decisions must be made by the assistant secretaries. This concept of authority is right out of the catalogue of "principles" associated with the hierarchical general staff system,[49] and it closely approaches the notion of command which developed in the Army before World War II.[50] The assistant secretaries were extensions of the personality of the secretary of defense. When they acted, they acted in his name. When they spoke, they spoke with his voice. When they exercised authority, they exercised his authority (even so, they never issued commands). Even these incantations can be accepted more readily than their corollary, namely, that the secretary could in fact control all of their actions.

Because of the Secretary's concept of authority and its method of implementation, denial of congressional access to service secretaries and their chiefs of staff followed logically. The highest appeal a subordinate could possibly have without "challenging" the authority of the secretary would be to the secretary himself. And since the assistant secretaries were to speak in the name of the secretary, appeals should really end

[47] *Ibid.*, p. 298.
[48] See *supra*, Chapter III, p. 40.
[49] See *supra*, Chapter III, pp. 45–46.
[50] See *supra*, Chapter II, pp. 22–23.

with them.[51] Since appeal to the secretary was looked upon with disfavor, appeals to Congress could not be tolerated.

DIRECTOR OF RESEARCH AND ENGINEERING

The President asked for the creation of a director of research and engineering. He would "perform such duties as the Secretary of Defense may prescribe. . . ." [52] In defending the need for the director, Secretary McElroy said that too many issues were coming directly to him for decision because the services could not agree on the proper assignment of responsibilities for new weapons systems. Furthermore, the secretary could not make decisions of such a technical nature. Commenting on this, Senator Russell conceded that "the Secretary of Defense is often in a dilemma, but do you think any law on earth that Congress passes is going to still the advocates of Talos, Nike, or any other weapon?" [53] An exchange between Secretary McElroy and Senator Henry Jackson revealed the Secretary's attitude on this very point:

SENATOR JACKSON. What is to prevent the Department of Defense from dealing with this problem now? That is what I am getting at. I am talking now specifically of research and development.

SECRETARY McELROY. One of our beliefs is that in the control of research and development we will be able to catch this kind of thing at the very early state which is where it could be settled.

In other words, who is to be given the assignment of doing this development job for a particular kind of mission.

SENATOR JACKSON. Don't you have authority on that now?

SECRETARY McELROY. In my judgment we do not have it to the degree that we will have it in the new legislation, which is the creation of the new position of Director of Research and Engineering.

SENATOR JACKSON. You now have an Assistant Secretary of Defense for Research and Development.

SECRETARY McELROY. *But he can't give orders.*

SENATOR JACKSON. Yes, but the Secretary of Defense can.

SECRETARY McELROY. You see, that is a good deal of the point that

[51] Secretary McElroy's statement that he expected assistant secretaries and service secretaries to "work things out" lends weight to this interpretation. Senate Committee on Armed Services, *Hearings, 1958,* p. 298.

[52] *President's Draft Legislation,* p. 7.

[53] Senate Committee on Armed Services, *Hearings, 1958,* p. 319.

we have made throughout here, Senator Jackson. The Secretary of Defense, if he made every decision in the Department, is not lacking in any authority he requires.

The problem is to get authority down to the levels where most of the decisions must be made. [Italics added.]

What an extraordinary admission! The Secretary was saying that he could not exercise all the authority he had. He was invoking the same argument used by advocates of decentralization—authority that cannot be exercised is a worthless asset.

Guided by the logic of organization folklore, the secretary could not permit authority to be delegated downward to operators. It must be kept at the top. According to organization folklore, authority exercised at the top by staff officers does not impinge upon secretarial authority, while authority exercised by line officers does.

Some such logic must have guided the Secretary, because he wanted to give the director of research and engineering not only authority, but also *operating functions*—purchasing and contracting power.[54]

This last proposal signaled a new and significant development in defense organization. Trapped in the contradictions of the hierarchical general staff concept, defense reformers were returning to a perverted form of the 1947 concept. Authority was to be shared; it *had* to be shared. But in 1958, it had to be shared not by those responsible for the operational performance of the armed services, but by an undetermined (if not unidentified) number of functional assistant secretaries and directors.

This new trend was obscured if not lost in the arguments for centralization. Despite the Secretary's admission of his inability to perform the functions already assigned to his office, the burden of the testimony in 1958 was in favor of giving him more functions.

CONGRESSIONAL ACTION

In reviewing the President's proposals, the congressional committees obtained ample evidence that the purpose of the proposals was to centralize the department. Nevertheless, Congress proceeded to approve most of the administration's proposals. As indicated previously, Congress insisted upon the continuance of JCS supervision of the Joint Staff, although they permitted the chairman to manage the staff on behalf of the Joint Chiefs.

[54] Senate Committee on Armed Services, *Report, 1958*, pp. 33–34.

After surprisingly little debate, Congress approved an amendment proposed by Representative John McCormack giving the executive extremely wide latitude to transfer, reassign, abolish, or consolidate functions of the armed services. In the matter of statutory functions (roles and missions), the secretary had to report "pertinent details" to the armed services committees thirty days before any change was to be effective. To prevent the change, either House of Congress had to pass a disapproving resolution.[55]

In the event of "hostilities" or threat of "hostilities," the President was authorized to make any changes he deemed necessary. Such changes would be effective until the termination of hostilities.[56]

The result of these provisions was to give the secretary much more freedom than previously to reorganize the Defense Department. Before 1958, the reorganization provisions of 1949 governed all departmental changes. The provisions of the 1949 act required the submission of *all* changes to Congress. The 1958 act was worded so that changes not involving statutory functions[57] could be made without seeking congressional approval. Furthermore, the act specifically provided for the reorganization of service and supply activities common to more than one military department at the discretion of the secretary.

Regarding the status of the service departments, the 1958 act specified that each of them would be "separately organized" under its own secretary, and that each would function under the "direction, authority, and control" of the secretary of defense.[58] The words "separately *administered*" were finally dropped.

The act permitted assistant secretaries of defense to issue orders to the military departments, providing they had authorization in writing from the secretary of defense. However, the civilian secretaries and service chiefs were still permitted direct access to Congress, if they first notified the secretary of their intention.

Legislative-Executive Relations

There was little question of Congress' primary concern with preserving its prerogatives in the formulation and determination of defense policy in 1958. In the words of Representative Carl Vinson:

[55] For full details of the secretary's authority see U.S., Statutes at Large, LXXII, 514, sec. 3. The purpose of the McCormack Amendment was made clear during the House debate. Congressional Record, Vol. 104, Part 8 (June 12, 1958), pp. 11031–35.

[56] U.S., Statutes at Large, LXXII, 514, sec. 3.

[57] *Ibid.*

[58] *Ibid.*, sec. 2.

Congress cannot abdicate the responsibility vested in it by the Constitution. It must continue to reserve to itself decisions as to the basic duties each of the four services [Army, Navy, Air Force, and Marine Corps] is to perform. This has the great advantage of insuring that matters of such vital import to the defense of the nation are not left to the Executive alone, but are subject to the collective judgment of Congress.[59]

Congress saw the problem in 1958 as one of giving the secretary the freedom and authority he insisted that he needed "without prescribing that the Congress abdicate or renounce its constitutional responsibilities." [60] And each instance where Congress denied or altered a request of the President can be explained in these terms. Once again Congress tried to draw the line beyond which it would lose effective participation in defense policy-making. And the line passed through two key points: continued existence of the service departments and of the JCS.

If Congress had permitted the elimination of the separate service departments either by removing any reference to their separate existence or by allowing the secretary to destroy them by transferring or consolidating their functions, Congress would lose its only meaningful tool for control, alternatives. Three separate departments with overlapping functions would generate alternatives. And Congress must discover alternatives in order to judge the secretary of defense's recommendations. Because of this requirement, Congress could not permit the denial to service secretaries, or their chiefs of staff, of direct access to itself.

The three requests denied the President (removal of the word "separate," unlimited freedom to alter service roles and missions, and denial of service access to Congress) can be explained primarily in terms of legislative-executive relations. The fourth request, dealing with the JCS goes beyond such relations. Congress wanted to insure both the existence of alternatives in defense policy and a hearing for them within the Defense Department. Therefore, the JCS had to maintain its service ties and its control over the Joint Staff. The services needed this access to the top policy-making machinery if they were to have any influence on policy.

In its attempt to preserve its own participation in the defense policy process, Congress missed the most significant aspect of the 1958 reorganization. Congress was still thinking of three service departments controlled by a central agency. Administration witnesses were speaking

[59] House Committee on Armed Services, *Report, 1958,* p. 36.
[60] *Ibid.,* p. 3.

of a centralized operating agency, of which the three services were small and not very significant parts. And because of this difference in approach, most limits which Congress designed to insure the continued existence of the services, and its own continued access to the services, were to prove ineffectual.

THE FOURTH SERVICE DEPARTMENT

The National Security Act of 1958 made possible for the Department of Defense the indirect accomplishment of what it had been specifically denied since 1947. It could indirectly merge the three services.

The secretary could consolidate and assign to any organizational entity he deemed appropriate all service and support activities common to more than one service. Furthermore, he could assign all combat forces to unified commands (or to a single unified command for that matter). And it was not long before the Secretary demonstrated the use he would make of these powers.

Defense-wide Agencies

Secretary of Defense Robert S. McNamara made especially vigorous use of the powers granted his office by the 1958 Act. He continued the practice of assigning combat units of the three military departments to unified and specified commands. By the end of 1961, with the creation of STRIKE Command, virtually all combat forces had been assigned to unified and specified commanders who report directly to the secretary through the JCS.[61]

He continued the practice of consolidating common service and supply functions under defense-wide agencies which his predecessor had begun. The Defense Intelligence Agency and the Defense Supply Agency were established in the fall of 1961. The Defense Communications Agency had been established in the spring of 1960. Together with the Defense Atomic Support Agency (heir to the Manhattan Engineering District) and the National Security Agency (first established under presidential order in 1952), these five agencies and the Defense Director

[61] In the seven unified commands there is a combination of forces from two or more services: Alaskan Command, Atlantic Command, Southern Command, Continental Air Defense Command, European Command, Pacific Command, and Strike Command. There is one specified command, Strategic Air Command, which consists entirely of air force units.

of Research and Engineering perform major support activities for the entire department.[62]

At present there are six assistant secretaries of defense, in addition to the General Council, who exercise responsibility in functional areas on a defense-wide basis. While it is difficult to determine the extent to which they are developing operating control over their areas of functional responsibility, the 1958 Act gave them permission to "issue orders" to the military departments if they had permission in writing from the secretary.[63]

The inauguration of the program budget has enhanced the legal authority of the assistant secretaries of defense by several orders of magnitude. Implementation of the program budget, the responsibility of the Office of Programming, assistant secretary of defense, comptroller, involves identifying program elements (for example, Polaris submarine forces and all associated support activities), and, regardless of their origin in military departments, combatant commands, or defense-wide agencies, relating them to one of nine major program categories.[64] Marginal utility analysis (as applied in this context, it is called cost analysis) then becomes the primary tool of selecting among program elements. Whoever makes the analysis gains enormous, if not virtually complete, authority over future DOD (that is, military department, defense-wide agency, and combatant command) programs as well as budg-

[62] A detailed account of the functions of these agencies and congressional reaction to them can be found in U.S., Congress, House, Committee on Armed Services, Special Subcommittee on Defense Agencies, *Report*, 87th Cong., 2d Sess., 1962. Cited hereafter as the *Hardy-Bates Report*.

[63] In practice, the charters defining the responsibilities of assistant secretaries authorize them to issue directives "on a one-time basis." At present there are over 900 directives listed in the DOD *Directive System Quarterly Listing*. All contact between the military departments and Congress has been centralized in the special assistant to the secretary of defense for legislative affairs. *Army, Navy, Air Force Journal* (November 18, 1961), p. 1. The separate service book and magazine branches, community and industry relations programs are being merged. *Army, Navy, Air Force Journal and Register* (February 8, 1964), p. 4. The most recent study of the extent to which assistant secretaries of defense and defense-wide agencies were becoming centralized operating agencies is the *Hardy-Bates Report*.

[64] Charles J. Hitch (the assistant secretary of defense, comptroller under Secretary Robert S. McNamara) and Roland N. McKean developed the application of economic analysis to military strategic programming embodied in the DOD program budget: Hitch and McKean, *Economics of Defense*, pp. 105–33. The nine programs and their elements used in the DOD budget are explained by Charles J. Hitch in his testimony before the Senate Operations Committee on July 24, 1961. U.S., Congress, Senate, Subcommittee on National Policy, Committee on Government Operations, *Hearings, Organizing for National Security, the Budget and Policy Process*, 87th Cong., 1st Sess., 1961, Part VIII, pp. 1004–36. A list of programs and program elements used at that time is in *ibid.*, pp. 1039–55.

Fig. 8

THE DEPARTMENT OF DEFENSE, 1964

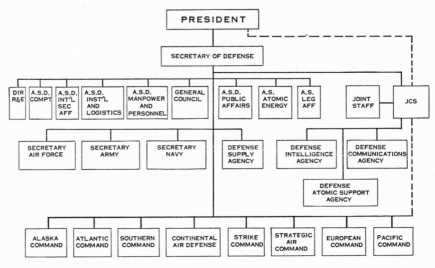

ets. Both the objectives to be accomplished (program) and the criteria for selecting among alternative methods for accomplishing the objectives (program elements) are in the hands of those making the analysis.

While the program budget was being introduced within the Department of Defense, primary responsibility for program integration was given to the defense comptroller. Subsequently, responsibility has been delegated to the appropriate assistant secretary of defense and the defense director of research and engineering.[65] The Secretary of Defense has chosen to use his civilian staff as his primary agents of policy control within the department. The OSD staff, not the subordinate operating units, are delegated program authority. The success of the system depends upon the ability of the secretary of defense to control his civilian staff and the success of his civilian staff in controlling the subordinate operating units. In sum, success depends upon the validity of the hierarchical general staff concept of organization.[66]

The military departments continue to be responsible for the training, supplying, and administering of their forces assigned to unified and specified commands. Review of major budgetary and program proposals, "wholesale supply" functions, intelligence gathering and evaluation, and communications have been removed from them and given to the

[65] *Hardy-Bates Report*, pp. 6629–30.
[66] *Supra*, Chapter III, p. 45–46.

defense super-agencies and the assistant secretaries of defense. Combat, of course, is the responsibility of the unified and specified commands. In short the military departments have been stripped of most of the functions which originally justified their existence. In the words of Professor Samuel P. Huntington, ". . . the castles of the services, like many of their medieval counterparts, will remain in existence, battered but untaken, long after the decisive battles—both political and military—have shifted to other fields." [67] The decisive battles have moved to the fields where assistant secretaries of defense, defense super-agencies, and unified and specified commands—not military departments—joust for the honors.

As mentioned previously, some aspects of the 1958 reorganization proposals resemble a perversion of the original 1947 concept. Recent trends confirm this interpretation. The defense-wide agencies are highly centralized operating agencies which exercise authority and responsibility much as the service departments were intended to in 1947. There are, however, two pronounced contrasts between the 1947 system and the one presently evolving. First, in the 1947 system, authority was allocated to match operational responsibility. The three services were responsible for the end product of the defense establishment—strategic plans and combat forces. The defense-wide agencies and the assistant secretaries of defense of today are troubled with no such responsibility. Because they have limited and highly specialized responsibility, they do not need to worry about criticisms for jeopardizing strategy or combat readiness. Highly specialized agencies are not judged in terms of over-all, end-product performance. They are subject only to management criteria such as costs. In short, they lose the very "national view" that was used to justify their creation. Second, the 1947 system provided for a series of co-ordinating devices to link and integrate service programs and to control their policy premises. Under the presently evolving system, no provision exists for lateral co-ordination or control among the defense agencies and assistant secretaries of defense except by the secretary himself. This is an impossible job for one man, as Marshall discovered in World War II.

When the current defense agencies are viewed collectively—the eight combat commands, the assistant secretaries who give orders, and the defense agencies—they bear a striking resemblance to the War Department before the Root organization of 1903. Under the bureau system, it will be recalled, combat forces were divided among a series of separate

[67] "Interservice Competition and the Political Roles of the Armed Services," p. 52.

units (Artillery, Cavalry, Infantry, and so on) assigned to "unified" commands (Department of the East, Department of Missouri, and so on), while support functions were performed by the special staffs or bureaus (Engineers, Quartermaster, Adjutant General, and so on). The secretary of war supposedly supervised the functional agencies while a commanding general supposedly directed the combatant arms.

The fatal weakness of the pre-1903 organization—lack of co-ordination and central control—was demonstrated only under the stress of the Spanish-American War. And this was the reason Root wanted a General Staff. But not even the General Staff was able to break the power of the bureaus.

The absence of a commanding general is a major contrast between the contemporary trend in the defense establishment and the pre-Root War Department. At present the secretary of defense commands the unified commands with the assistance of the JCS. However, in November, 1961, a special study group appointed by the Secretary of Defense submitted a report which recommended the creation of a commanding general for all unified commands.[68]

Fantastic though it may seem, defense reformers have succeeded in turning the calendar back sixty years and are ready to face the demands of "modern warfare" with a bureau system similar to one that failed to meet the test of the Spanish-American War!

[68] *New York Times*, November 29, 1961, p. 1. More recently, former Deputy Secretary of Defense Roswell L. Gilpatric made a similar recommendation: "An Expert Looks at the Joint Chiefs," *New York Times Magazine*, March 29, 1964, pp. 11, 71–72.

.

XI

TRENDS, ALTERNATIVES, AND PROSPECTS

CONTEMPORARY TRENDS

Authority of the Secretary of Defense

When considered in the context of attitudes and events during the past fifteen years, attempts to "clarify" or "strengthen" the authority of the secretary of defense appear to have been unrecognized attempts to banish disagreement. The secretary of defense felt awed by the scope of the decisions he had to make. But worst of all, in his view, his chief military advisers could not agree upon the course of action he should take. Moreover, the disagreement of his military advisors seemed to stem from partisan service motives.

The early reactions of the secretary of defense were attempts to push the decision (and the disagreement) downward. He tried to force the JCS to come to a decision by interposing either a board or an individual between the JCS and himself. After the creation of the chairman in 1949 and his strengthening in 1953, the secretary came to realize that pushing the decisions downward was not enough to end disagreement or to prevent challenges to his authority when he arrived at decisions. The real sources of disagreement—the services and Congress—had to have their power source taken into account. In 1958, therefore, the secretary proposed changing the basic nature of the services and reducing congressional contact with them.

Although these attempts to end disagreement were largely unsuccessful, they resulted in centralizing the department. Hierarchy replaced decisional and co-ordinating mechanisms. A large staff was created at the department level. Functional specialization was stressed, and operating agencies began to reflect the specialization that took place at the top. Service departments were replaced with special purpose agencies. And there is absolutely no reason to believe that the new agencies, if not the assistant secretaries, will not become the vested interests of tomorrow. Since vested interest is promoted by special interest, these agencies are fully capable of gaining a congressional power base sufficient to challenge the authority of the secretary of defense. Far from ending disagreement, centralization merely changes its emphasis.

Centralization and Control

After the department was centralized, in 1958, the secretary's authority was no more clearly established than in 1947 when the department was decentralized. Yet those who study defense organization continue to urge more centralization. As recently as December, 1960, a committee appointed by President-elect John F. Kennedy urged complete merger of the three services and a single chief of staff.[1] And why did it recommend this?

> The end result should be to accomplish what the Committee believes to be a major objective in any change of Defense structure, namely, to make the Secretary of Defense the civilian official in the Department of Defense with unquestioned *authority and control* over all elements of the Department of Defense at all levels.[2] [Italics added.]

Centralization means control. This slogan has been and continues to be the dogma of every defense reorganization proposal. It is so imbedded in the folklore of organization that nothing, even the experience of the preceding fifteen years, can shake the faith of those who believe in it.

Ironically, devotion to the administrative mechanics of centralization has so preoccupied the civilian administrators that even the military has developed a sensitivity to management forms and overlooks the political consequences of policy issues. And because political consequences are ignored so are political issues. The result is increased inter-

---

[1] *New York Times,* December 6, 1960, p. 1.
[2] *Ibid.*

service rivalry.[3] A major issue of defense policy was aired and settled the one time the political consequences of a policy decision were considered (the B–36 hearings). But these happenings seem to hold no lessons for defense reformers. And the cycle of centralization, emphasis on management forms, interservice rivalry, and more centralization seems as regular as the change of the seasons.

Control and Authority

If control does not mean centralization, what does it mean? It is important to notice that the control sought is not simply control, but civilian control. The authority to be clarified is the authority of the secretary of defense, not the authority of the JCS, or even of the chairman of the JCS. But if civilian control means anything, it means that military policy (means) must serve broader foreign policy goals (ends). And if such is the case, what meaning is there in devising relationships between civilian and military members of the Department of Defense? Military policy, whether it is made personally by the secretary of defense, the JCS, the assistant secretaries, the unified commands, the defense agencies, or a single chief of staff must be subordinate to and in support of larger foreign and national policy objectives. In the complex world of the 1960's, fraught with change and uncertainty, there is little possibility that anyone—the Congress or the President and the National Security Council combined—can map out a "clear, unambiguous national policy." And even if they could, which of the various possible military means will accomplish it?

If military policy is to be subject to civilian control, military force and military capabilities must be adjusted to broader national objectives. But these objectives have meaning only in terms of the specific military (and other) means selected to support them. When those who are politically responsible turn over questions of means to those who are politically irresponsible (whether military or civilian) civilian control is lost. Civilian control involves only two factors: political responsibility and final choice of means. And for a politically responsible official to make a decision "stick" involves political power and not hierarchical position or administrative centralization.

Centralization may beget uniformity, but it will never of itself produce unity. Unity is gained, not imposed. The most perfect strategy or defense posture that does not gain the understanding and support of

[3] Janowitz, *The Professional Soldier,* p. 348.

those who must finance it (Congress) and those who must execute it (the services, at least up until 1958) is worthless. The authority of the secretary of defense depends not upon the amount of uniformity he can impose within the department, but upon the agreement that he can find hidden beneath the disagreement of those who have the knowledge, the expertise, and the responsibility to qualify for participation in the ends-means adjustment of policy-making. The authority of the secretary of defense depends upon skill in negotiation.

If the secretary's authority depends upon political power and negotiation, the most obvious and the most misunderstood characteristics of the defense establishment since 1947 have been those resulting from centralization. In Chapter III, the real price of centralization was seen to be loss of central control. And the real price of the three reorganizations in the defense establishment has been precisely this—loss of central control. Between 1947 and 1949, the real power centers in the defense establishment were easily identified—the three services and the secretary. If the secretary had used his power sources, he could have led the services through the means-ends adjustment that results in real civilian control. After 1949 (if not before), however, the services were reduced in power. But the services' loss was not the secretary's gain. Power became diffused and harder to pinpoint. Certainly the defense comptroller became a power to be reckoned with. It was extremely difficult, after 1953, and virtually impossible, since 1958, to determine the location of real power within the department. In their areas of specialization, assistant secretaries and unified commanders seemingly have developed significant power. If the various assistant secretaries, defense agencies, and unified commands develop into the vested interests which their counterparts in the prewar Army became, it may eventually be possible to answer the question of control. But the answer will not be pleasant because control will have no relation to political or operational responsibility.

The relationship between centralization and loss of control is well illustrated in an incident related by Admiral Hyman Rickover before the Senate Armed Services Committee in May, 1958:

> The purchase of nuclear cores . . . [involved] a six months delay. Even though the Chairman and the General Manager of the AEC [Atomic Energy Commission] were for it, it wound up with the necessity for an official request from the Navy to the AEC via the Secretary of Defense. The matter was handled by General Loper, the Chairman of the Military Liaison Committee. I went over to see General Loper with the draft of the letter which he agreed to

and which he initialed. After that it took the initials of 15 or 20 officials in the Pentagon and a month's delay before the letter got out of the Pentagon.

So it took 6 months just because one staff person with no responsibility but with authority had on his own decided that the policy was wrong.[4]

Control is lost because authority is dispersed and exercised without responsibility.

Defense Policy

The concentration of effort throughout the entire defense establishment on ways and means has been the most undesirable consequence of equating centralization and control. Whether one considers the Forrestal struggles with the JCS in 1947–48,[5] the Lovett difficulties in 1951,[6] or the recent complaints of generals Ridgway and Taylor,[7] means—military force levels, service roles and missions, defense budgets, and allocations of new weapons systems—are all treated as though they had little or no political or policy implications. The results of these actions are assumed as "givens," essentially unambiguous, even obvious. The Defense Department's decision-making machinery is viewed as a tool whose goals are externally determined.

Too often the secretary has acted as though he should play no role in the formulation of ends. And having separated ends and means, he has acted at times as if he had no role in even the development of means.[8] The result has been a history of uncontrolled, opportunistic adaptations of strategy to force levels and budgets.

When the secretary eschews any role in the policy process, whether it be in formulating ends or in judging means, he is simply abdicating his role. He is attempting to substitute staff work for thought and decision. Staff work is important. It is a device for collecting data. It provides the materials for thought and decision. But it can never be a substitute for decision. Attempts by the secretary and the President to

---

[4] U.S., Congress, Senate, Committee on Armed Services, the Preparedness Investigating Subcommittee, *Hearings, Inquiry into Satellite and Missiles Programs*, 85th Cong., 2d. Sess., 1958, p. 1435.

[5] See *supra*, Chapter VII, p. 115.

[6] See *supra*, Chapter IX, p. 149.

[7] As Ferdinand Eberstadt predicted (see *supra*, Chapter VIII, p. 134) JCS members were unwilling to take responsibility for policy that they had neither made nor approved. See Ridgway, *Soldier*, pp. 288–89; and Maxwell D. Taylor, *The Uncertain Trumpet* (New York: Harper and Bros., 1959), pp. 78ff.

[8] See *supra*, Chapter VII, pp. 115–16.

get the JCS to reach unanimity guarantee that its recommendations will be so vague and general as to be useless as guides to action. "Completed staff work" had become a substitute for thought, decision, and responsibility.

The attempt to separate ends from means and to substitute staff work for thought and decision has led the defense establishment to develop what has been called a "premature technological orientation." [9] Defense policy ends are viewed as externally provided, and the sole job of the department is to develop capabilities. Cost analysis, requirements, probability factors, and other quantitative measurements are used to select among capabilities. Capabilities thus are judged, not in terms of ends, but in terms of some measurable, but extraneous, index.[10] And ends, subtly and at times imperceptibly, become subordinate to means.[11]

The problems, then, of defense policy, as well as those of civilian control and secretarial authority, have more to do with the way executives behave and the use they make of their organizational tools than with organizational structure. At the present time, however, reorganization may be necessary because power has been so diffused by attempts to centralize the department. But if the department should be reorganized again, the purpose of the reorganization must be to consolidate power centers and make them manageable. To bring about power consolidation, the department would have to be *decentralized*. However, it is unlikely that those who have so ardently clung to the dogma of centralization would now abandon it.

SOME ORGANIZATIONAL ALTERNATIVES

A New View of Defense Organization

Since civilian control involves political responsibility and final selection of means, organization has significance only insofar as it relates to these two elements. But this relationship is not the only factor that

[9] Philip Selznick, a well-known student of organizational behavior, has used this expression to describe the "means" orientation which develops within an organization that attempts to separate policy from administration. *Leadership in Administration* (Evanston: Row, Peterson, and Co., 1957), pp. 74ff.

[10] In the words of Peter M. Blau, "To administer a social organization according to purely technical criteria of rationality is irrational, because it ignores the nonrational aspects of social conduct." *Bureaucracy in Modern Society*, p. 58.

[11] See Robert K. Merton's comments on the displacement of ends by means. *Social Theory and Social Structure* (Glencoe, Ill.: The Free Press, 1949), pp. 154–55.

defense reformers must consider. The military establishment, regardless of its structural configuration, will reflect the greater whole of which it is a part. It will be forced to conform to the processes which operate in a democratic society to adjust and reconcile conflicting values and purposes. This process involves slippage and lost motion, duplication and waste. It is designed for accommodating an infinite number of varieties and variables and not for efficiency. It makes great decisions slowly and tentatively, and always subject to later revision. The process is as uncertain as the feelings and knowledge of the humans who operate it. But out of the process sufficiently exact national inclinations evolve to serve as premises for policy and military decisions. And those who wish to control defense policy must remember that they are but a part of the larger political process.

Defense policy, especially in peacetime, must adjust and reconcile conflicting ideas, values, and premises. And adjustment can take place only when responsible officers operate within the power structure and use the power sources that constitute the larger political process. Ignorance or unsophistication about the political system dooms officials to meaningless appeals for more legal authority—an asset they continue to waste because they do not know how to use it.

If the secretary of defense wishes to exercise real control, he must learn from the experience of the defense establishment over the past fifteen years. And this experience involves not just the behavior of organizational elements within the defense establishment itself but also relationships between the defense establishment and other parts of the national policy machinery, both executive and legislative. Above all, he must be astute in the political process.

The Political Process

The first and most important understanding for the secretary of defense is that the Constitution does not establish a government of "separated powers." Policy and administration, legislation and execution, means and ends are not separated into neat categories and parceled out to various governmental branches. The Constitution has provided that *separated institutions shall share power*.[12] Federalism adds other separated institutions, and Congress adds still others (for example, the agencies created under the National Security Act of 1947). And the separation of these institutions determines the basis for exercising power.

[12] For further elaboration see Neustadt, *Presidential Power*, pp. 33, 39.

The only *national* policy worthy of the name is a policy agreed upon and subscribed to by a majority of those who share power. There is no reason to believe those sharing power will view all policy questions identically. Differences will occur. And these differences do not appear because some individuals have the "right" or the "truly national" view while others have the "wrong" or "parochial" view.[13] On the contrary, differences occur because of the different duties of those who share power. Duties to office, duties to constituency, duties to organization, duties to knowledge, and duties to self are different.

The key to effectively exercising power within this environment is to persuade others to a course of action by convincing them it is in their interest. Others must be convinced their duty to office or constituency requires following the proposed course of action. If the elements of effective power resemble bargaining and negotiation more than an intellectual exchange between philosopher kings, it is because persuasion deals in the coin of self-interest and men have the right to reject counterfeit.[14]

The role of leadership among those who share power is the role of a negotiator.[15] The demands of leadership are not levied by the National Security Act nor any law of Congress. They are levied by the larger whole—the political process—of which the Defense Department is only a part. These demands will continue to exact bargaining as the price of leadership whether the department is centralized, decentralized, or abolished. Regardless of what the folklore of organization prescribes, leadership and control have a political rather than a statutory base.

The Policy Process and Instruments of Secretarial Control

The secretary must dismiss the myth that policy originates at the top and flows down to lower echelons. Certainly vital decisions should

[13] Indeed, "national interest" is usually a metaphysical cloak for the particular values of one or another interested party. Norton E. Long elaborates this point in "Organizations as Political Systems," *Concepts and Issues*, Mailick and Van Ness, eds., pp. 116–17.

[14] Analysis based on *ibid.*, pp. 38–43. Cyert and March suggest that bargaining over "side payments" is the usual method of defining goals within organizations. Furthermore, it is quite common to try to keep bargaining concealed under the façade of analysis. R. M. Cyert and J. G. March, "A Behavioral Theory of Organizational Objectives," *Modern Organizational Theory*, Haire, ed., pp. 79–83; and March and Simon, *Organizations*, p. 131.

[15] See Huntington's discourse on the "legislative" nature of defense strategy in *The Common Defense*, pp. 168–72.

be, and often are, made at the top (when they are not made by events), but policy—the sum of many decisions—is the product of all levels of organization. In the words of Dean Acheson, "the springs of policy bubble up; they do not trickle down." [16]

In practice, decisions are made at all levels. Managers at every level of organization interpret and apply policy declarations in the process of executing them. And policy is modified in light of what is *feasible* as well as desirable. Regardless of what the organization chart may show, managers at all echelons create, modify, even veto policy. Directives, chain of command, subordination, staff supervision—none of these formal controls can alter this fact of organizational behavior.

There is another, even more important aspect to the *de facto* decentralization of policy-making. The only persons who can and do translate policy—statements of aspirations—into operational reality are those charged with performing the various tasks constituting the performance or output of the organization. Conversely, they are the only ones in the organization with the information, ideas, and suggestions necessary for strong, imaginative, and *effective* policy. When the entire thinking and planning function is assigned to a "think group," or a planning staff, there is a question that these groups simply are not qualified to answer: Is the policy or plan adapted to reality?

If the secretary hopes to answer the question of feasibility, he must be willing to deal directly with his major operating subordinates. These are (at least were, before 1958) his chiefs of staff and his service secretaries. On troublesome issues, where sharp differences occur among subordinates, no substitute exists for the consideration of opposing views, ably argued.[17] The secretary must be able to examine the proponents carefully, convince them he is familiar with the full consequences of the decision, is intolerant of superficiality, and is willing to use his political power, fully if necessary, in resolving the issue.

The procedure through which the secretary does this must be orderly. All parties involved should be present to state their case and to hear it criticized by others. They should also hear, as well as read, the decision. Nothing equals direct confrontation between subordinates and their chief when he makes a decision involving them. They must have confidence that decisions are those of the "boss." The curse

---

[16] Dean Acheson, "Thoughts About Thought in High Places," *New York Times Magazine*, October 11, 1959, p. 20.

[17] One student of organization, Ernest Dale, argues, "the greatest single bane of management today is its growing absolutism, its refusal to discuss or listen to different opinions." "The Social and Moral Responsibilities of the Executive in the Large Corporation," *American Economic Review*, LI, No. 2 (May, 1961), 545.

of this confidence is the chief of staff, the special co-ordinator, the favorite, who emerges from the "Presence" with the "Word." It is the "Word," but whose word? Does it really have the "boss's" authority or will a protest or a leak to the press reverse it? These prescriptions are rather obvious, even trite, but those who have served in government testify as to their rarity.[18]

These comments are not meant to imply that this process must be set in motion for every decision to be made. On the contrary, detailed and technical decisions should be, and in fact will be, made by lower echelons. As the testimony by Admiral Rickover indicated,[19] top echelons can not implement operating decisions, they can only delay them. Working levels must be delegated the legal authority and must be encouraged to make the kinds of decisions they alone are capable of making. Only by clearing the detail from his office will the top official have time to make the important decisions that he should make.

When serious differences arise, when new courses must be charted, and when (the cynic might add) congressional displeasure is threatened—these are the matters that should concern the secretary. And then he must be more than concerned; he must be immersed in the issue, willing to exercise his political bargaining power to the fullest.

When the secretary acts to develop new policy or resolve ambiguities in current policy, he must be willing to confront the advocates of conflicting solutions among his subordinates, but even more important, he must remember the nature of the political process. He shares power to resolve these issues with the President, Congress, his subordinates, interest groups, the press, industry, and others. Neither he nor the President has exclusive power, or, one might add, the wisdom to make such a decision in his own right. But if he is going to influence and control the final outcome of the decision, the secretary has to be willing to bargain with these others who share power. And as the secretary discovers common threads in the ravel of conflicting interests, he will be able to negotiate a decision that will "stick." When his decisions are supported by allies in Congress, the White House, and the press, then and only then is the secretary's authority clear and complete.

An additional benefit accrues from this wedding of the political and the policy processes. If subordinates participate in the decision-making process, and if they know the secretary has ample political support for his decision, the homogeneity that begets real unity will begin to emerge. When subordinates understand the premises upon which de-

[18] See Acheson, "Thoughts About Thought in High Places," p. 20.
[19] *Supra*, pp. 196–97.

cisions are based and when they have complete confidence in the commitment of political leadership to the decision—only then can delegation and decentralization take place without loss of control.

The vital interrelations between policy, decentralization, control, and the political process are conspicuous in defense establishment experience by their complete absence. Secretaries of defense have too often behaved as though defense decisions were completely unrelated to the political process. And they have wondered why their control was subject to constant and frequently successful challenge. Nothing better demonstrates the enormous bargaining power of the secretary and the President, or both, in defense policy than the Army's failure to challenge the defense budgets of 1954 and 1958. In each case its plight was worse and its case was better than that of the Navy in 1949, but there was no "revolt of the generals." The Army, if not the secretary, had understood the lesson of 1949.[20] Real power is political bargaining power, and on those occasions, the secretary had the edge, even if he did not realize it.

Bargaining and negotiation in the political arena is much easier and less exacting than bargaining in other arenas. The values, interests, and actors involved constitute a complex and tangled skein of interactions. The negotiation between Faust and the devil was simplicity itself compared to the complexities of even the most routine defense policy action, for no defense action is limited to only two parties. Whether awarding a TFX contract to General Dynamics or closing down a military installation in Schenectady, the secretary of defense affects several local, regional, and national interests and actors, thereby involving them—whether he wishes to involve them or not. Whatever an issue starts out to be, it eventually becomes political. Defense issues are not immune from the forces that transform all governmental issues into political issues.

The political environment he inhabits forces the secretary of defense to employ political as well as strategic and economic criteria to defense policy. His control is as much (if not more) a function of his political powers as of his legal authority or hierarchical position. His political power is directly proportional to the number of allies he can attract and keep. His most valuable ally is the President who can bring negotiation to a favorable conclusion by inviting a congressional committee

[20] A description of the issues of the 1953 budget can be found in Ridgway, *Soldier*, pp. 287–90. The story of the 1958 budget can be found in Taylor, *The Uncertain Trumpet*, pp. 47–79.

chairman for a walk in the White House rose garden.[21] Congressmen, military chiefs of staff, industries, interests groups—every actor in national politics is a potential ally or opponent. And it is crucial to his power that the secretary see them for what they really are. They are not just aliens inhabiting a co-ordinate branch of government, nor subordinates within a hierarchical structure, nor greedy agents of a "military-industrial complex," nor self-serving parochial interests. To some extent they may be all of these things, but they are much more. They are potential partners or opponents who will eventually determine the long-run course of defense policy. But because their values and objectives overlap and intermingle with his own, the secretary of defense is invited to enlist their support for his objectives by convincing them it is in their interest to do so. In short, he must bargain with them.

Policy and Organizational Structure

Decentralization seems to be a fact of large organization.[22] Whether the organization chart reflects delegation of decisional authority, decisions will be made, policy will be adapted, and discretion will be exercised at operating levels. The sole alternative open to top management is determining whether decentralization will be orderly. In the prewar Army, decentralization was random. Bureaus gained authority on the basis of their bargaining power. During the war, army decentralization was orderly and bargaining power was rationed among three major organizational subdivisions. Beginning in 1953 and especially since 1958, Defense Department decentralization has threatened to be disorderly. However, frequent and direct contact between the President and Congress and certain unified commanders indicates the beginning of a discernible power structure. The next wave of budget reductions should more clearly reveal those who have succeeded in gaining substantial bargaining power.

Whether the three military departments continue to be merged indirectly or whether they are completely abolished, the Defense Department will eventually break down into units of manageable size. If no large semi-autonomous agencies are created to replace the three

[21] The "rose garden" agreement on the RS–70 between President John F. Kennedy and Congressman Carl Vinson is described in the *Army, Navy, Air Force Journal-Register* (March 31, 1962), pp. 3, 47.

[22] Decentralization and the group consensus model of organization need not be defended in terms of central control as has been done here. Morris Janowitz defends it in terms of evolving military technology. *Sociology, passim.*

services, there is a real possibility of a system similar to the old War Department bureau organization finally emerging. The similarities between the present organization and the bureau system have already been considered,[23] but there is another element common to both deserving consideration. Highly specialized agencies like the army bureaus and the present defense agencies can be co-ordinated only by a large staff at the top. Every act requiring the efforts of more than a single agency must be channeled through a co-ordinating agency. This very requirement prevents the system from succeeding. As General Marshall discovered in 1941 and as Admiral Rickover testified in 1958, elaborate channels of co-ordination and decision result at best in delay and at worst in "command failure." [24] Students of bureaucracy have discovered organizational stability to be inversely proportional to the number of "links" (levels of hierarchy) in an organization.[25] Finally, when the specialized agencies begin to develop power independent of the central co-ordinating and decisional agency, they will start to deal directly with one another and with other parts of government, as did the army bureaus.

The problem of co-ordinating staff action and subordinating staff to line becomes severe when specialized staff services are organized into separate agencies. Consider the following comment on the War Department bureau system:

> This condition of things is highly unsatisfactory ... each of the ten unrelated bureaus holds, thru its chief, direct communication with the Secretary of War, who cannot fittingly represent the line. . . . In some of the bureaus, though apparently working under high pressure, much of the time of the officers is frittered away, on the one hand with the consideration of small details in purely routine matters that do not legitimately belong in the War Department at all ... and on the other hand by the attention they are required to give to oral requests of a personal nature coming from men in high station, or to the schemes or proposals more or less visionary pressed upon the Secretary or Assistant Secretary and which they feel bound to have investigated and reported upon. Under the circumstances questions vitally affecting the policy or the welfare of the Army at large have little chance to receive just consideration and in many cases must be and are allowed to

---

[23] See *supra*, Chapter X, pp. 191–92.
[24] See *supra*, Chapter II, pp. 23–24.
[25] Robert Dubin, "Stability of Human Organization," *Modern Organizational Theory*, Haire, ed., pp. 218–53.

"drift." . . . Let the War Office be held by the tallest and strongest man living, and he would stagger or be crushed under the weight. This lack of unity, this pulling and hauling at cross purposes, cannot justly be laid at the door of the bureau chiefs, each of whom in his own way, according to his own lights, is continuously striving to work out the destiny of his specialty.[26]

Although written over sixty-five years ago, this comment is relevant in contemporary defense organization. As indicated in Chapter III, to create separate staff agencies is to emphasize staff activities.[27] Moreover, the continuing growth of staff agencies in both size and number, reporting directly to the executive, absorbs his time with management as opposed to operating policy.

Presently there are five staff agencies (bureaus?) reporting to the secretary of defense in addition to the JCS, the assistant secretaries, the service secretaries, and the unified commanders. Who co-ordinates them? Can the secretary of defense personally prevent the staff from "frittering away" its time on detail? Can he represent the line? Can he see to the "welfare of the Army at large?" Can he be sure that questions "vitally affecting policy" are not being allowed to "drift?" Or will the next reorganization call for a super-staff to control the staff?[28] These questions, unfortunately, are as relevant today as they were sixty-five years ago.

If subordinate agencies are less specialized and staffs are integrated into operating agencies, there is no need for a large overhead co-ordinating machine. For example, until April, 1964, the three service ministries in Great Britain were co-ordinated through the Ministry of Defense, an organization of less than 300 persons.[29] Since they contain most of their own support agencies, the service ministries can meet their own requirements without funneling a flood of minutiae to the top.

Another advantage of continuing diversified agencies, such as the existing military departments, involves the nature of defense policy itself. In peacetime, especially during the present conditions of the Cold War, it is vital to develop and reconsider constantly policy alter-

[26] Brigadier General Theodore Schwan, "The Coming General Staff," *Journal of the Military Services Institution of the United States*, p. 4, quoted in Nelson, *National Security*, pp. 18–19.
[27] *Supra*, Chapter III, pp. 38, 42.
[28] Super-staffs and super-agencies, of course, have already been recommended. For an example of the premises and the logic that produces such recommendations see Hans Morgenthau, "Can We Entrust Defense to a Committee?" *New York Times Magazine*, June 7, 1959, p. 9.
[29] Howard, "Central Defense Organization in Great Britain, 1959," p. 66.

natives. This is particularly true during the present period of rapid technological change. The greatest threat to adequate defense comes from gaps in defense capabilities, not from duplication. The existence of several agencies with overlapping missions encourages competition in determining alternative ways of doing the same job and provides the incentive to find gaps that need filling. Competition, far from being extravagant, is probably the surest and cheapest insurance that can be purchased against a fatal gap in defense capabilities. Even if gaps do not occur, the single way is often the most expensive way. The costs are the undiscovered cheaper ways of developing the same capability.[30]

Those who argue for a functional development of the services into even a few highly specialized commands (such as strategic, limited war, and home defense) are seeking to resolve the problem of choosing among alternatives by developing a system that will have little incentive to develop alternatives at all.

There is an apparent advantage to the proposal, however. One can argue that if the services are organized in terms of the teleology of war—limited, all out, and defense—service missions will be brought into harmony with the nature of weapons systems—tactical, strategic, and defensive. According to the argument, the problems of interservice rivalry would be solved and our military posture improved. Attractive as this agrument may be, it overlooks the cost mentioned earlier, that is, it will reduce the incentives to develop alternative methods and weapons. Furthermore, it assumes that weapons systems are single purpose and that they will automatically fall into one category or another—a position that might be hard to defend. But finally, and perhaps most important, if weapons systems or even the teleology of warfare are allowed to determine military organization,[31] means are determining ends. This argument really stems from the premature technological orientation discussed earlier.

If the secretary is to exercise any control in the political bargaining process, he must deal with services that represent a broad spectrum of interests. Services dedicated to a single value or strategic concept are in no position to seek common ground with the secretary if the issue involves their sole claim to organizational existence. For example, the

[30] Alain Enthoven and Henry Rowen develop this point in "Defense Planning and Organization," esp. pp. 4–5.

[31] The expression "military organization" is used rather than "combat deployment," because it may be entirely logical to deploy forces in terms of weapons systems, that is, strategic bomber wings, tactical air forces, artillery, and so on. However, the problems of force application are entirely different from the problems of resource allocation to create force. This distinction is frequently overlooked.

Air Force can consider the equities of sharing its strategic functions with the Navy and Army if it can expect to share in their tactical and transport functions. But if its sole mission were strategic, every attempt to get it to share this function is not simply a threat to its force levels and share of the budget, it is a threat to its very existence. Organization must be structured to encourage, not to prevent, bargaining.

The Form of Decentralization in the 1960's

The legislative changes of the past seventeen years and the practices of the various secretaries of defense have produced a central civilian operating staff which is seeking to "run" the Department of Defense from the top down. Any organizational adjustment designed to relieve the press of detail mounting within the office of the secretary of defense must take into acount these changes accomplished and consolidated since 1947.

The realities of "modern warfare" seem to have dictated, and, more significantly, Congress has accepted, creation of the unified command system, establishment of six centralized operating agencies, and reduction of the three military departments to "administrative" agencies.

If decentralization is to take place, it will have to take place within the context of these trends. There would seem to be no question of returning to the tri-service system of the post-World War II period. In the minds of both Congress and the public, the three-service system is associated with "waste, duplication, and senseless rivalry." Furthermore, there is no reason to expect the commanders of the unified and specified combat arms to relinquish willingly their recently acquired direct access to the secretary of defense and the power that accrues to them as its by-product. Finally, there is little logic in making the operating commands submit to the direction of a JCS which represents training and administrative establishments, not combat units.

Within contemporary organizational realities, the most promising direction for decentralization might be to consolidate the eight existing unified and specified commands into no more than three or four mission oriented services and have them absorb the existing military departments. The JCS could then be manned by the chiefs of staff of these newly formed commands. Such a transformation should satisfy those who feel that "integrated" and "functional" commands are required by the changed nature of "modern warfare," but should also provide sufficient flexibility of mission responsibility to provide incentives for seeking out and filling any "gaps" in combat capabilities (that is, generating alternatives).

If the unified commands are consolidated and the JCS-military department structure altered in keeping with it, the various support activities now performed by separate, centralized, operating agencies and the assistant secretaries of defense might also be consolidated under a support command similar to the Army Service Forces of World War II.[32] However, the military commander of this agency would then have to be given membership on the JCS to insure the responsiveness of support activities to operational requirements. Although such an arrangement would still have the defect of separating support from operational functions (that is, staff from line), it would have the partially offsetting characteristic of acquiring the advantages of centralized purchasing and distribution and their associated dollar savings.

Although decentralization through the old tri-service system would have the advantage of placing all resources necessary for support of operational missions under the control of each military department, it would have the disadvantage of providing this control at the cost of some duplication, and, consequently, waste among the three services. However, and perhaps more relevant, the organizational realities of the 1960's and especially the new-found power of the unified commanders seems to render any return to the old tri-service system out of the question. Future decentralization will have to take place within the existing power structure. And the rising power of the new combatant commands cannot be ignored.

PROSPECTS FOR CHANGE

There are only three sources from which the impetus for reversing the trend toward greater centralization can be expected to originate. These sources are the Defense Department itself, the military departments and other students of military organization, and Congress. Yet none of these sources has given any indication that it perceives anything but a positive correlation between centralization and control. Indeed, even those who are critical of centralization oppose it not because it threatens central control, but because they think it will result in too much central control. The dogma of centralization appears to be universally accepted.

[32] See *supra*, Chapter II, p. 30.

The Defense Department

The secretary of defense, and possibly even his assistants, may realize their isolation, their vulnerability, and their tenuous control. However, the forces operating on them must surely buttress their desire to "run" the entire organization. Congress, the public, the press, and possibly even the President, expect the secretary to take personal responsibility for everything that happens within the defense establishment, especially when things go wrong. They make it clear that the secretary must know everything about his department. In light of this pressure, what secretary could be so courageous (or foolhardy) as to refuse accountability on this basis?

Furthermore, there is a reward for becoming immersed in detailed operating decisions. They are easier to deal with and easier to make. No one likes to risk the onus that accompanies protracted negotiations and decisions involving B–52's and B–70's, Polaris and Minuteman, or whether air cover should be provided for a Cuban counterrevolution. No decision, at worst, results in failure, but wrong decision brings blame. In sum, it is easier and safer, if not healthier, to make minor operating decisions than the ones that are really called for at the top. And this provides an attractive incentive for top echelons to absorb themselves in the minutiae that floods upward in a centralized organization.

Finally, for the secretary to decentralize the department so that he could have time, opportunity, and assistance to cope with major decisions would require him to make a decision unheard of in bureaucracy. He would have to decrease rather than increase his staff.

Service Departments and Students of Defense Organization

Within the three military departments there is surprisingly little critical analysis of centralization. What criticism there is has been generated by service members who feel there has not been enough centralization, or that the present degree of centralization concentrates more power in "civilians" than in the military.[33] The one service that has consistently criticized the trend toward greater centralization, the Navy, has done so because too much control would be given to those

---

[33] The typical treatment of planning and staff in articles by military officers deals with adjusting the general staff concept to modern technology and communications. See, for example, Anthony L. Wermuth, "A General Staff for America in the Sixties," *Military Review*, XXXIX, No. 11 (Feb., 1960), 11–20; and William H. Hubbard, "The Staff and Modern War," *Military Review*, XXXIX, No. 11 (Feb., 1960), 52–69.

who do not have the proper appreciation for the role of sea power.[34] But so far all service critics have one point in common. They equate centralization with control. Perhaps this is because they are educated in operational tactics where "unity of command" has proven applica- tion. Combat calls for decision and discipline. The commander gives an order and his subordinates are to obey. And it is at least understand- able if the military tends to apply these principles to defense organiza- tion and the political process in general.

With respect to other students of defense organization, aside from the governmentally-appointed study groups such as the Hoover Com- mission and the Rockefeller Commission, remarkably few scholars have even tried to analyze organizational developments within the defense establishment and none recommends anything other than centraliza- tion.[35]

In the field of public administration, the last decade has witnessed an ever-growing volume of material that is highly critical of centraliza- tion and its accompanying "principles of administration." [36] Few scholars will still unequivocally defend administrative centralization. But this development seems to have made little impact on the national administration in general, and the Defense Department in particular.

Congress

Finally there is Congress. Congress has consistently and persistently resisted attempts to centralize the Defense Department, but it has usually just as consistently given in to executive pressure. During all reorganization hearings since 1947, Congress succeeded in focusing on the crucial issues: the chairman of the JCS, the authority of the assist- ant secretaries, the power of the secretary over service roles and mis- sions, the difference between legal authority and control, and the provi- sion for separately administered services. Yet Congress itself gives evidence of accepting the positive correlation between centralization and control. However, Congress does realize that increased executive control involves decreased legislative control. And when Congress

[34] See for example, Phillip B. Brannen, "A Single Service: Perennial Issue in National Defense," *U.S. Naval Institute Proceedings*, LXXXIII, No. 12 (December, 1957), 1280–87; George F. Elliot, "How to Lose a War," *U.S. Naval Institute Proceed- ings*, LXXVI, No. 7 (July, 1950), 707–14; and Arthur O. Salzberger, "Concept for Catastrophe," *U.S. Naval Institute Proceedings*, LXXIX, No. 4 (April, 1953), 398–407.

[35] Most works on the Department of Defense deal with evaluations of particular strategies or describe the history of events and decisions.

[36] The citations in Chapter III contain a short bibliography of materials critical of centralization.

attempts to draw the line beyond which centralization is not to go, it is also drawing the line beyond which effective congressional participation will be lost. In view of the trends since 1958, there is serious question whether Congress really succeeded in drawing the line in the proper place.

In the congressional insight that centralization limits legislative participation lies a seed from which a new type of Defense Department reform may eventually grow. Congress does seem to be aware that its control lies in choosing among alternatives and hearing criticism, not in approving the single recommendation of others. It may eventually apply this insight to the administration. Furthermore, Congress gives evidence of appreciating the dynamics of policy development in a way that members of the defense establishment have never done. Speaking of defense strategy, Carl Vinson has remarked that decisions must represent the "divergent views of several military experts, not the doctrine of one individual." [37] The choice of words is significant. He did not say that the decisions must be a *compromise* among divergent views, but *representative* of divergent views.

Mr. Vinson then went on to pinpoint the organizational requirements of a system that could take divergent views into account. There must be "responsible chiefs of military services," subject to the control of the secretary, but free from "domination by any of the others," who are "free to express and to advocate . . . views and to present and press for the full, proper, and efficient employment of their respective services' capabilities." He concluded that "when a plan is arrived at, those who have themselves made the plan—subject always to final civilian control—are responsible for carrying it out." [38] The truly remarkable aspect of such statements is the attempt to get the Defense Department to consider alternatives. Congress is not trying to get the secretary of defense to accept its own notion of what strategy should be.

But as Congress discovered in 1949, merely establishing the organizational machinery is not enough. The attitudes of those who man the organization are more important than the machinery. The secretary of defense can not afford to stay "out of politics." But only his sense of power and purpose will determine whether he will continue to depend upon hierarchy and legal authority, or whether he will start using his political tools. The best organizational machine imaginable will not function if its levers are left unpulled. Organizations do not function by themselves. They are what they are made by the men within them.

[37] House Committee on Armed Services, *Report, 1958*, p. 2.
[38] *Ibid.*, p. 36.

BIBLIOGRAPHY

BOOKS

APPLEBY, PAUL H. *Policy and Administration.* University: University of Alabama Press, 1949.

ARGYRIS, CHRIS. *Interpersonal Competence and Organizational Effectiveness.* Homewood, Ill.: The Dorsey Press, Inc., 1962.

BERNARD, CHESTER I. *The Functions of the Executive.* Cambridge: Harvard University Press, 1938.

BLAU, PETER M. *The Dynamics of Bureaucracy, A Study of Interpersonal Relations in Two Government Agencies.* Chicago: University of Chicago Press, 1955.

————. *Bureaucracy in Modern Society.* New York: Random House, 1956.

———— and SCOTT, W. RICHARD. *Formal Organization: A Comparative Approach.* San Francisco: Chandler Publishing Co., 1962.

BRODIE, BERNARD. *Strategy in the Missile Age.* Princeton: Princeton University Press, 1959.

CATER, DOUGLASS. *The Fourth Branch of Government.* Boston: Houghton Mifflin Co., 1959.

CHILDS, MARQUIS. *Eisenhower: Captive Hero, A Critical Study of the General and the President.* New York: Harcourt, Brace and Co., 1958.

CLINE, RAY S. *Washington Command Post: The Operations Division.* Washington, D.C.: Department of Army, 1951.

DONOVAN, ROBERT J. *Eisenhower: The Inside Story.* New York: Harper and Bros., 1956.

DRUCKER, PETER F. *Concept of the Corporation.* New York: The John Day Co., 1946.

————. *The New Society: The Anatomy of the Industrial Order.* New York: Harper and Bros., 1949.

ETZIONI, AMITAI. *A Comparative Analysis of Complex Organizations.* New York: The Free Press of Glencoe, 1961.

FESLER, JAMES W. *Area and Administration.* University: University of Alabama Press, 1949.

FINLETTER, THOMAS K. *Power and Policy: U.S. Foreign Policy and Military Power in the Hydrogen Age.* New York: Harcourt, Brace and Co., 1954.

GAVIN, JAMES M. *War and Peace in the Space Age.* New York: Harper and Bros., 1958.

GINZBERG, ELI and REILLEY, EWING W. *Effecting Change in Large Organizations.* New York: Columbia University Press, 1957.

GOULDNER, ALVIN W. *Patterns of Industrial Bureaucracy.* Glencoe, Ill.: The Free Press, 1954.

HAIRE, MASON (ed.). *Modern Organizational Theory: A Symposium of the Foundation for Research on Human Behavior.* New York: John Wiley and Sons, Inc., 1959.

HAMMOND, PAUL Y. *Organizing for Defense: The American Military Establishment in the Twentieth Century.* Princeton: Princeton University Press, 1961.

HANKEY, LORD. *Government Control In War.* Cambridge: Cambridge University Press, 1945.

HITCH, CHARLES J. and MCKEAN, RONALD N. *The Economics of Defense in the Nuclear Age.* Cambridge: Harvard University Press, 1960.

HITTLE, J. D. *The Military Staff: Its History and Development.* Rev. ed. Harrisburg: Stackpole, 1960.

HUNTINGTON, SAMUEL P. *The Soldier and the State.* 2d ed. Cambridge: Harvard University Press, 1959.

———. *The Common Defense: Strategic Programs in National Politics.* New York: Columbia University Press, 1961.

HUZAR, ELIAS. *The Purse and the Sword: Control of the Army by Congress Through Military Appropriations, 1933–1950.* Ithaca: Cornell University Press, 1950.

HYNEMAN, CHARLES L. *Bureaucracy in a Democracy.* New York: Harper and Bros., 1950.

ISMAY, LORD. *The Memoirs of General The Lord Ismay.* London: Hinemann, 1960.

JANOWITZ, MORRIS. *Sociology and the Military Establishment.* New York: Russell Sage Foundation, 1959.

———. *The Professional Soldier: A Social and Political Portrait.* Glencoe: The Free Press, 1960.

JESSUP, PHILIP C. *Elihu Root.* 2 vols. New York: Dodd, Mead and Co., 1938.

JOHNSON, FRANKLIN A. *Defense by Committee: The British Committee of Imperial Defense, 1885–1959.* London: Oxford University Press, 1960.

KAHN, HERMAN. *On Thermonuclear War.* Princeton: Princeton University Press, 1960.

KAUFMAN, HERBERT. *The Forest Ranger: A Study in Administrative Behavior.* Baltimore: The Johns Hopkins Press, 1960.

KINGSTON-MCCLOUGHRY, E. J. *The Direction of War: A Critique of the Political Direction and High Command in War.* New York: Praeger, 1955.

———. *Defense Policy and Strategy.* New York: Praeger, 1960.

KINTNER, WILLIAM R. *Forging a New Sword: A Study of the Department of Defense.* New York: Harper and Bros., 1958.

KISSINGER, HENRY A. *Nuclear Weapons and Foreign Policy.* New York: Harper and Bros., 1957.

———. *The Necessity for Choice.* New York: Harper and Bros., 1960.

LASSWELL, HAROLD D. and KAPLAN, ABRAHAM. *Power and Society.* New Haven: Yale University Press, 1950.

LAWRENCE, PAUL R. *The Changing of Organizational Behavior Patterns: A Case Study of Decentralization.* Boston: Harvard University Press, 1958.

LEACH, W. BARTON. *The New Look.* Maxwell AFB, Alabama: Air Command and Staff College, Air University, 1954.

LILIENTHAL, DAVID. *TVA—Democracy on the March.* New York: Harper and Bros., 1953.

MAASS, ARTHUR. *Muddy Waters: The Army Engineers and the Nation's Rivers.* Cambridge: Harvard University Press, 1951.

MAILICK, SIDNEY and VAN NESS, EDWARD H. (eds.). *Concepts and Issues in Administrative Behavior.* Englewood Cliffs: Prentice-Hall, Inc., 1962.

MARCH, JAMES G. and SIMON, HERBERT A. *Organizations.* New York: John Wiley and Sons, Inc., 1958.

McCLENDON, R. EARL. *The Question of Autonomy for the United States Air Arm, 1907–1945.* Maxwell AFB, Alabama: Documentary Research Division, Air University Library, 1950.

MERTON, R. K. and others. *Reader in Bureaucracy.* Glencoe: The Free Press, 1952.

————. *Social Theory and Social Structure.* Glencoe: The Free Press, 1949.

MILLIS, WALTER and others. *Arms and the State, Civil-Military Elements in National Policy.* New York: The Twentieth Century Fund, 1958.

———— (ed.). *The Forrestal Diaries.* New York: Viking Press, 1951.

MORGANSTERN, OSKAR. *The Question of National Defense.* New York: Random House, 1959.

MORISON, ELTING E. *Turmoil and Tradition: A Study of the Life and Times of Henry L. Stimson.* Boston: Houghton Mifflin Co., 1960.

NELSON, OTTO L. *National Security and the General Staff.* Washington, D.C.: Infantry Journal Press, 1946.

NEUSTADT, RICHARD E. *Presidential Power: The Politics of Leadership.* New York: John Wiley and Sons, Inc., 1960.

PARSONS, TALCOTT. *The Social System.* Glencoe: The Free Press, 1951.

PETTEE, GEORGE. *The Future of American Secret Intelligence.* Washington, D.C.: Infantry Journal Press, 1946.

PFIFFNER, JOHN M. and SHERWOOD, FRANK P. *Administrative Organization.* Englewood Cliffs: Prentice-Hall, Inc., 1960.

RIDGWAY, MATTHEW B. *Soldier: The Memoirs of Matthew B. Ridgway.* New York: Harper and Bros., 1956.

SAMPSON, ROBERT C. *The Staff Role in Management.* New York: Harper and Bros., 1955.

SCHILLING, WARNER R., HAMMOND, PAUL Y. and SNYDER, GLENN. *Strategy, Politics, and Defense Budgets.* New York: Columbia University Press, 1962.

SELZNICK, PHILIP. *TVA and the Grass Roots.* Berkeley: University of California Press, 1949.

————. *Leadership in Administration.* Evanston: Row, Peterson and Co., 1957.

SIMON, HERBERT A. *Administrative Behavior: A Study of Decision-Making Processes in Administrative Organization.* New York: The Macmillan Co., 1951.

————, SMITHBURG, DONALD W. and THOMPSON, VICTOR A. *Public Administration.* New York: Alfred A. Knopf, 1950.

SINGER, J. DAVID. *Deterrence, Arms Control, and Disarmament.* Columbus: Ohio State University Press, 1962.

SNYDER, GLENN H. *Deterrence and Defense.* Princeton: Princeton University Press, 1961.

STANLEY, TIMOTHY W. *American Defense and National Security.* Washington, D.C.: Public Affairs Press, 1956.

STEIN, HAROLD (ed.). *American Civil-Military Decisions, A Book of Case Studies.* New York: The Twentieth Century Fund, 1963.

STERNBERG, FRITZ. *The Military and Industrial Revolution of Our Time.* London: Stevens and Sons, Ltd., 1959.

STIMSON, HENRY L. and BUNDY, MCGEORGE. *On Active Service in Peace and War.* New York: Harper and Bros., 1947.

TAYLOR, MAXWELL D. *The Uncertain Trumpet.* New York: Harper and Bros., 1959.

TRUMAN, DAVID B. *Administrative Decentralization.* Chicago: University of Chicago Press, 1940.

VAGTS, ALFRED. *A History of Militarism.* Rev. ed. New York: Meridian Books, Inc., 1959.

WALLACE, SCHUYLER C. *Federal Departmentalization: A Critique of Theories of Organization.* New York: Columbia University Press, 1941.

WASKOW, ARTHUR I. *The Limits of Defense.* Garden City: Doubleday, 1962.

WATSON, MARK S. *Chief of Staff: Prewar Plans and Preparations.* Washington, D.C.: Department of Army, 1950.

WEBER, MAX. *Theory of Social and Economic Organization.* Glencoe: The Free Press, 1949.

WHEARE, K. C. *Government by Committee.* Oxford: Clarendon Press, 1955.

WHITE, LEONARD D. *Introduction to the Study of Public Administration.* 3d ed. New York: The Macmillan Co., 1950.

——. *The Republican Era: 1869–1901.* New York: The Macmillan Co., 1958.

ARTICLES

ACHESON, DEAN. "Thoughts About Thought in High Places," *New York Times Magazine,* October 11, 1959, p. 86.

ALBION, ROBERT G. "The Administration of the Navy, 1798–1945," *Public Administration Service, Report No. 95 (The Navy: A Study in Administration),* 1946.

APPLEBY, PAUL H. "Organizing Around the Head of a Large Federal Department," *Public Administration Review,* VI, No. 3 (Summer, 1946), 205–12.

BENSON, GEORGE C. S. "A Plea for Administrative Decentralization," *Public Administration Review,* VII, No. 3 (Summer, 1947), 170–78.

BRANNEN, PHILLIP B. "A Single Service: Perennial Issue in National Defense," *Proceedings, U.S. Naval Institute,* LXXXIII, No. 12 (December, 1957), 1280–87.

CAPLOW, THEODORE. "Organizational Size," *Administrative Science Quarterly,* I, No. 4 (March, 1957), 484–505.

CLINE, RAY S. and MATLOFF, MAURICE. "Development of War Department Views on Unification," *Military Affairs,* XIII, No. 2 (Summer, 1949), 65–74.

CONNERY, ROBERT H. "Unification of the Armed Services—The First Year," *American Political Science Review,* XLIII, No. 1 (February, 1949), 38–52.

———— and DAVID, PAUL T. "The Mutual Defense Assistance Program," *American Political Science Review*, XLV, No. 2 (June, 1951), 321–47.

CUTLER, ROBERT. "The Development of National Security Policy," *Foreign Affairs*, XXXIV, No. 3 (April, 1956), 441–58.

DALE, ERNEST. "Contributions to Administration by Alfred P. Sloan Jr., and G.M.," *Administrative Science Quarterly*, I, No. 1 (June, 1956), 30–62.

————. "The Social and Moral Responsibilities of the Executive in the Large Corporation," *American Economic Review*, LI, No. 2 (May, 1961), 540–48.

DALTON, MELVILLE. "Conflict Between Staff and Line Managerial Officers," *American Sociological Review*, XV, No. 3 (June, 1950), 342–51.

DRUCKER, PETER F. "Politics for a New Generation," *Harpers*, CCXX, No. 1321 (June, 1960), 29–36.

DUFFIELD, EUGENE S. "Organizing for Defense," *Harvard Business Review*, XXXI, No. 5 (Sep.–Oct., 1953), 29–42.

ELLIOT, GEORGE F. "How to Lose a War," *Proceedings, U.S. Naval Institute*, LXXVI, No. 7 (July, 1950), 707–14.

EMERSON, WILLIAM. "Franklin Roosevelt as Commander-in-Chief in World War II," *Military Affairs*, XXII, No. 4 (Winter, 1958–59), 181–207.

FESLER, JAMES W. "Administrative Literature and the Second Hoover Commission," *American Political Science Review*, LI, No. 1 (March, 1957), 28–37.

GIBNEY, FRANK. "The Missile Mess," *Harpers*, CCXX, No. 1316 (January, 1960), 38–45.

GILPATRIC, ROSWELL L. "An Expert Looks at The Joint Chiefs," *New York Times Magazine*, March 29, 1964, pp. 11, 71–72.

GOULDNER, ALVIN. "Metaphysical Pathos and the Theory of Bureaucracy," *American Political Science Review*, XLIX, No. 2 (June, 1955), 496–507.

GUMZ, DONALD G. "The Bureau of the Budget and Defense Fiscal Policy," *Proceedings, U.S. Naval Institute*, LXXXV, No. 4 (April, 1959), 80–89.

HAMMOND, PAUL Y. "The National Security Council as a Device for Interdepartmental Coordination: An Interpretation and Appraisal," *American Political Science Review*, LIV, No. 4 (December, 1960), 899–910.

HAYDON, FREDERICK S. "War Department Reorganization, August 1941–March 1942," *Military Affairs*, XVI, Nos. 1 and 3 (Spring, 1952, and Fall, 1952), 1–11 and 97–114.

HENRY, A. F., MASLAND, J. W. and RADWAY, LAWRENCE I. "Armed Forces Unification and the Pentagon Officer," *Public Administration Review*, XV, No. 3 (Summer, 1955), 173–80.

HENSEL, H. STRUVE. "Changes Inside the Pentagon," *Harvard Business Review*, XXXII, No. 1 (Jan.–Feb., 1954), 98–108.

HOGAN, WILLIAM N. "A Dangerous Tendency in Government," *Public Administration Review*, VI, No. 3 (Summer, 1946), 235–39.

HOLLIS, SIR LESLIE. "Britain's Defense Organization—A Survey," *Brassey's Naval Annual, 1956*, ed. H. G. Thursfield. New York: The Macmillan Co., 1956, pp. 24–36.

HOWARD, MICHAEL. "Central Defense Organization in Great Britain, 1959," *The Political Quarterly*, XXXI, No. 1 (Jan.–Mar., 1960), 66–70.

HUBBARD, WILLIAM H. "The Staff and Modern War," *Military Review*, XXXIX, No. 11 (February, 1960), 52–69.

HUBBELL, ROBERT L. "Techniques of Making Committees Effective," *Public Administration Review*, VI, No. 4 (Autumn, 1946), 348–53.

HUGHES-HALLET, J. "The Control of Armed Forces," *Brassey's Naval Annual, 1956*, ed. H. G. Thursfield. New York: The Macmillan Co., 1956, pp. 15–23.

HUNTINGTON, SAMUEL P. "Interservice Competition and the Political Roles of the Armed Services," *American Political Science Review*, LV, No. 1 (March, 1961), 40–52.

HUZAR, ELIAS. "Notes on the Unification Controversy," *Public Administration Review*, VI, No. 4 (Autumn, 1946), 297–314.

IRVINE, DALLAS D. "The Origins of Capital Staffs," *Journal of Modern History*, X, No. 2 (June, 1938), 161–79.

JACKSON, HENRY M. "To Forge a Strategy for Survival," *Public Administration Review*, XIX, No. 3 (Summer, 1959), 157–63.

JORDAN, HENRY D. "The British Cabinet and the Ministry of Defense," *American Political Science Review*, XLIII, No. 1 (February, 1949), 73–82.

KAUFMAN, HERBERT. "Emerging Conflicts in the Doctrine of Public Administration," *American Political Science Review*, L, No. 4 (Dec., 1956), 1057–73.

KLEIN, BURTON. "A Radical Proposal for R and D," *Fortune*, LVII, No. 5 (May, 1958), 112–226.

KNIGHT, ARCHIE J. and HERZBERG, ALLEN F. "A Proposal for the Next Step in Defense Reorganization," *Air University Quarterly Review*, XII, No. 2 (Summer, 1960), 53–90.

LEACH, W. BARTON. "Obstacles to the Development of American Air Power," *The Annals of the American Academy of Political and Social Sciences*, CCXCIX (May, 1955), 67–75.

LEE, F. G. and STEVENS, ROGER. "Coordinating Policy and Operations in Government of the United Kingdom," *Public Administration Review*, VI, No. 4 (Autumn, 1946), 354–61.

LEE, GUS C. "The Organization for National Security," *Public Administration Review*, IX, No. 1 (Winter, 1949), 36–44.

LIPSET, SEYMOUR. "Bureaucracy and Social Change," in R. K. MERTON, and others, *Reader in Bureaucracy*. Glencoe: The Free Press, 1952, pp. 221–32.

LYONS, GENE M. "The New Civil-Military Relations," *American Political Science Review*, LV, No. 1 (March, 1961), 53–63.

McCAMY, JAMES L. "Analysis of the Process of Decision-Making," *Public Administration Review*, VII, No. 1 (Winter, 1947), 41–48.

MILLETT, JOHN D. "The Organizational Structure of the Army Service Forces," *Public Administration Service, Report No. 10 (Administrative Management in the Army Service Forces)*, 1944, pp. 14–27.

MOORE, LEO B. "Too Much Management, Too Little Change," *Harvard Business Review*, XXIV, No. 1 (Jan.–Feb., 1956), 41–48.

MORGENTHAU, HANS. "Can We Entrust Defense to a Committee?" *New York Times Magazine*, June 7, 1959, pp. 9, 62ff.

MORTON, LOUIS. "Army and Marines on the China Station: A Study in Military and Political Rivalry," *Pacific Historical Review*, XXXIX (Feb., 1960), 51–73.

MYLANDER, WILLIAM H. "Management by Executive Committee," *Harvard Business Review*, XXXIII, No. 3 (May–June, 1955), 51–58.

PFIFFNER, JOHN M. and MASON, FRANK K. "Personnel Management at The Grass Roots," *Personnel Administration*, XX, No. 3 (May–June, 1957), 25–33.

RAY, JOSEPH M. "Reflections of a Professor Turned Bureaucrat," *Public Administration Review*, XIX, No. 4 (Autumn, 1959), 238–42.

ROBINSON, C. F. "British Organization for Defense," *Public Administration Review*, VIII, No. 3 (Summer, 1948), 181–87.

SALTONSTALL, ROBERT. "Who's Who in Personnel Administration," *Harvard Business Review*, XXXIII, No. 4 (July–Aug., 1955), 75–83.

SALZBERGER, ARTHUR O. "Concept for Catastrophe," *Proceedings, U.S. Naval Institute*, LXXIX, No. 4 (April, 1953), 398–407.

SIMON, HERBERT A. "Notes on the Observation and Measurement of Political Power," *Journal of Politics*, XV, No. 4 (Nov., 1953), 500–16.

———. "Staff and Management Controls," *The Annals of the American Academy of Political and Social Sciences*, CCXCII (March, 1954), 95–103.

THOMPSON, JAMES D. "Authority and Power in Identical Organizations," *The American Journal of Sociology*, LX (November, 1956), 290–92.

THURSFIELD, H. G. (ed.). "The United States Defense Structure," *Brassey's Naval Annual, 1956*. New York: The Macmillan Co., 1956.

URWICH, LYNDALL F. "The Manager's Span of Control," *Harvard Business Review*, XXXIV, No. 3 (May–June, 1956), 39–47.

VERRIER, ANTHONY. "Defense and Politics After Nassau," *The Political Quarterly*, XXXIV, No. 3 (July–Sept., 1963), 269–78.

WERMUTH, ANTHONY L. "A General Staff for America in the Sixties," *Military Review*, XXXIX, No. 11 (February, 1960), 11–20.

WORTHY, JAMES C. "Organizational Structure and Employee Morale," *American Sociological Review*, XV, No. 2 (April, 1950), 169–79.

PUBLIC DOCUMENTS

Great Britain, Ministry of Defense. *Central Organization for Defense*. Cmd. 6923. Reprinted in *Brassey's Naval Annual, 1947*, ed. H. G. THURSFIELD. New York: The Macmillan Co., 1947.

Great Britain, Ministry of Defense. *Central Organization for Defense*. Cmd. 476, 1958.

———. Cmd. 2097, 1963.

U.S., The Commission on Organization of the Executive Branch of the Government. *Task Force Report on Departmental Management (Appendix E)*, 1949.

———. *Task Force Report on National Security Organization (Appendix G)*, 1949.

———. *Subcommittee Report on Special Personnel Problems in the Department of Defense*, 1955.

U.S., Office of the Secretary of Defense. *First Report of the Secretary of Defense*, 1948.

U.S., The President's Committee on Administrative Management. *Report of the Committee*, 1937.

U.S., President. *Reorganization Plan No. 8 of 1949, Presidential Message.* H.D. 262. 81st Cong., 1st Sess., 1949.

——. *Message Accompanying Reorganization Plan No. 6 of 1953, Relating to the Department of Defense.* Committee Reprint. H.D. 136. 83d Cong., 1st Sess., 1955.

——. *Message from the President of the United States Transmitting Recommendations Relative to our Entire Defense Establishment.* H.D. 366. 85th Cong., 2d Sess., 1958.

——. *State of the Union Message.* H.D. 251. 85th Cong., 2d Sess., 1958.

U.S. Congress, House. Committee on Expenditures in the Executive Departments. *Hearings, National Security Act of 1947.* H.R. 2319. 80th Cong., 1st Sess., 1947.

——. *National Security Act of 1947.* House Report 961, to accompany H.R. 4214. 80th Cong., 1st Sess., 1947.

——. *National Security Act of 1947.* Conference Report, to accompany S. 758. 80th Cong., 1st Sess., 1947.

——. Committee on Armed Services. *Hearings, To Convert the National Military Establishment into an Executive Department of Government, To be Known as the Department of Defense.* 81st Cong., 1st Sess., 1949.

——. ——. *Hearings, To Reorganize Fiscal Management in the National Military Establishment; To promote Economy and Efficiency, and for other purposes.* 81st Cong., 1st Sess., 1949.

——. ——. *Hearings, H.R. 5632, Conference Report.* 81st Cong., 1st Sess., 1949.

——. ——. *Unification and Strategy: A Report of Investigation.* H.D. 600. 81st Cong., 2d Sess., 1950.

——. *National Security Act Amendments of 1949.* Conference Report, to accompany H.R. 1142. 81st Cong., 1st Sess., 1950.

——. Committee on Government Operations. *Hearings, Reorganization Plan No. 6 of 1953: Department of Defense.* 83d Cong., 1st Sess., 1953.

——. ——. *Providing for the Taking Effect of Provisions of Reorganization Plan No. 6 of 1953.* Report 633, to accompany H.J. Res. 264. 83d Cong., 1st Sess., 1953.

——. Committee on Armed Services. *Communication from the President of the United States Transmitting a Draft of Legislation.* 85th Cong., 2d Sess., 1958.

——. ——. *Hearings, Reorganization of the Department of Defense.* 85th Cong., 2d Sess., 1958.

——. ——. *Department of Defense Reorganization Act of 1958.* Report 1765, to accompany H.R. 12541. 85th Cong., 2d Sess., 1958.

——. *Department of Defense Reorganization Act of 1958.* Conference Report. 85th Cong., 2d Sess., 1958.

——. Special Subcommittee on Defense Agencies. *Report.* 87th Cong., 2d Sess., 1962.

U.S. Congress, Senate. Committee on Military Affairs. *Hearings, Department of Armed Forces, Department of Military Security.* 79th Cong., 1st Sess., 1945.

——. *Report to Hon. James Forrestal, Secretary of the Navy. Unification of the War and Navy Departments and Post War Organization for National Security.* Committee Print. 79th Cong., 1st Sess., 1945.

——. Committee on Naval Affairs. *Hearings, Unification of the Armed Forces.* 79th Cong., 1st Sess., 1946.
——. *Department of Common Defense.* Report 1325, to accompany S. 2044. 79th Cong., 2d Sess., 1946.
——. Committee on Armed Services. *Hearings, National Defense Establishment, Unification of the Armed Services.* 80th Cong., 1st Sess., 1947.
——. *National Security Act of 1947.* Report 239, to accompany S. 758. 80th Cong., 1st Sess., 1947.
——. Committee on Armed Services. *Hearings, National Security Act of 1949.* 81st Cong., 1st Sess., 1949.
——. *National Security Act Amendments of 1949.* Report 366, to accompany S. 1843, 1949.
——. Committee on Armed Services. *Report of the Rockefeller Committee: Department of Defense Organization.* Committee Reprint. 83d Cong., 1st Sess., 1953.
——. Committee on Armed Services, the Preparedness Investigating Subcommittee. *Hearings, Inquiry into Satellites and Missiles Programs.* 85th Cong., 1st Sess., 1958.
——. ——. *Hearings, Department of Defense Reorganization Act of 1958.* 85th Cong., 1st Sess., 1958.
——. ——. *Department of Defense Reorganization Act of 1958.* Report 1845, to accompany H.R. 12541. 85th Cong., 2d Sess., 1958.
——. Committee on Government Operations. *Hearings, Organizing for National Security.* Parts I, IV, V, and VI. 86th Cong., 2d Sess., 1960.
——. ——. *Organizing for National Security, the National Security Council. Report.* 86th Cong., 2d Sess., 1960.
U.S. Congressional Record, 85th Cong., 2d Sess., 1958, CIV, Part 8, 11031–11035.
U.S. Statutes at Large. LXI, 253.
U.S. Statutes at Large. XLI, 759.
U.S. Statutes at Large. LXIII, 109.
U.S. Statutes at Large. LXXII, 514.

NEWSPAPERS

Army, Navy, Air Force Journal. November 18, 1961, p. 1.
Army, Navy, Air Force Journal and Register. February 8, 1964, p. 4.
The Economist. CCVIII, No. 6256 (July 20, 1963), 237–38.
New York Times. December 6, 1960, p. 1.
New York Times. November 29, 1961, p. 1.
The Times (London). March 4, 1963.

UNPUBLISHED MATERIALS

ENTHOVEN, ALAIN and ROWEN, HENRY. "Defense Planning and Organization (P-1640)." Santa Monica: The RAND Corporation, 1959.

GREEN, MURRAY. "The First Secretary of the Air Force and Unification." Ph.D. dissertation, Department of Political Science, American University, 1959.
LEGERE, LAWRENCE J., JR. "Unification of the Armed Forces." Ph.D. dissertation, Harvard University, 1951.
LINDBLOM, CHARLES E. "Bargaining: The Hidden Hand in Government (RM–1434–RC)." Santa Monica: The RAND Corporation, 1955.
SMITH, WILLIAM Y. "The Search for National Security Planning Machinery, 1900–1947." Ph.D. dissertation, Harvard University, 1960.

INDEX

Adams, Sherman: example of "principles" of command, 23
Administrative control: meaning in War Department, 34. *See also* Control in organization
Ainsworth, F. C., Army Adjutant General, 45
Air Force: Department of, 27, 89, 95, 105, 120, 172; created, 25; and 70–groups, 115, 116, 117, 127, 144. *See also* Military departments
Air power: autonomy of, 3; and unification, 4
Army, Department of, 4, 16, 28, 34, 89, 95, 105, 125, 142, 172, 183, 203
Army Air Forces, 4, 5, 26, 125: functions of, 25
Army bureaus: relationship to secretary of war, 19; National Defense Act of 1920, 21; power base, 21, 22; consolidation, 30; congressional alliances of, 45; and policy process, 204–6
Army chief of staff: alliance with secretary of war, 17; relation to general staff, 19; functions according to Simpson board, 32; and War Department reorganization, 1946, 34; authority of, 45
Army general staff: origin of, 16, 17; bureau rivalry, 18; and National Defense Act of 1920, 21; power base, 22; power during World War II, 24; functions of Operations Division, 25, 26; changes in 1942, 25–29; size during World War II, 29n; functions proposed by Patch Board, 31, 32; functions proposed by Simpson Board, 32, 33; and War Department reorganization of 1946, 33; a symbol of control, 35
Army ground forces: functions of, 25, 27

Army service forces, 25, 27, 209: and bureau independence, 30; and Patch board, 31
Arnold, Henry H., 4, 27, 62
Assistant secretaries of defense: origin, 141, 143, 158, 160, 165; policy role after 1953, 170; and separately administered military departments, policy role after 1958, 182–83; 181–85; responsibilities, 189, 191
Assistant secretary of defense, international security affairs: staff size, 43
Authority: myths of, 22; types distinguished, 45; distinguished from power, 45n; separated from responsibility, 180

Bradley, Omar M., 116, 132, 175
British-American defense organization: contrasted, 76–77, 158, 161, 180, 206
British defense organization: origin of, 69; Committee of Imperial Defense subcommittees, 70; War Cabinet, 70, 71, 75; Committee of Imperial Defense, 71, 74, 75, 77, 79, 94; Chiefs of Staff Committee, 72, 79, 81, 82, 84; Defense Committee, operations, 72, 75, 76, 86; War Cabinet Secretariat, 73; minister of defense, 74, 76, 78, 79, 80; rejection of general staff, 75, 78; Defense Committee, 78, 79, 80, 81, 83, 84; Committee on Defense and Overseas Policy, 81; Defense Staff, 82; concept of defense policy-making, 83–85; Secretariat, 86
Brownlow, Louis, 35
Bureau of Budget: 168; staff size, 42–43; and 1949 defense reorganization, 128, 129

Centralization in organization: as a

223

THE MANAGEMENT OF DEFENSE:
ORGANIZATION AND CONTROL OF THE U.S. ARMED SERVICES
by John C. Ries

designer:	Edward D. King
compositor:	Waverly Press, Inc.
typefaces:	Baskerville, Bodoni ✠375
printer:	Waverly Press, Inc.
paper:	Perkins and Squier, SM
binder:	Moore and Co.
cover material:	Columbia Riverside Linen